Discourse on
Covid-19 Pandemic and
Fiscal Federalism in India

About the Editors

Prof. K.J. Joseph is the Director of GIFT, Secretary General of Globelics (www.globelics.org) and The Founding Editor-in-Chief of Innovation and Development published by Taylor and Francis, London. Earlier positions that he held include Ministry of Commerce Chair Professor at Centre for Development Studies, Visiting Senior Fellow at RIS, New Delhi, Professor Jawaharlal Nehru University, IT Policy Consultant of UNESCAP for Cambodia, Laos, Myanmar, Vietnam, Thailand and the Yunnan Province of China, Expert in Innovation studies at Tianjin University of Finance and Economics, China, selected under the program of search for global experts. He has also been a consultant to UNCTAD. Gold Medalist of the Calicut University for MA Economics, he earned M Phil and PhD Degrees from Jawaharlal Nehru University (Centre for Development Studies, Trivandrum) and undertook post doctoral research at Yale University as a Ford Foundation Fellow. Apart from over 80 research papers and a number of policy-oriented reports, he has six books published by five leading international publishers (Sage publications, Oxford University Press, Palgrave Macmillan, Routledge and Edward Elgar) to his credit. He has delivered invited lectures, keynote addresses and presented papers in over 80 seminars/conferences held in 35 countries and over 150 seminars/workshops/conferences in India.

Pyaralal Raghavan is a journalist who has worked in different national newspapers. He has also worked as an economist with some of the industry lobby groups. Trained as an economist he did his doctorate from the Centre for Development Studies, Thiruvananthapuram.

Discourse on Covid-19 Pandemic and Fiscal Federalism in India

Editors

K.J. Joseph
Pyaralal Raghavan

Published on Behalf of

GIFT GULATI INSTITUTE OF FINANCE AND TAXATION

Concept
Since 1974

ISBN: 978-93-5594-663-8

First Published 2023

Published and Printed by

Concept Since 1974

Concept Publishing Company Pvt. Ltd.
A/15-16, Commercial Block, Mohan Garden,
New Delhi-110059 (INDIA)
T : +91 11 41101460
E : publishing@conceptpub.com; *W* : www.conceptpub.com

Cataloging in Publication Data--Courtesy: D.K. Agencies (P) Ltd. <docinfo@dkagencies.com>

Seminar on Covid 19 and Fiscal Federalism (2020 : Online)
Discourse on Covid-19 pandemic and fiscal federalism in India / editors, K.J. Joseph, Pyaralal Raghavan.
pages cm
"Papers presented at an online Seminar on Covid 19 and Fiscal Federalism, organized by Gulati Institute of Finance and Taxation in 2020.
Includes index.
ISBN 9789355946638

1. COVID-19 Pandemic, 2020- --Economic aspects--India--Congresses. 2. COVID-19 Pandemic, 2020- --Economic aspects--India--Kerala--Congresses. 3. Intergovernmental fiscal relations--India--Congresses. 4. Intergovernmental fiscal relations--India--Kerala--Congresses. I. Joseph, K. J., 1961- editor. II. Raghavan, Pyaralal, editor. III. Gulati Institute of Finance and Taxation (Trivandrum, India), organizer. IV. Title.

LCC HJ1338.S46 2020 | DDC 336.1850954 23

In memory of
Professor Abhijit Sen and V. Bhaskar IAS
who were with us for this discourse
But no more with us

Foreword

In the last few years, we have been compelled to confront a series of unprecedented and difficult situations. As is generally understood, the adverse outcomes of demonetisation left hardly any sector of the economy or section of society untouched. The hardest hit perhaps was the informal sector which is the major source of livelihood for almost 90% of the labour force. This was followed by the rather unprepared and unplanned implementation of the goods and services tax (GST) and consequently making the worst out of something which could have had an excellent outcome if implemented cautiously. While the country was faced with this double whammy, Kerala had to confront three other crises. We were confronted with the Nipah virus followed by the historic deluge of 2018 that almost devastated the state's economy. This was followed by yet another flood in 2019. As we are about to recover from these manmade and natural disasters, we were again caught in the grip of a once in a century pandemic due to the spread of coronavirus disease.

Although the news about the outbreak of a deadly virus in the Wuhan province of China has been in the media, it was really shocking when the first incident of COVID 19 was reported in Kerala when a student returning from China was tested COVID positive. Having been familiar with the literature on the plague outbreak in the previous century and hardly any vaccines in place to hold the virus, it was rather easy to visualise what is in the making.

However, the strong health system of the state, confident with the experience in effectively handling Nipah virus, was fully alert and equipped to handle any plausible crisis conditions. Evidently, Kerala's record in handling the virus under the Minister for health, Smt Shailaja Teacher, attracted much global acclaim. With the Chief Minister, Shri Pinarayi Vijayan, himself directly taking over the task of monitoring and handling the crisis, the confidence of the entire system was amplified. Along with health machinery at all levels, the entire institutional architecture of decentralised governance adapted quickly to the task of dealing with the virus. Social distancing, which was considered as the only option in the short run to contain the spread of the virus, was strictly implemented by the authorities concerned and monitored on a daily basis by the Chief Minister.

Since the virus posed a serious threat to the lives and livelihoods, the government had to step in by initiating urgent measures not only for saving the lives but also livelihoods. The announcement of abrupt lockdown of the economy on 24 March 2020 caused misery to the entire population and especially to the migrants. Being a state with the largest number of guest workers, we realised the perils in following the strategy of the union. Hence, on 19 March 2020, we announced, for the first time in the country, a COVID package of Rs 20,000 crore. This ensured the delivery of all the necessaries of life at the door steps of the people apart from offering liberal financial assistance to the health and the other badly affected sectors. The opening of community kitchens meant for all, especially the guest workers, helped them remain safe and protected in their place of residence.

It was our conviction that the states, being closer to the people, have the greater responsibility to undertake measures for saving the people from the pandemic. However, given the existing fiscal federal relations in our country the states, which account for only 32% of the total revenue while shouldering 62% of the expenditure, are fiscally constrained to step in any significant manner to address the challenge. The severity of the situation seems to have aggravated as the union government has been firm on adhering to the FRBM and fiscal prudence despite the crisis. No wonder, there was hardly any effort by the union government to help states in addressing the mounting challenge, especially the severe fiscal constraints, to effectively address the crisis. It was our perception that the union and the states should urgently reconcile with the gravity of the situation and realise the imperative of working together.

The issue was not simply confined to financing the war against the virus; of course, that was important. There was an urgent need for a better understanding on how the different states are positioned to fight the pandemic and the nature and extent of deficit in the existing systems and capabilities of states and above all for evolving a collective approach. Further, the 15th Finance Commission, which came up with its interim report should be induced to reconcile the implications of the pandemic such that that the final report is cognizant of the predicaments of States. At the same time, there is an imperative of adhering to the FRBM Act and given the pandemic induced economic setback, it is also timely to deliberate on the future of the FRBM. There are other related issues like what could be learned and unlearned from Kerala's strategy to contain the COVID-19 apart from delving with livelihood strategies and above all the role of media.

By keeping these and other issues in mind, I encouraged GIFT to organise a webinar with the active involvement of the leaders of political parties, finance ministers of states, scholars of eminence, health experts and practitioners and of course the captains of the media. I am extremely happy that the Hon'ble Chief Minister of Kerala, Shri Pinarayi Vijayan, appreciated the need for such a dialogue and readily came to inaugurate the webinar.

Unlike the usual workshops with long presentations by experts, the webinar was organised as a rich dialogue between eminent personalities and specified issues. The collective outcome of the discourse turned out to be incredibly insightful thanks to the vast experience and rich expertise that each of the speakers brought to the table. We have benefitted immensely from this conversation and it provided much confidence in proceeding with Keynesian type interventions to address the pandemic and its fall outs.

I am extremely happy to see that this book has been conceived in an innovative manner by effectively imbibing the form and content of the discourse. I consider it very useful read for those concerned with fiscal federalism in India in general and those interested in the role of the state in confronting challenges like the COVID-19 pandemic.

T.M. Thomas Isaac

Contents

Preface

It was during the last week of March 2020 when the pandemic was sweeping across the country and we were keeping ourselves away from all our friends and colleagues, that our chairman, Professor T M Thomas Isaac called me for a meeting. Professor Isaac suggested that GIFT should consider organising an online seminar on COVID 19 and fiscal federalism. The list of eminent persons whom he suggested was indeed a very long one, including almost all prominent personalities with such expertise. Since Kerala's performance in handling the pandemic was attracting global attention, Prof Isaac also wanted us to invite the Minister for health Smt Shailaja Teacher and the health experts. We were also assured that the Chief Minister, Shri Pinarayi Vijayan, will inaugurate the event. Since the online platforms like WebEx and Zoom were yet to be very popular in those days, I was apprehensive, the Chairman was persuasive and encouraging. Next day, in the Faculty Committee meeting, I put forward the proposal and my colleagues readily took up the challenge. We subscribed to the WebEx platform and our IT team familiarised themselves with its operations.

All the experts whom we invited, that included political leaders, finance ministers of states, scholars of eminence, and media stalwarts responded promptly and positively to our invitation. In fact, it was the first exposure to the WebEx platform not only for us but also to many of the speakers. The online event was highly successful with 55 speakers deliberating on various issues of relevance organised in 10 different sessions spread over two days with over 400 participants who were also actively involved. To the best of our knowledge, this turned out to be the first of its kind large scale online event.

As the online transcription was not available at that time, we had to transcribe the event. Dr Pyaralal Raghavan took up this challenge. The manuscript made it abundantly clear that all the speakers individually and collectively brought to the table immensely insightful ideas. Hence, we thought it should be published. We sent the manuscript to a publisher who politely returned it because the form and content were distinctly different from the usually published books. We had to keep the dream of publishing in the cold storage.

After some time, we revisited the idea of publishing as we felt that the whole manuscript, in the form of a seamless discourse among highly knowledgeable and experienced, contributing towards informed policy making in our country should see the light of the day. Hence, we copy edited it once again and returned to each of the speakers for their approval. Almost all of them, despite their busy schedule, highlighted the relevant part of their contributions. However, some of the contributors, given their other preoccupations, could not return to us. Hence, in this book, you will note that in the case of some of the contributions, it is shown as reported by us on the basis of their presentations.

In accomplishing this task, we have developed a string of indebtedness to a number of persons. To begin with, we acknowledge the patronage and guidance in the whole process received from our Chairman, Prof. T.M. Thomas Isaac. We are happy and feel highly obliged to Shri Pinarayi Vijayan, honourable Chief Minister of Kerala, who inaugurated the webinar. Most importantly, this book would not have been possible without the active involvement and insightful inputs offered by all the eminent personalities. Without naming anyone specifically, we record our sincere appreciation and thanks to all of them. Our IT team led by Sheeja with the support of Shaiju, Abhilash and Varun made the event a reality. My faculty colleagues Anitha, Thomas, Ramalingam, Jenny offered unconditional support as always. The newly joined faculty, Parma, Santosh, Anoop, Kiran, Renjith and Zakaria cheerfully took up the challenge of thoroughly reading through the transcript and checked it with the audio clips. Finally, we thank the Concept Publishing Company Pvt. Ltd. for associating with us in the publication.

We sincerely hope that this unique publication will be a useful read for the policy-makers, academia, journalists and those concerned with the role of institutions and individuals in addressing development challenges.

K.J. Joseph
Pyaralal Raghavan

Section 1

Fiscal Crisis of State Governments

Pinarayi Vijayan

Fiscal federalism in India is at cross-roads. Why do we say so? To briefly explain this, we need to look back at the last three decades of the Indian economy. Since the past two and a half decades, we have witnessed the winds of liberalisation and privatisation flowing in full speed. Many economic activities undertaken by the state have been considered as unnecessary and avoidable. The propaganda was that most of these activities could have been done better outside the government. A natural corollary of this ideology is that governments need not have larger fiscal powers, especially on the taxation front. Tax less and spend less is the philosophy behind reforms in our country, as well as abroad since the 1990s.

In a federal set-up, it meant that the domain of the states has to shrink and uniform fiscal policies are implemented throughout the country. The ideology of economic reforms further shrank the already limited fiscal space of the state. Taxation policies became uniform and spending domain was restricted by requiring the states to pass the Fiscal Responsibility Act. States were compelled to keep fiscal deficit within 3% of their gross state domestic product, through the awards of the successive Finance Commissions since the 11th FC. The

---

Pinarayi Vijayanis an Indian politician who is the current Chief Minister of Kerala, serving since 25 May 2016. A member of the Politburo of the Communist Party of India (Marxist), he is the longest-serving secretary of the Kerala State Committee of the CPI(M) (1998 to 2015). He also served in the government of Kerala as Minister of Electric Power and Co-operatives from 1996 to 1998. Vijayan won a seat in the May 2016 Kerala Legislative Assembly election and was selected as the leader of the Left Democratic Front (LDF) and became the 12th Chief Minister of Kerala.

centre too passed such laws but the targets laid down seldom became a reality.

Under the constitutional division of powers, states have limited revenue raising powers and more expenditure obligations in the social sectors especially in education and health. This created a situation of vertical imbalances, which were sought to be resolved through tax devolution and grant disbursement by the Finance Commission which is a constitutional body. It is this constitutional mechanism that has become the vehicle for monitoring implementation of the Fiscal Responsibility Act by the states, whereas the Centre is free from any such monitoring mechanism. This is not in tune with the structure of cooperative federalism, which conceives the Centre and States as equal partners.

The above process started with the 11th Finance Commission, which imposed conditionalities on states for adhering to fiscal targets. Successive Finance Commissions have continued this. However, the 14th Finance Commission brought about a change by not making any conditionality in its recommendations. But, there are indications that conditionalities may come back if we go by the terms of reference of the 15th Finance Commission. States including Kerala, have submitted a joint memorandum to the Honourable President of India in this regard. We hope that in the forthcoming report of the 15th Finance Commission, there will not be any imposition of conditionalities on the states.

This is not the time for fiscal conservatism. Countries across the world are spending to energise their economies which are afflicted by weak demand and supply side disruptions. We too cannot afford to stand apart. Mechanical deficit and debt targets cannot be the prime aim at this juncture. We have to come out of a big crisis. For this more spending and borrowing are needed. Once the demand and supply side problems abate, we can go out of the debt. This is a fundamental economic principle. Public and private borrowings are not similar. When governments borrow money and spend on physical and social infrastructure, the economy will grow faster.

The saying, "private vice can be a public virtue," has been proved right more than once in history. This is not the time to hesitate. We need to pause rules and raise the borrowing power of states from 3% to 5% of the GSDP. This has been the consistent demand of states like Kerala in the post-pandemic situation. Empowered states, strong Centre and functional local governments are pillars of cooperative federalism. In periods of natural calamities and unprecedented challenges like Covid-19, all these have to act in unison. Kerala has a decentralised governance system which has helped us a lot in our fight to combat Covid-19 and the earlier natural calamities.

The Government of India should move for a paradigm shift in fiscal policy by implementing cooperative federalism in its full spirit. It is unfortunate that it required a pandemic like Covid-19 to make believers of fiscal conservatism rethink their ideas. But better late than never. I hope the discussions here will lead to wider acceptance to the policies, which advocate state intervention in the social sector for a more inclusive development. We need a strong public health care system to guard against the pandemics like Covid-19 and other exigencies. A truly federal structure of governance is the best to meet such challenges. With these introductory remarks, I inaugurate this program.

Thank you

Manpreet Singh Badal

We are in extremely challenging times. We are facing a struggle on two fronts: one is life and the other, livelihood. They appear to be two words but are deeply interconnected.

As a student of history, I perceive this situation as nothing less than a world war. While the earlier world wars were fought by a one dozen or two dozen nations, we now have around 200 nations fighting the pandemic. We are in stage two of the lockdown. In the words of Churchill, one of the greatest wartime leaders, "this is not the end, not even the beginning of the end, it is perhaps the end of the beginning." We are actually meeting in these challenging circumstances when our resources are very strained.

The combined fiscal deficit of the Centre and the states budgeted for the current fiscal year is about 6% of the GDP. It must be noted that even if we don't spend an extra rupee for Covid-19 relief during this year, our fiscal deficit is likely to go up and touch about 10%. Almost all economic activity in the country has come to a complete standstill. In Punjab, I have targeted a 2.9% deficit for the current fiscal year, but my rough calculations indicate that it is likely to go up to almost 6.5% by the year's end.

Manpreet Singh Badal is an Indian politician and leader of the Indian National Congress (INC). He is the Finance Minister of Punjab. He has been a member of Punjab Legislative Assembly five times (1995, 1997, 2002, 2007, 2017), and has been finance minister twice. He has presented the Punjab budget a record nine times — the maximum for any minister in Punjab. He is credited to have stabilised the state finances, and his stint saw an increase (a 30 per cent increase) in Punjab GDP. In 2011, he formed a new political party called People's Party of Punjab and later (2016) merged with INC.

7
Fiscal Crisis of State Governments

In many states, both individuals and entities will not be able to withstand the damage that has already been done. With reputed banks looking for cover, it will be foolish for us to believe that adequate funds will be available for different sectors of the economy. It is not just one or two sectors that are getting affected but several, and we will have to spend some time to put the list together. It includes airlines, hotels, banks, non-banking financial companies (NBFC), mutual funds, oil and gas, start-ups, transportation, real estate, retail and also automobiles. It is believed that about 75% of micro, small and medium enterprises (MSMEs) are actually facing existential crisis.

Funds from the Central Government to the states have been very little so far. All we have got, to date, is largely the freedom to borrow and front load some of the revenue. Punjab has got GST arrears of over Rs 1000 crore now, pending for three years, apart from compensation for shortfalls brought about by the Goods and Services Tax (GST).

I was also hoping for some relaxation of the rigid fiscal deficit targets, but, all these resources are not much when compared to the crisis caused by the pandemic. Today, India requires two different kinds of doctors—medical doctors and also those who can solve the impending economic crisis. I do not know whether such people are readily available in India or have migrated abroad.

Today, the job of a state finance minister is more difficult than that of the health minister. I don't have a vaccine available to prevent a financial crisis, no mask to hide revenue shortfalls, no sanitation for my hands, or mass immunisation, which is the need of the hour. This in short is the backdrop of our gathering here today. We have 90 minutes in this session with 10 minutes for questions and answers. So, let each panellist make introductory remarks for 5-6 minutes and then we shall have more rounds. I first call upon the deputy chief minister of Delhi, Sisodia Saheb.

Manish Sisodia

Delhi is today one of the worst affected cities. The revenue impact of the lockdown has been bad as Delhi is a totally consumption-based economy. In April 2019, we collected Rs 3500 crore as Goods and Services Tax but, during April this year, we were able to collect only Rs 326 crore. We are not covered by the Finance Commission since we are still categorised as a Union Territory in their list. Hence, we can't directly borrow from the market and the Government of India has to borrow for us. We have now written to the Government of India to mobilise some debts.

The situation is so grave that we have no money to pay salaries. I spoke to the Union finance minister too. Delhi has been adversely affected and really needs immediate help. We have no clue if the markets will reopen on May 3. I don't know how this situation can be handled. We are going through very tough times. The Government of India is not allowing us to be categorised as a state under the finance commission. That would have allowed us to participate in discussions and help get more funds.

Manish Sisodia is an Indian politician and Deputy Chief Minister of Government of Delhi since February 2015. He is also an elected (third consecutive term) MLA from Patparganj constituency. In Government of NCT of Delhi, he holds the portfolios of Education, Finance, Excise, Vigilance, Tourism, Land & Building, Art, Culture & Language. Previously, he was a cabinet minister in the Government of NCT of Delhi between December 2013 and February 2014. Prior to active politics, Sisodia was a social activist and journalist. He is a member of the National Executive Committee of the Aam Aadmi Party (AAP), and is also a founding member of the AAP. Sisodia has written a book Shiksha: My Experiments as an Education Minister, has received wide acclaim.

9
Fiscal Crisis of State Governments

Manpreet Singh Badal

This crisis has to be fought not just by the governments but also by the entire people. It is sometimes a crisis like this, which brings out the character of a nation and even that of an individual. The world is grappling with scarce resources and money and given our limitations, India will have to fight with discipline and determination. On a recent visit to my village, someone told me, "Manpreet, you are our finance minister and we sympathise with you, but this battle cannot be won easily. If it were so, Europe, which has no shortage of doctors, Trump with all his finances or the Arabs with their oil wealth, would have easily dealt with the situation." This is indeed unprecedented. There are no easy solutions.

T.M. Thomas Isaac

Please refer to the e-version of the second edition of my book "Challenges to Indian fiscal federalism", which I sent you yesterday. It will provide a backdrop for the issues we are now discussing. Everybody accepts that the Centre has control over most of the revenues. There is a serious mismatch of revenues and expenditure at the state level. My first point is that, over the post-independence period, this mismatch has become more and more acute. Statistics in this direction show that in 1950-51, the pre-devolution gap of states was just 2.41% of the GDP which increased to 10.01% in 2015-16. The post-devolution gap of the states, even after the finance commission devolution, increased from 1.95% in 1950-51 to 6.1% in 2015-16.

From 1991 onwards the realm of Centre-state financial relations has tended to undermine states' rights. There are two major issues to consider. One is the Goods and Services Tax (GST). Unfortunately, the GST has undermined the fiscal space of states. We won't discuss it in detail, as we have discussed it in the GST council several times in the past. Though revenues have not been buoyant,

---

T.M. Thomas Isaac, Minister of Finance and Coir, Government of Kerala has been a member of Kerala Legislative Assembly for 20 years. He held the finance portfolio during 2006 to 2011 as well. He is also the Central Committee Member of Communist Party of India (Marxist). During his tenure as a Member of the Kerala State Planning Board, he spearheaded the People's Plan Campaign. Ph D from JNU (CDS), prior to entering full time politics, he was a Professor at Centre for Development Studies and currently the Distinguished Professor at GIFT and Honorary Fellow at CDS. He is a prolific bilingual on a wide range of economic and social issues, and has a large number of books to his credit published by national and international publishers including Cornell University Press.

we have been reducing rates. The Central Government had said we would be compensated for GST shortfalls. A GST growth rate of 14% was guaranteed, but they have now backtracked. That was a solemn promise. When Haseeb Drabu raised this issue and Manpreet Singh Badal intervened, the Union finance minister, Arun Jaitley had stated that it was not an issue, as the states would be compensated for the shortfalls. He had even said if the compensation fund had no money, it would be borrowed and repayments done by extending the cess for a year or two till the money could be fully recouped. This change of stance to deny the agreed compensation, has been a very serious blow to the right of the states.

The second is the FRBM Act, which has also severely restricted the fiscal domain of states. It was in this situation that the 15th Finance Commission was formed with its terms of reference loaded against the states. For the first time, there was even an attempt to turn back the recommendation of the previous Finance Commission, especially the award of the 42% devolution of the total central tax pool. There was a serious attempt to make transfers to the state more conditional and bring in defence as a third claimant to the Central tax resources. They wanted to indirectly reduce the tax share of states by reducing the shared tax pool, by first deducting the money for defence and internal security from the total Central tax pool even prior to the devolution. This is unconstitutional. This book elaborates on each of these processes.

The first report of the 15th Finance Commission for 2020-21 has almost confirmed our worst fears. For, there are sufficient hints that the full report will consider a review of the FRBM Act to make it more difficult for the states to borrow. They were also going to address the problem of financing defence. We were concerned about this when the pandemic came. The crisis brought out the fragile nature of state finances. All of a sudden, our entire revenue evaporated. Kerala could only collect around Rs 200 crore of revenues a month, instead of Rs 2500 crore that we normally get and Central transfers have also declined. As Manpreet Singh Badal said, the only help that we have received was that we were permitted to front load our borrowings.

Some states like Punjab opted to borrow smaller amounts and were able to get a rate of 7-8%. We in Kerala, were committed to a Rs 20,000 crore package which would enable us to provide income transfer and welfare payments, and hence had to borrow at 9%. This is terrible. Our economy will contract this year. It will lead us to a serious situation, as it is the surest road to a debt trap. This is a very serious situation and this is the background in which we are bringing scholars, academicians, journalists, state finance ministers and others concerned to come together and discuss the impact of the pandemic on state finances. Thank you.

Manpreet Singh Badal

We have to collectively pool in our resources of experience and intellect to tackle the situation.

Haseeb A Drabu

First, a comment starting off from where Isaac left. I think that the federalism battle has changed. For the last 20 years, globalisation, reforms and constitutional changes have shrunk the fiscal space of states, which Isaac referred to. The Centre has been squeezing the states from the top and the panchayats have been nibbling at their heels resulting in the contracting of the fiscal space of states. However, the design or architecture of fiscal federalism in India is not or should not be the real issue today.

The real issue today is how the Centre is using the current pandemic to create a new form of federalism, which I call cannibalistic federalism. We are actually cannibalising the states using the pandemic as a tool for that. Having said that about fiscal federalism, I really want to focus on the kind of situation we are in today because going by the trends we have seen in recent times, we will not be concerned with fiscal federalism or any such thing anymore as we will all be more concerned about our very survival.

The real problem as I see from outside the government today, fortunately, is that we have to do away with binaries. There are three kinds of binaries in the national discourse today. One binary is not about lives versus livelihoods, but

---

Haseeb A Drabu was the finance minister in the state of Jammu & Kashmir and the Former Chairman Jammu & Kashmir Bank. He has also been the economic adviser to the Jammu and Kashmir government between January 2003 and 2008. Haseeb Drabu started his career in 1990 with the Planning Commission of India and then served as consultant to the Economic Advisory Council of the Prime Minister. Drabu was also associated with the Tenth Finance Commission and was a consultant to multilateral organisations like Asian Development Bank. Drabu is a prolific writer contributing regular columns to National and International media.

lives and livelihood as Manpreet Singh Badal said. It is not about Centre versus states. It is about Centre and states and ultimately it is not about lockdown and no lockdown, but of a smart lockdown as referred by the chairman. We have to do away with these three binaries and try to find a way forward by combining these three and find a middle ground.

The fact that it is a global pandemic does not mean that it is a universal phenomenon where there is a one size fits all solution either globally or within the country. There is a local context to it and a major point that emanates from this is that, states have to get the flexibility to manage the problem in terms of managing, policy, operations and also financing as it affects those areas which are in the domain area of the state governments as per the constitution primarily. Take for example, health. It is a state subject. While there can be a guideline or a template at the Central level, for instance on how to standardise a lockdown, at the ground level it has to be left to the individual district magistrates. You will have particular success stories emerge and the district magistrate will have to decide on which model to adopt. It could be a Bhilwara model or something else. Unless this flexibility is provided for, there will be a huge centralization and it will impair the efficacy of how things are handled in the crisis.

Thirdly, today there is a lockdown and people can't go to work. Tomorrow if you lift the lockdown can the people go to work? Will it solve the problem? It will not happen, as there is a massive supply chain disruption. You will have to have this as another aspect of policy. That is, how to restore the supply chain disruption even when there is a lockdown. The lockdown is preventing people from going from one part of the country to another, but there is a much bigger structural problem of a supply chain breakdown.

Finally, even if the supply chain is restored, there is a serious demand problem. For example, agriculture markets have been opened up in some areas like Karnataka or Kashmir, but there is no demand for exports. So, what will you do with the produce? You can't sell those. Thus, there are three layers of constraints that are not being addressed. That is because you are more concerned with the optics of management and not at the substantive parts of management. This will happen only when you give the states more flexibility because they are managing the crisis. In terms of policies, on the basis of these things you can look at a relief policy, a revival policy and a recovery policy.

There has not been much of a relief activity and the policy initiatives are not very grand. Two initiatives come to mind immediately. Instead of starting MGNREGA, which will again cause a health crisis, the best thing would be for some states to convert MGNREGA to a universal basic income scheme by taking the last year's list of users and give out money so that people will have some cash in hand. In today's crisis situation cash is the most critical thing for the state governments, companies and individuals. How will I keep all of them and the economy liquid? When Isaac talks of a cash crisis, he is talking of liquidity management of his own thing.

I heard the chairman talk of raising fiscal deficit. How will the fiscal deficit be financed? Debt markets are looking very bad and the banks are not going to lend. One simple solution that comes to my mind is that the state governments should ask for an automatic increase in ways and means advances from the RBI within a 12 month period. Today, ways and means advances are five times your cash balance converted into 20 times your cash balance. At least you will have a certain liquidity profile within your states.

Secondly, what about doing a complete public expenditure policy restructuring and completely cutting down or stopping capital expenditure works. I would suspend the capital budget completely and divert resources to revenue expenditure, maybe to three important sectors, instead of waiting five years or ten years for the capital expenditure to fructify. Divert money to health and education. You can at least target some priority sectors like health. Both states and the Centre should also do the same.

Another part where I find fiscal federalism has taken a different meaning altogether is how the institutionalised network of panchayats is not being used by the Central Government. It is only about DM and DC. Panchayats are not mentioned anywhere, even though they are in the Disaster Management Act and should be in the forefront of crisis management and democratic response to the crisis. This leads to huge centralization and minimised political engagement in a crisis.

I don't see any talk of panchayats being used in the crisis. The current dispensations seem to think that institutions that have been built in the last 70 years do not matter or are just not there. The states should talk of under leveraging institutions built up over the last 70 years. I would imagine the real crisis is also in some ways about not seeing the totality of the potential of the large institutional network to respond effectively. This is resulting in a very ad hoc, top-down approach to pandemic management driven by brownie points rather than more substantive issues. With this I shall stop.

Manpreet Singh Badal

Haseeb Drabu, it is always enlightening to listen to you. I appreciate your point of under leveraging our institutions. In this crisis there are opportunities. We have to repair our ruptured polity at any cost, as the repercussions will otherwise be disastrous. I now call on Jairam Ramesh to join in.

Jairam Ramesh

To me the one issue that we have to grapple with as we come out of the lockdown progressively, is that the entire fiscal and political architecture is going to be transformed. The last 30 years have seen decentralisation of power to states and also to some extent to panchayats and 'nagarpalikas,' though not as much as envisaged in the 73rd and 74th constitutional amendments. Nevertheless, the movement has been towards political decentralisation along with economic liberalisation. I am afraid that economic liberalisation will not be a causality, but political decentralisation will definitely be a causality.

The clamour for liberalising the environment, land and labour laws will intensify with the pressure to revive the economy, but, the real danger is that we are going back to a Centralised polity mode. All of us and the other finance ministers should really put our heads together. I have always maintained from the beginning that the 15th Finance Commission was a political exercise. It is going to be even more political than before. What really bothers me is that the architecture is going to completely change. The Central Government is going to go back and become all-powerful politically, administratively and fiscally. That is what we should be really bothered about as we collectively move out of the crisis.

Jairam Ramesh, Distinguished Fellow, GIFT, is an Indian economist and politician belonging to Indian National Congress and the Member of Parliament. In July 2011, Jairam Ramesh was elevated to the Union Council of Ministers of India and appointed Minister of Rural Development and additional charge of the Ministry of Drinking Water and Sanitation. He was previously the Minister of State (Independent Charge) at the Ministry of Environment and Forests from May 2009 to July 2011 and the Minister of State for Commerce. Apart from being a regular columnist for Business dailies, he has authored eight books published by leading publishers like Penguin.

I suggest that the states should collectively demand the presentation of a revised budget in mid-July. Clearly, the budget of February 1, has been made completely irrelevant by the events of the last few weeks.

Manpreet Singh Badal

One thing that we can derive from this is that, there is a need for a separate Covid-19 budget or maybe even a new budget for the states. The sanctity of the old budget does not exist any more. Panellists should now contemplate whether it is prudent to raise taxes, when addressing demand is the actual need of the hour. As it is, the Centre now controls GST. So, what is the scope for raising tax on petroleum, real estate, vehicle taxes etc.? What about non-tax revenues? Raising taxes will only aggravate the problem.

Manish Sisodia

The problem is that the taxpayers are also in a very difficult situation. There are no jobs and no profits. Industries and markets are all looking for relief. It will not be possible to raise taxes including oil taxes. Non-tax revenues have its own merits and demerits. We have to now rethink our entire economic framework. You spoke about reworking budgets, but it has to be more than that. A tax increase will not work. It has to be fair. I have no clue how this problem can be solved.

Thomas Isaac

The issue raised by Badalji is very relevant. The budgets of the Centre and the states have been made irrelevant by the changes in the economic situation. Last year, soon after the budget, many important proposals were changed in what many described as mini budgets within weeks. Take the case of the present budget. There was not even a reference to the demand collapse in India and we have to think of bringing in a new budget.

In the new budget the first challenge will be to raise revenues. It is not a good idea to tinker with tax rates. *The Economic Times* and *Business Standard* have carried two reports speculating opposite views about the Central Government raising or reducing taxes. Since raising taxes is not at all an option, what about tax reductions? The Centre has already cut corporate taxes to the tune of Rs 1,75,000 crore with no positive results. Investment has not responded. The only thing is profits have increased, share prices shot up and cash balances increased in the hands of companies. Tax as an instrument to influence the macro-economic situation is not useful now.

How do you then finance expenditure? That is where Haseeb's comments are important. But ways and means advances won't work. That would be inadequate. The Bank of England has allowed unlimited ways and means accommodation to the British Government. The 60% increase allowed now in India is a paltry increase, and it won't help close the gap between revenue and expenditure of state governments. The alternative would then be to increase ways and means. However, even this will not be enough. A probable solution would be to increase fiscal deficit ceiling to 5% and allow states to monetize the debt. According to N K Singh, the present laws don't allow higher deficit. He suggests an escape clause as a solution, which I feel will not work. These are unusual times, and we need to resort to extraordinary actions. Pandemic borrowing, I suggest, should be over and above the 3% fiscal deficit. The RBI should consider opening a new window of opportunity with a pandemic bond.

Monetizing the debt won't result in price increases. The only reason why prices are not crashing is that you are not allowing the reduced international oil prices to be passed on to consumers. You reduce tax on petrol and diesel. There are enough food stocks. Oil prices are low. There are enough foreign exchange resources. So, monetizing of debt will not raise inflation.

I don't understand why nobody in Delhi has protested against India voting against the IMF proposal for issuing 500 billion in SDR. India would have got something like Rs one lakh crore in foreign exchange and this would not even have to be paid back. India should be demanding not 500 billion SDR but a 2 trillion SDR creation by the IMF. I can understand Trump vetoing it, but why should India support it? 102 nations have approached the IMF for emergency aid and 25 poorest countries have already got 0.4 billion dollars. These countries would have got 0.8 billion dollars if the extra 500 billion SDR proposal was accepted, that is double the amount, free without conditions and with minimal interest, say 0.005% or so.

The Indian Government would have to give up the obsession with rules framed in very different times. What is the sanctity of a 3% fiscal deficit? Look at what other countries are doing. So, I am against tinkering with taxes. You have no choice. We can't raise the rates. By now we are quite experienced in GST. Forget taxes for the time being. As it is, no taxes are being collected as no sales are taking place. The only way to finance the budget is to monetize debt. We should take a united stand on it.

Jairam Ramesh

I am so happy. In 1991 it was Jyoti Basu and his colleagues of the ideological brotherhood of Thomas Isaac who were resisting when Manmohan Singh went for an IMF loan. Now in 2020 Isaac has become an advocate of the same.

Thomas Isaac

Let me counter your statement. Stiglitz' book on 'Globalization and its Discontents,' in which he talks about how the IMF managed the third world fiscal crisis in the last decades of the 20th century, is a fine example of how even experts change their stance according to the prevailing situation. Stiglitz has done a complete volte face now and changed his stance under the present circumstances. Even the IMF has been frightened by the pandemic and forced to change its stance. Then why should I stick on to the position I held in 1991?

Manish Sisodia

The Government has been sending out hints of new packages and concessions to different sectors and industries. I have been getting such notifications on my mobile. Apparently, they are experimenting with such ideas.

Haseeb Drabu

This is really the core issue. Since there are friends here, I will tell Isaac that the route you are proposing to take will ensure you are headed towards the declaration of a financial emergency, which will be the end of state finances in totality. So be very careful. It will be the end of fiscal federalism. Let us not push it.

Let us look at separating the issues. There is the short-term current funding problem. I proposed ways and means advances to alleviate the current problem faced by everybody. Funding is different. My WMA suggestion was to resolve the current liquidity problem faced by everybody. I won't think of a separate Covid budget or fresh budget. I will seek solutions from within that which has been approved by the legislature. We can think of reallocations from the current budget. Restructuring budgets without getting into legislative approval, will be enough to take you through the next 6-8 months. Raising issues of monetizing of state debt etc., will have the threat of creating a situation of financial emergency. You can certainly seek a 1% increase in FRBM limits from 3% to 4% or 5%. Do not get into monetizing of state debt which will lead to other problems like funding of fiscal deficit will then arise as a primary issue.

This is a phase for fiscal expansion. There is no space for raising taxes in this phase. There is bound to be a stimulus package, reductions in GST and so on. I am aware that this is happening. The Central Government is seeing this crisis as a two-year phase. Setting up a joint corpus for the Centre and the states is crucial. It will have to be made by leveraging foreign exchange reserves for a three-year period. This will be an alternative to borrowing from the IMF.

At the end of the day there are no free lunches. We can only defer economic liabilities. A two-year lockdown will continue in some form or other. There will be many sectors in distress. You cannot think of raising taxes. It will become a retail crisis. It will have an impact on banks.

My biggest worry really is from now on, we will see the fragility of the economic system and collapse of the banking sector. You have already seen what has happened. Look at the corporates. They are in a mess. Prices of their services have fallen so much. Fiscal expansion is required, increase the FRBM limit from 3% to 4% or to 5%, don't think of a tax raise, don't ask for monetizing state debt and cause fiscal emergency, look at leveraging the foreign exchange reserve to present a package that has a time horizon for three years.

Jairam Ramesh

Do you think that a government that announced demonetization can't go in for declaration of financial emergency?

Haseeb Drabu

That is my biggest worry. The constitutional provisions of financial emergency will ride roughshod over every state government. Isaac should navigate this path very carefully. A financial emergency will signal the end of the story. Try and find a path, which cannot give a reason for financial emergency.

Thomas Isaac

Haseeb is correct. A financial emergency should be avoided by all means. A bad idea, which should be rejected outright. This situation has to be met through mutual consultations with no emergency powers to the Centre.

Manpreet Badal

What about pruning expenditure? Wasteful expenditures can be cut. However, there are limits to doing that. Maximum gain will be some 20%. Some states have cut government salaries. A financial emergency will only allow salary cuts. But there is another view that this can also happen through legislative action. A financial emergency will allow salary cuts through executive action. What is the scope of pruning expenditure, particularly salaries?

Thomas Isaac

We are opposed to salary cuts. So, what Kerala has done is to defer a part of the salary for a brief period. For example, salary for 5 days a month is deferred. The time of repayment will be decided later depending on the situation. This is simply because my revenue, including Central transfers, cannot even meet salary demands. I require Rs 2500 crore for salaries and excluding pensions. My total revenue income including Central transfers is around Rs 2000 crore. Hence the suggestion to defer repayment until a better situation emerges. This is just deferment. The timing of repayment will have to depend on the situation. This could possibly happen by July.

If the pandemic extends for a whole year, this may be prolonged further. What else can one do? It is a bad idea to cut salaries in these times of recession. It will reduce demand. In Kerala, the deferred salary has almost entirely been passed on as income transfer to the people. About 60 lakh families, that is, around 70% of our population, will have income transfers from a minimum of Rs 1000 to Rs 8500. So, the deferred amount is entirely used as an income transfer. I would never argue for salary cuts, but, under these circumstances, there is no other option.

Manpreet Badal

During the American civil war and even the First World War, soldiers were given interest free bonds redeemable after two or three years. Would such bonds be a solution now?

Manish Sisodia

The Central Government has decided to cut DA till July. Are you doing something similar? A government is not only for paying salaries. People expect much more. We will have to have a relook. Everything will have to be put on hold. We will have to do something about salaries. How can we cut welfare funds? The problem is nobody knows how long it will last.

Manpreet Badal

Uttar Pradesh has followed the Government of India. After 29th we will have a clearer picture.

Haseeb Drabu

Manish, don't look for a fresh budget. That will not be in the best interest. I think the basic guiding principle would be to defer payments. It is not a July game. It is certain that the crisis will have at least a two-year frame and recovery will be U-shaped. Freeze the capex budget. It does not matter. Increase transfer payment through welfare schemes. Impound dearness allowances. Make forced savings. Government servants are privileged. They have no loss of income. Make it a forced saving which can be drawn after three years.

The bond idea that Manpreet suggested is not bad. You can look at some non-interest-bearing liability. The RBI does it. You can do it for a period of three years. Legislative powers allow you to do that. Impound the dearness allowances and put it into GP. You will have increased future liabilities. The real part would be deferring interest payments to the Central Government.

You can defer interest payments to banks for six months. I am not sure if RBI moratorium is applicable to states. That needs to be clarified. If it is then it may be even extended up to a year. Make sure that the tenure of the loan is elongated. This will help you to tide over. Finally, cuts in unnecessary expenditure alone will not solve the problems. It will just reduce 5% of the expenditure at the maximum. Just freeze the capex, impound the dearness allowances, defer interest payments and increase income transfers. That should be the strategy of state governments.

Thomas Isaac

I think a simpler way would be to defer dearness allowances or part of salaries and put it into the provident fund. This, I think, will be better than bonds. You can do it with a lock in period of a year or even allow them to borrow. Only people in need will borrow from the provident fund.

Haseeb Drabu

Impound dearness allowances and put it into the provident fund. Then there would not be a defined period. It won't hurt it in the long run. Don't see this as a policy of 'either or'. It is within your powers. Your withdrawals will be staggered over the next 20 years. You create a lot of buffer for yourself.

Manpreet Badal

I would suggest that answers will be given at the end of the day. Let the panellists sum up.

Thomas Isaac

To sum up. Firstly, there is no solution other than the Indian Government or the state government directly borrowing from RBI and raising the ceiling on fiscal deficits. Secondly, GST compensation should be paid. Thirdly, Central devolution is going to decline. So, a special Covid grant should be provided. I am just repeating what the chief minister of Punjab said in his letter to the Prime Minister. These, I think are the three important issues. We can also demand that allocation for public health be dramatically increased. Presently this is only Rs 15,000 crore, of which only half is to be distributed this year. Therefore, there can be some kind of common minimum program. Every state finance minister should write individually to the Centre.

Jairam Ramesh

A fourth point is a ruthless review of capital expenditure. Cutting out a large part of capex will provide immediate relief.

Thomas Isaac

I think in the case of capital expenditure, we are only applying administrative sanctions now and payments will come two or three years later. Right now, your capex is for bills pending on works completed. That has to be paid. No cuts are possible. The sanctions you impose now will create buoyancy.

Haseeb Drabu

This is an important operational issue. There are two parts to your capex. One is the liabilities in your treasury which should be cleared, as it is a good way of actually putting money into business. Failing this, their CC limits with banks will be breached. Therefore, the basic decision should be to increase the flows to business and use this opportunity to clear liabilities.

Freezing capex means that every capex that you do is funded and tied to it is a certain resource, which you can utilize. This does not mean projects should be stopped. Tied to every capex project is a certain funding from NABARD, LIC, REC and the likes. This money can be used for transfer payments. That fund will not be available to you if capex is not done.

Second is an important point you referred to. What will happen in the next few months? Your devolution will drop. You built the budget on the assumption of devolution. According to me, a Covid grant is no solution in my mind. Where will they get the money from? The solution is to seek a minimum guaranteed devolution this year. Once you see the gap, you can think of ways to fund the rest. I believe that the FRBM limit will be raised to 5%. Ensure a minimum guaranteed devolution. The GST council can be used to solve the funding issue. States will have to fund the gaps including non-redeemable non-interest-bearing security from the RBI. So, let us also frame these policies in a doable manner.

Manish Sisodia

It was a very interesting session. Presently we all are clueless about the next course of action. Some solutions have also been suggested. They are very important for us. Thank you very much.

Jairam Ramesh

It is necessary that finance ministers of each state should discuss ideas in detail. We should not wait for the Centre to announce anything.

Section 2

Covid-19 Pandemic: The Context and the Way Forward

Sitaram Yechury

Fiscal federalism in the larger sense has always been a very important and contentious issue. Very often it was an issue on which the opposition had to rally together, demanding it as a prerequisite for better Centre-state relations. Now we are discussing it in the background of this serious pandemic, which has affected the whole world, and we need to take proper steps to contain the pandemic and ensure that people's livelihood is not disrupted beyond repair.

If these have to be fulfilled, the country has to recognize that the state governments which are on the battlefront have to be strengthened. They are on the frontlines. Unless they are strengthened, it is not possible to win the battle. The PM has been meeting the chief ministers. However, only a few CMs can speak. The others are to be spectators. These CMs will articulate the state position. Strengthening the states will require a large dose of financial assistance.

Sitaram Yechury is an Indian politician. He is currently the general secretary, politburo member and Parliamentary group leader of the Communist Party of India (Marxist). He has headed the CPIM's international department and the party used to depute him as fraternal delegate to the party conferences of most socialist countries. He studied B.A. in Economics at the St. Stephen's College, Delhi and M.A. in Economics, from Jawaharlal Nehru University (JNU), achieving first class in both. He joined the JNU for a Ph.D. in Economics, which was aborted with his arrest during The Emergency. He was elected to Rajya Sabha from West Bengal in July 2005. He has made a mark in the Upper House, becoming one of the most prominent voices of opposition. A prolific writer, he has authored many books and writes the fortnightly column *Left Hand Drive* for *Hindustan Times*.

This is inevitable in the present context and the government package of Rs 1.7 lakh crore for the pandemic is less than 1% of the GDP, a pittance. We should immediately increase it up to at least 5%. Many countries have announced such a package, which is 15%, 20% or even 25% of the GDP. We cannot start without at least 5%. Now state finances are down by 80%. There is no money to pay salaries. There is a deduction of one day's salary to the PM cares fund, which provides a lot of incentives. But why is this special trust non-auditable? What is the amount collected till now? What is it going to be used for? It has to be disbursed to the states.

Doctors, health workers are succumbing to the virus. There is a need to increase the testing as we now have one of the lowest levels in the world. I have pointed out in a letter to the Prime Minister, that we are lower than even Pakistan in terms of testing. We have to test, identify and isolate. The Kerala government has done a meticulous job, a tremendous effort in location and isolating hot spots. South Korea, Singapore have done it. You need funds for this. Now the health ministry has put out the results of its survey saying 44% of Indian people have curtailed their food intake. They will push people into malnutrition. It is going to be a serious problem.

Regarding migrant labour, how can you announce a nationwide lockdown with just a 4-hour notice period, without alerting the states beforehand? Now the Centre is asking the states to take care of the migrant workers. States will have to fund this job, which is not their making. You should have allowed them to get back. Indians abroad were brought back with chartered planes. Why not trains and buses for migrant labour? But that was not done.

Survey itself shows that only 31% of migrant workers, except in states like Kerala, are receiving any assistance in terms of money or food. Most are going hungry. Can we afford a situation when there are more non-Covid deaths in the country than Covid deaths? The state governments have to be liberally assisted. Their ways and means of assistance have been increased; but then the states have to pay back.

States are not being paid the GST dues. Such a situation will mean losing the battle against Covid. While funding the states the Central Government should give at least Rs 7500 for next three months, to all workers who lost their jobs. There is large-scale retrenchment. CMIE estimates that nearly 14 crore people lost jobs after the pandemic began. Immediate funds are needed. There should be free distribution of foodgrains. You have 77 million tons of foodgrains in the godown. The grains from the new harvest are coming in. What will you do with the entire stock? Release it free to the states so that people can be fed. If we cannot take care of the people, we are undermining the Covid fight, as malnutrition and fall in immunity levels will only allow the Covid to strike harder.

I suggest and hope that the panellists would enlighten us, that we should immediately on behalf of all states ask the Central Government to transfer the PM cares fund to the states immediately and liberally finance them to procure PPEs for health workers, as well as test kits, and give immediate cash transfers, free supply of food and make arrangements for transportation of migrant workers back home as soon as it can be done. Some relaxations have been given and more can be done.

Eminent panellists will continue with the discussions. In short, the demand should be very clear. Fund the state governments who are on the battlefront very liberally. Their own resources have fallen by nearly 80%. A fiscal package for fighting the Covid should be raised from less than 1% of the GDP now to at least 5% of the GDP to start with, and then allow it to go up to 10%. I would now request Jairam Ramesh to speak.

Jairam Ramesh

You have expanded the scope of the debate but I am going to restrict myself on issues relating to fiscal federalism. You raised larger issues, which Sonia Gandhi has taken up with the Prime Minister regarding providing relief to large sections of society. I am going to keep that aside and focus on fiscal federalism. It is very clear to me that as we emerge progressively out of the lockdown in a graduated manner, the architecture of fiscal federalism will see a radical transformation.

In the last 30 years, the move has been for greater political decentralisation. States have got power from the Centre, but most states were unwilling to carry forward decentralisation to the third tier. Broadly speaking the trend was towards political decentralisation, accompanied by social empowerment and economic liberalisation of the economy. My great fear is that political decentralisation will take a huge knock and the politics of centralisation will become much stronger now. The Centre will become much more pivotal than it ever was in our history. This is the outcome of the impact of the events of the last few weeks. We have to take pre-emptive action as a collective entity.

One of the lessons of the crisis is that political decentralisation works and is preferable to a top-down command and control "talibajao" and "diyajalao" approach. On this, Sitaram, we need really to recognize that fiscal federalism is going to take a knock and we have to be sure that we are in a position to deal with the inevitable clamour and put up an all-out resistance against the movement towards greater centralization of political and financial authority.

Our biggest concern is what should be done in the short term. In the short run, there is absolutely no alternative to increasing the FRBM ceiling and people have speculated about it. The time has come to recognize that without any increase in FRBM ceiling to around 5% immediately, it will not be possible for us to move ahead in a meaningful manner.

The second requirement is a ruthless review of capital expenditure. Isaac points out that capital expenditure is spread over a period of time. There are immediate implications. The February 1st budget has provision for a large capital expenditure, which would fructify in 2020-21. This has to be deferred and substituted by transfer payments to sections of society and devolution to states. The capital expenditure issue has to be dealt with immediately.

Thirdly, I see no alternative to the Government presenting a budget in the month of July, as it was earlier done in 1999, 2014 and 2019 as well. I think the budget of February 2020, was based on extremely fraudulent and unrealistic assumptions, and now it has been made completely irrelevant. That is the reason why I would argue that there has to be a clearer delineation of the budget and its architecture, especially revenue and expenditure in the middle of July, by the Central Government to be followed by the states. I think it is absolutely inevitable.

There was a large number of other issues flagged by state finance ministers. Haseeb wanted minimum guaranteed devolution to the states. I find that an attractive proposition. The devolution shouldn't fall below a minimum level. In any case the legitimate demand of states, like GST compensation must be provided for on time, so that states can deal with this crisis both from a social and economic point of view. I think we can also discuss a large number of other issues, like how to revive the economy, protect livelihoods and migrant labour.

Right now, we are discussing only issues of fiscal federalism, which refers to the Centre, state and 'nagarpalika' relations. We have a tendency to look at it from only a Centre-state perspective. But, we must remember that it also has a state-panchayat-'nagarpalika' perspective. There are two dimensions to the fiscal federalism issue. In the long run this is what really bothers me a lot. Let me share with you another of my concerns. When I look at remedies for economic revival, I find standard remedies that have been there even before. Liberalise land, labour and environment laws. Sitaram, these in your words are standard new neo-liberal orthodoxies. And it seems to me that the clamour for this is going to increase because we need to restore economic growth. So, let us now put land, labour and environment laws on the back burner. These arguments will happen. We shall have to be careful. I disagree with this approach. In many ways I have argued that in 1991 the necessity was that the state had to give way to private enterprise and initiative, but, in 2020 this crisis shows us that the state has to re-enter. A smarter, meaner and a more focused state has to re-enter particularly in areas like health, which has to receive absolute priority. There is no alternative to public investment and expenditure, but, current system of delivery will not deliver goods from enhanced public investment. We have to think about it in the medium term. These are my initial thoughts on the issue of fiscal federalism. I think that we should really be worried that the gains in the last three decades of greater fiscal and administrative and political decentralisation are not lost and frittered away by a Government itching and waiting to centralise political, administrative and financial authority.

Sitaram Yechury

The session is on pandemic and fiscal federalism. We are on the same boat on the larger issue of federalism. You know the position CPM has taken and we have implemented it much before the central law. It goes back to the 1950s. We have debated on federalism and fiscal federalism many times. My focus was in the context of Covid and the way forward.

D. Raja

I broadly agree with the larger issues on which Sitaram and Jairam spoke. Our economy was already sick for some time and it is now facing a new sickness called the Corona pandemic. It is in this context that we discuss the broader questions like fiscal federalism, mass unemployment and so on. This brings us to the question of fiscal federalism. Since our independence, we have kept discussing how adequate devolution of economic and political power can be ensured. Thus, in the present context, it becomes essential to discuss fiscal federalism.

I think there are some fundamental questions. Since 2014 we have seen repeated assaults on federalism in various forms. The dismantling of the Planning Commission and the constitution of the Niti Aayog was a part of such efforts. Now we have the 15th Finance Commission recommendations on how the Centre and states are to share revenues. It is being implemented in the context of the Corona pandemic. The Tamil Nadu government has been asking the centre for more money as the 15th Finance Commission has recommended

---

D. Raja is an Indian politician. He is currently the General Secretary of the Communist Party of India (CPI). He is a two-time Rajya Sabha member from Tamil Nadu and his second term at the Upper House comes to end on 24 July 2022. He started out as a student leader and rose through the ranks to become the CPI's national secretary in 1994. He was the first graduate in a predominantly Dalit village and completed B.Sc and B.Ed. His major works include *Dalit Question: The Way Forward* (2007) and *Marx and Ambedkar: Continuing the Dialogue* (2018)

that Tamil Nadu be given a revenue deficit grant of Rs 4025 crore, but they are not getting it.

Another general point to note is that the Union Government in its budget has allocated only Rs 30,000 crore against the Financial Commission recommendation of a total grant of Rs 74,340 crore as post-devolution revenue deficit grants to the states. That includes all states from Manipur, to Maharashtra and Tamil Nadu to Jammu & Kashmir.

The general tendency today is to centralise everything. Just consider the budgetary allocation on public health. It is not even 2% of the GDP. The CPI has demanded that at least 6% of the GDP be spent on public health. That is not happening. Again, in the context of the pandemic, I should say democracy is also under threat. The Prime Minister announced the lockdown without proper consultation with state governments, or adequate preparedness for such a lockdown. This is what I am questioning. The Centre should not grab all powers and decide everything for the whole country when there are elected state governments to be taken into confidence. They are working on the ground to face the pandemic crisis. That is one point we should try to understand.

Jairam referred to the GST. I was in the joint parliament committee, which discussed GST. Even then I could sense dissent. Just consider what is happening today. Why are state governments complaining that they are not getting their due share? That is an issue we have to discuss. There is a National Disaster Relief Fund. What is this PM Cares Fund? What does it mean and what are the details of its manner of functioning? Does it mean that the PM should decide everything? This is what is undermining the Federal principles of our country.

We all agree that panchayats and municipalities should get adequate funds. But the provision of adequate funds to local bodies would be possible only if states get ample funds from the Centre's pool. But is this happening? These are just some of the issues amongst many, which Sitaram has already pointed out.

Now we are discussing the concerns and threats to federalism in the context of Corona. When we discuss fiscal federalism, it is important that issues relating to the National Disaster Management Authority, Disaster Relief Fund and PM Cares Fund, are all discussed in totality. Then there are also questions about the recommendations of the Finance Commission and why states are not getting their dues. It is necessary to discuss why states should literally beg for their dues from the GST Council. These are certain fundamental questions we need to address. We will have to find solutions as the present system cannot help to address these challenges we face today.

We are not able to discuss the optimal sharing of powers among states and Centre. There is no opportunity to discuss in the absence of a relevant forum. And if you discuss, your patriotism is questioned. If you question the Government your nationalism is questioned. The pandemic has brought new questions, new challenges and more financial difficulties, which will all have to be discussed in the context of fiscal federalism. That needs to be discussed along with what we are going to propose to the Government.

The Government has to give more money for which the government will have to find money and generate revenues. Why should the Government allow corporate houses to have all concessions in the name of revenue forgone? Since the present Government came to office, Rs 7 lakh crore is the revenue forgone. These corporate houses do not share profits. Corporate houses will not share anything.

Unless such issues are taken up, there is no point discussing fiscal federalism and proposing measures for implementation by the Central and state Governments. That is my perception of how these issues should be tackled. We have to know what is happening in the country and take a public position on issues. We will also have to ensure that the Union Government meets its obligations to the states, particularly when the country is facing such a grave crisis. This is what I think we should stress.

Sitaram Yechury

To bring in some perspective, the issues we are discussing include large issues, fundamental issues as well as concrete and immediate issues. As far as large issues are concerned Article 1 says India, that is Bharat, is a Union of states. Without states there is no Union. This is a recognition that is unfortunately weakening in the consciousness of both political leaders and the people. Why is it coming under strain today? Raja is correct. There was a crisis happening even prior to the pandemic. I am sure Jairam, you will agree that we were bordering on a recession before the pandemic hit. It will be worse after the pandemic. The final figures after all the doctoring of GDP might actually show a negative growth rate. If that is the case what will be devolution of resources for the states? Already it is very little and will fall further. We have to think hard about tackling these fundamental issues and chalk out a way forward in these Covid times.

Jairam Ramesh

Sitaram, I agree with you that there was a free fall even before this crisis. Investment was sluggish, six consecutive quarters of GDP growth deceleration, stagnant exports and the atmosphere of fear and harassment and tax terrorism. All these were indicators of the pre-Covid crisis. Now the Prime Minister has a perfect excuse for a negative GDP growth. He says he is helpless. We have to recognize that even before the Covid crisis, devolution to states was far lower than what was promised.

If you look at data for the last three years, even before the Covid crisis, it was not 42% of the total Central taxes as the Prime Minister grandly claimed. It was only 31-32%. Even before the crisis the economy was sputtering and more importantly devolution to states was far lower than what was recommended by 14th Finance Commission and accepted by the Government.

The Covid crisis will accentuate the economic turmoil and distress, and I don't think any section of society is going to be immune to the impact of this economic and financial crisis. Economists will argue and they will continue to argue whether it is going to be a 'V' recovery or 'W' recovery. I think as people in the political arena, our priority should be to identify what short- and medium-term steps can be taken.

I think we should not abdicate all thinking to the Central Government. This Government's policy resorts to announcing first and discussing real issues later. We have to put our heads together and make demands from the Central Government. The reason why GIFT has organised this seminar, is to discuss how we could bring back fiscal capacity of states, which was being eroded even before the Covid pandemic and will now be decimated in the name of the Covid pandemic. That will be the real issue.

Sitaram Yechury

Covid is the mother of all excuses for the Prime Minister right now. As responsible political leaders each one of us has to answer the people. It is not merely accountability or charity, but responsibility. How will we meet the challenge now? I think the current response is completely inadequate. We need to succeed in this battle.

D. Raja

It is the Centre, which is abdicating its economic responsibilities. It wants all political power in its hands. It can announce lockdown or even a financial emergency. The Centre can announce all things, but when it comes to devolution of funds, we cannot avoid questioning the Centre.

States have the responsibility of containing the virus. They have to do everything on the ground. So, what is the role of the Centre? It has very large powers under fiscal federalism, which is why we are asking them for more funds. I raised two issues, namely, the provisions of the National Disaster Relief Fund and now the PM Care Fund. How will the funds be distributed to the states and what has happened to the recommendations of the 15th Finance Commission?

The Centre should act fast and be broad minded enough to share whatever available resources it has with the states. We are now talking of rapid testing and there are reports that the kits are not functioning well. How will we tackle all these issues?

The economy is sinking, but big corporate houses are making money by plundering National resources, as well as labour power. All that the Government is thinking of, is taxing the poor and adding to their burdens. The Government will now have to think innovatively of ways to increase resources. That is what I am pleading for. What are the ways to generate money? We will decide that collectively.

Sitaram Yechury

A 2% tax on the 'super rich' will give much more resources than promised in the current fiscal package that the Government has announced. This is something that everybody is debating in the world today.

Jairam Ramesh

One thing is certain. The neo lib discourse will not change because of the crisis and neither will the discourse of the left. One of the things this crisis has shown, is the complete hollowness of the so-called Gujarat model. If you notice what is happening today, as a student of political economy, both Kerala and Tamil Nadu models have been far more superior both in terms of economic growth and social development. The number of testing done in Gujarat is less than half of Maharashtra and even lower than in Tamil Nadu.

Since you raised the issue of testing, Sitaram, I was told that currently we are conducting approximately 40,000 tests daily and we have the capacity to increase testing by 3 times and to do more than 100,000 tests a day. South Korea has tested around 1% of its population. I was told very reliably that we could easily, with our existing whereabouts, increase our test numbers to 100,000. The question is, why are we not doing it? Is it because the PM is afraid that he won't be able to face the fallout?

Sitaram Yechury

Yesterday ICMR was saying that the kits we have will not last for more than a week. But I will be glad if we have the capacity.

Jairam Ramesh

We are not utilising the capacity of 100000.

Sitaram Yechury

Fewer tests will show that you have contained Covid and hence you become a world leader. Why is Kerala on the front page of *Washington Post*? Why is China, Cuba, Vietnam, South Korea, Singapore or Kerala implementing it more effectively? Give the devil its due.

Why is it not possible elsewhere? That is the larger question. Look at the spread of hate and insecurity that has been growing. Why is that happening? The objective is to replace the Secular Democratic Republic of India with a Hindutva Rashtra, which is a fascist agenda. For that, you need a unitary state structure where the power lies primarily with the Centre.

D. Raja

The Gujarat model has failed in every respect and the Kerala model is being appreciated. The way Kerala has handled migrant workers is also very commendable. However, look at what happened in Surat. That is why we are talking of Kerala. Also, your liberal structure cannot provide solutions to our financial problems and to the pandemic. In the name of democracy, there is an attempt to dismantle it.

Sitaram Yechury

The basic issue all over the world during this pandemic is basic universal public health. Spain has nationalised the health sector and announced a basic minimum income. They have done both.

Jairam Ramesh

In the CMP, in which we were involved in in 1996, the centrality of Government investment in health has been recognized very upfront. The Covid crisis has exposed the class and character of the Indian state and society. We are bringing Indians from abroad, but ignored the domestic migrants. The Prime Minister has talked about students, Indians abroad and others but is not prepared to deal with the problems of migrant labour. That is the single biggest failure of the Indian state as well as Indian society.

Sitaram Yechury

This entire Islam phobia is going to affect federalism. Just consider what will happen in Kerala if you disturb communal amity. That is also a very important aspect. Not a word by the Government or Prime Minister to condemn it. But, can a pandemic be the reason for demonising an entire community? Only a united India and a united people can deal with these issues.

Thomas Isaac

I want to underline a point you raised. If there is anything to take home from Kerala's experience, it is the importance of the public health system. Perhaps even Tamil Nadu has a comparable public health system. Kerala's uniqueness is basically the local governments. I don't want to dilate. There is a talk of a financial emergency in India, which is not just a threat but a real danger. I would like to know the political response. It is a big danger to Indian fiscal federalism.

Jairam Ramesh

This point came up in the previous session. My personal view is that the declaration of financial emergency will be completely detrimental to fiscal federalism. It will destroy the economic power of state governments. For a Prime Minister who can thoughtlessly announce demonetization, announcing financial emergency is not improbable. We have talked of alternatives to meet the contingencies. But under no circumstances should a financial emergency be allowed. It will be detrimental to our interests. This is my personal opinion.

D. Raja

I referred to a financial emergency. If that happens, it will redraw the entire Governmental structure and will be no less than a political emergency. Already across the world, people are attracted to strong men. Modi is called a strong man in India. The very fabric of democracy will be threatened. Saving people and democracy will then become our primary task.

Jairam Ramesh

The Inter-state Migrant Workers Act, which was an important legislation, has got subsumed in the labour court. Considering the plight of migrant workers, it is time we revisited this issue. There should be a strong Inter-state migrant Workers Act, which is not subsumed in any labour court.

D. Raja

Jairam was the pioneer of the MGNREGA to discourage migration from rural to urban areas. Now we are driving away migrant workers from urban areas.

Thomas Isaac

Responding to Jairam, I want to point out that interstate and international migration is in the Central list. Everything is the responsibility of the Centre. Protection, food, accommodation, and transport of these migrants is the responsibility of the Centre, but they have done nothing except saying SDRF can be used for assisting migrants.

Coming to financial emergency, it will institutionalize certain arbitrary trends, which are already visible. The Union Government has unilaterally declared that it cannot give GST compensation. There is a constitutional provision. They are advising states to accept reduced devolution and bringing in a third claimant in the distribution of the Finance Commission award. There are these attempts to scuttle the whole fiscal domain of the states. Any attempts at declaring financial emergency will institutionalize this. This is a major danger arising from this pandemic.

Sitaram Yechury

Financial emergency will usher in a totalitarian regime and end federalism. The resistance to that will have to come from political parties who have state governments. If you can waive loans that have turned into non-performing assets, which amounts to Rs 7.76 lakh crore, you cannot seriously justify any financial emergency. Where is all this money, which should have been collected? Add to this the revenue-forgone numbers, which Raja has pointed out. If you stop crony capitalism, we will have no financial crunch or no dearth of resources in our country. The number of Indian billionaires has increased at the expense of the poor and marginalised. Now, you are only squeezing the poor further.

Just consider the scenario. How many lakhs of children were deprived of their vaccination so crucial for the rest of their life? Women in their postpartum phase are not getting food which is very important for the health of the mother and child. As many as 3.5 lakh diabetics and more than 1 lakh cancer patients have not got the needed attention. You cannot simply blame deaths on comorbidity.

Coming back to financial emergency it is something we will have to resolutely oppose. There is no basis for it. It is an excuse for rolling out an authoritarian system. The *London Observer* recently brought out a feature on countries ruled by Right Wing governments. All these countries are giving out huge bailout packages. It is not financial, it is political. We have to recognize that. Financial emergency is only an excuse to advance a political agenda. It is a real danger, which has to be relentlessly opposed.

D. Raja

I again refer to a financial emergency. It is something that we should oppose strongly. It will redraw the entire political structure. The threat to democracy indeed looms large. The immediate need is that the Centre should give adequate funds to states. In the long term we need not even visit Marxist thought. Let us revisit the economic thoughts of Ambedkar on education, health, employment and housing. All these should be made fundamental rights. How can we do this? That will be the biggest challenge.

Thomas Isaac

I am not going to argue or request for a common minimum program. There are no differences between state governments regarding demands. The common demands are payment of GST compensation, raising the fiscal deficit ceiling and additional grants. I don't think there will be any difference of opinion regarding the income transfer that Comrade Sitaram elaborated on.

It is possible to work out a package for MSMEs and farmers. It is important that opposition parties bring out a program on how to meet the challenge, and not leave it to the Central Government's thinking, which makes no economic sense at all. It is important that a program on what is to be done during the pandemic be put forward, so that it will not lead to ad hoc decisions and declarations. Why are political parties hesitating to do that?

Sitaram Yechury

There are limits. You are absolutely right. Political parties will have to put their heads together and decide. The Left has always been making a case for it. We are now saying that all committed people should move jointly. I wish many more finance ministers had participated, even in this Webinar. What Isaac said is right. They have independently written about the same things that we are talking about now. That will happen only if the political leadership comes forward.

As the biggest opposition party, the Congress could take the lead in bringing together all political leaders who are committed to the Constitutional order and welfare of the people. A discussion among opposition parties is absolutely necessary for which, the political leadership will have to give direction. Unless they do it, their state governments will not respond. That is what seems to be happening now. That needs to be corrected immediately. I wonder what Jairam thinks about it.

Jairam Ramesh

I agree with you. An initiative of like-minded parties should happen. The points that Thomas Isaac is talking about, will have support from across the spectrum. Finance ministers of West Bengal, Telangana, Andhra Pradesh and Bihar should all agree. The common program should have section on both what should be done, and also on what should not be done. In the section on what should not be done there must be a demand against any declaration of financial emergency.

Sitaram Yechury

Would you agree on a Constitutional amendment to remove the Constitutional provision for declaring any financial emergency?

Jairam Ramesh

We should seriously consider it. Thomas Isaac and his colleagues should bring you to parliament so that you can pilot the bill.

Thomas Isaac

The threat is very real. A statement by the political leadership in India on this danger, as well as other things on which we agree about, is most relevant. Even BJP leaders like Sushil Kumar Modiji have distributed a note in the GST council. Do not allow these things to drift.

Sitaram Yechury

Many finance ministers agree in private on what you are saying. Jairam, we will have to take it up seriously. There is no point right now in petty quarrels. They will continue. That is the strength of democracy. There are always much larger issues. If the country is not safe, you and I will not be safe. I would appeal to the Congress party to understand this and come on board to meet the challenge we are now facing. That is important.

Jairam Ramesh

In addition to states interacting among themselves, Central Government political parties who are concerned about the future and redrawing the architecture of Indian polity, both from a fiscal and administrative point of view, must also get together.

The threat to fiscal federalism is not purely an economic threat, but a political threat, and as important political parties, we must all be concerned. A dialogue must take place now. I hope I am here as a scholar, not as a politician. You should take this forward.

Sitaram Yechury

I will make the effort. I require help from all of you for a joint effort.

D. Raja

We all should oppose fiscal threats and discuss ways of generating revenue in the coming days, purely in the interests of the country and its future.

Sitaram Yechury

Since the session has titled the way forward, I notice that there is an agreement on at least 3 issues which could definitely be the way forward. These refer to paying the GST dues, increasing borrowing limits of states to meet the crisis, release funds to the states to meet the challenge and ensuring that the huge amount in the PM Cares Fund also gets transferred to the state governments.

Another issue on which there is general agreement is that financial emergency is something we have to resolutely oppose. Finally, let us make efforts to get together to ensure that we beat the pandemic and resolve the problems from which our brethren are suffering, and further strengthen and safeguard existing Constitutional order from greater assaults.

Jairam Ramesh

It is not necessary to declare a financial emergency. This Government has even now taken on powers without declaring a financial emergency. It is far more dangerous. An undeclared financial emergency is far more dangerous than a declared financial emergency.

Sitaram Yechury

Anyway, let us all persuade political parties who are willing to come together on these issues. Financial emergency empowers the Executive and as Jairam said, you can do it even without declaring financial emergency. But,we have to immediately highlight these three points as I mentioned before, namely, ensure GST payments, increase borrowing limits, provide liberal finance to states and fight against usurping their financial authority. Let us all try to take the movement forward on these bases and try to fulfil the process together.

Section 3

Covid -19 Pandemic and the First Report of the 15th Finance Commission

M. Govinda Rao

The Union Finance Minister tabled the first report of the Fifteenth Finance Commission on February 1, 2019, covering the recommendations for the year 2020-21. Although the initial terms of reference (TOR) issued in the Presidential Order required the Commission to cover the period 2020-21 to 2024-25, the later developments resulted in the revised Presidential Order requiring the Commission to submit two reports – one for the year 2020-21 and the second from 2021-22 to 2024-25. The abolition of Statehood to Jammu and Kashmir and a sharp decline in the growth of nominal GDP posed difficulties in the projections of revenues and expenditures of the Union and the States

---

M. Govinda Rao, Distinguished Fellow, GIFT, is a former member of the 14th Finance Commission and Non-resident Senior Fellow, NCAER. He was the Director of the National Institute of Public Finance and Policy and Institute for Social and Economic Change. Currently, he is a Counsellor to the Takshashila Institution and the *Chief Editor* of bi-monthly public finance journal *Indian Public Policy Review*. He was a Member of the Economic Advisory Council to the Prime Minister of India; a Member of Financial Sector Legislative Reforms Commission and High-Level Expert Committee on Universalising Healthcare, Member, High-Level Expert Committee on Efficient Management of Public Expenditure, Advisory Group of Eminent Persons to advise the Finance Minister on G-20 matters. His past advisory roles include Chairman of the Committee for the Implementation of Value Added Tax and Chairman, Expert Group on Taxation of Services. He is a Member, Board of Governors in Institute of Economic Growth, Institute for Social and Economic Change and Madras School of Economics. Dr Rao's research interests include fiscal decentralization and federalism, state and local finances, tax policy and reforms, public expenditure management.

required normalisation, and hence, it was decided to give the Commission more time to make recommendations for the medium term of five years. Moreover, the goods and services tax (GST), a major consumption tax reform, is yet to be firmly settled and giving more time to the Commission would help in making more realistic projections.

There were apprehensions that the Commission may change the approach and methodology particularly as the TOR had indicated, "The Commission may also examine whether revenue deficit grants be provided at all". However, the Commission did well to allay the apprehensions on this and continued with the approach and methodology adopted by the previous commission. After projecting revenues and revenue expenditures of the Union and individual States, it has applied selective norms and recommended revenue deficit grants for the States with post-devolution gaps. Even on tax devolution, the recommendations mark continuity as one percent lower than that was recommended by the Fourteenth Commission was attributed to Jammu and Kashmir becoming a Union Territory. However, the report has cautioned, "Our recommendation in the final report would undergo changes and adjustments as appropriate, in the light of subsequent data and analysis".

The shares of individual States, however, undergo changes due to change in the distribution formula and changes in the values of the variables used in the formula. On the much debated issue of using population of 2011 for distribution, the Commission has also given 12.5 per cent weight for demographic change which essentially is a change in fertility. A small weight has been assigned to tax effort, which is not likely to make much difference.

The comparative picture from the previous Commission's recommendations on the shares of different stats shows that the biggest loser is Karnataka followed by Uttar Pradesh, Kerala, Telengana and Andhra Pradesh. Kerala and Andhra Pradesh have post devolution gaps and hence qualify for revenue gap grants. The major reason for Karnataka and Kerala losing on devolution is that their per capita income has grown faster than most other states. In the case of Karnataka and Telengana, as the projected transfer (devolution and revenue-gap grants) in 2020-21 was lower than in 2019-20, the Commission recommended a special grant of Rs. 5495 crore and Rs. 723 crore respectively. However, the government has not accepted this and has asked the Commission to reconsider it stating that it introduces a new principle which is a little unusual as generally, there is a tradition of accepting the recommendations made on Article 275 of the Constitution.

For 2020-21, the Commission has recommended Rs. 7735 crore for improving nutrition based grants for the number of children in the 0-6 age group and a number of lactating mothers. It has also proposed to recommend sectoral grants for police training, modernisation, and housing, railways to meet additional funding of projects taken on cost sharing basis with states, maintenance of PMGSY roads, strengthening the judicial system, and improving the statistical system. The important challenge will be to design and dovetail all these sectoral and performance grants with the existing plethora of Centrally Sponsored Schemes.

On the whole, the Finance Commission has done a reasonable job and the report itself was not too disadvantageous to the States. However, the events subsequent to the presentation of the report have presented a very different picture of state finances. The budget estimate of tax revenue of the Union Government is much lower than the Finance Commission's estimate. Therefore, the States are likely to receive much lower revenues by way of tax devolution.

With these opening remarks let me invite Prof Abhijit Sen.

Abhijit Sen

There are a number of takeaways from the morning sessions. The first obvious takeaway is that the pandemic has thrown public finances in turmoil and we don't know where we are heading. As a corollary from this, there might be an argument to redo budgets of the Centre and the states. It is most likely that the Finance Commission's term also would be probably extended, given the context we are in.

This particular webinar and the way we are conducting is because of the pandemic. The first thing is, I would like everyone to acknowledge the impact. Somehow, we have converted a pandemic into a sort of scare that people are too scared to even think what would happen. And, there is really, as Haseeb said in the morning, no trade-off between life and livelihood. We should move forward with both the issues in mind.

In this context the first thing we should, as a group, agree is that these lockdowns, which have come at a huge economic cost, are not going to hurt Covid. All it will do is to flatten the curve, and in certain cases that flattening

---

Abhijit Sen, a former Professor at Jawaharlal Nehru University (JNU) and a former member of the Planning Commission (disbanded), Government of India. He has a PhD in Economics from the University of Cambridge. Before joining JNU in 1985, he held various teaching positions at the Universities of Sussex, Cambridge, Oxford, and Essex. He has served on the Senate or Executive Council of several academic institutions such as IIT Delhi and Universities of Allahabad and Delhi and was involved with several official policy-making bodies in India between 1997 and 2012. He also consulted many international organisations, including UNDP, ILO and UNU-WIDER. Prof. Sen has been awarded the Padma Bhushan, recognizing his distinguished service in Public Affairs in 2010

will hold the burden on the health infrastructure, within tolerable limits. In certain cases, like Kerala, the peak has been reached and active cases are coming down. States like Tamil Nadu and even Chhattisgarh and certain other states are coming fairly close to it, whereas, there are others who are far from it.

States will have to handle this situation differently. It brings back an important message from the morning, which is that the states should have the space to do what they have to do, as far as the epidemic is considered. The Centre's role should be restricted to things like international travel, those that involve spill over from one state to another and those other aspects, which is not an institutional responsibility of the states. It is the only way of dealing with Covid. That message has to be emphasised.

A number of panellists in the morning warned that the situation might possibly cause the declaration of a financial emergency. Having said that, I think it is important to recognize some dimensions of this situation. The longer we have this lockout, the costs of the lockout are also going to mount at a frightening rate. We already heard at least three finance ministers in the morning talking of the level to which state revenues have fallen and what has to be done. We also had some discussion on what to do in case of expenditure and in terms of the Reserve Bank of India stepping in.

In the long run of course, the issues would have to come back to Centre-states relations and the Finance Commission in particular. These issues will remain important at least in the short run, and it is for the Finance Commission to deal with this. I think something must be done for the states, whether it is in terms of RBI ways and means advances, or a substantial increase in the FRBM limits.

The minimum number that was thrown around was on an increase in the fiscal deficit of the states from 3% to around 6% of the GDP. As far as the longer run is concerned, an important issue that emerges is that in areas such as health, the disaster relief mechanism is simply not big enough, or not designed well enough to deal with major setbacks.

Secondly, I think as a number of speakers pointed out in the morning, the states themselves have done very little to ensure that the benefits of the decentralisation go down to the panchayat level, which is where finally beyond the ventilators of the ICU, the whole problem will have to be dealt with. Kerala is an example. These are my thoughts in this first round.

Sudipto Mundle

It is appropriate that Kerala has taken the initiative in holding this conference, given that it is leading the pack with its achievements on the Covid front. I have to say that even at the National level though the pandemic is still spreading, the curve has been flattening in terms of the number of deaths nationwide. There is some light at the end of the tunnel.

Of course, the lockdown could have been handled much better. It should not have led us to the terrible humanitarian disaster that these measures caused on the people at large, especially the daily wage and migrant workers. We are therefore facing three crises—the pandemic, the humanitarian crisis and the economic crisis. There is no question that the main action has to be taken by the state governments. The centre can only play a supportive role. The frontline action has to be taken by the states.

Let me focus on the specifics of the first report of the fifteenth Finance Commission. I have to say the first report is pretty much on the same lines as

---

Sudipto Mundle, Distinguished Professor NCAER, is also an Emeritus Professor, NIPFP and Chairman of CDS Governing body. He is also the Member of the Governing body of the National Institute of Public Finance and Policy (NIPFP), New Delhi. He has served as a member of the Fourteenth Finance Commission, constituted by the Government of India. Before this, he has also served as the Acting Chairman of the National Statistical Commission, Government of India; Member of the Monetary Policy Advisory Committee of the Reserve Bank of India (RBI); Member of the Board of Governors of the Institute of Economic Growth, New Delhi; and Chairman of the Research Advisory Committee of RIS, a think tank of the Ministry of External Affairs. He has also been a part of two steering committees of the Planning Commission for the 12th Five Year Plan. His research areas include macroeconomic policy modelling and rating the governance performance of Indian states.

the 14th Finance Commission. It is funny because the 15th Finance Commission had been asked to review the award of the 14th Finance Commission. It has mostly supported the 14th Finance Commission report. Of course, there are some differences. There is a one percent reduction in devolution to 41%, because Jammu and Kashmir and Ladakh have been taken away from the states and their funds have to now come through the Central budget.

As far as the devolution formulae is concerned, they are pretty similar on most counts. They had forest, floods and ecology, while we had forests in the 14th Finance Commission. The population part was split up into two in the earlier report, now there is one. The main difference is the 5% reduction in the income distance component from 50% to 45% now and the 5% difference is now reallocated to tax effort, forest and ecology.

If you actually come up to the final devolution allocation to the states, we find that the differences are really marginal. The main big change is in the case of a few states. Kerala has the largest difference, with its share going down by more than 0.5%, and the biggest gainer is Maharashtra whose share has gone up by 0.69%. Barring that the allocations have been similar.

As Dr Abhijit Sen mentioned that the award of the first report and the budget of state and Central government has completely gone out of whack. They have become completely outdated, because of the economic shock. As pointed out, the taxes of states like Kerala, Punjab and others have gone down by 90%. Also, the NCAER estimates for the country as a whole show that first quarter revenue will come down by 33% and it will be down by 15% for the year as a whole. These are all just guess estimates. What do you do in response? Clearly the budgets need to be reworked.

As Haseeb pointed out, there is a possibility of the government declaring a financial emergency. But I don't think that is needed. We have had plenty of interim budgets and budgets have been revised in the past. I don't know why that can't be done now. The Centre and states can have revised budgets. This is also applicable to the Finance Commission. The first report of the 15th Finance Commission has also to be revised. All that has to be done is that the President makes a request to the Finance Commission to have a second look, given the changed circumstances.

The question is how much is at stake and what do we need to do. Overall, in the macroeconomic sense, the West Bengal chief minister has talked about increasing public expenditure by 6% of the GDP to take care of the humanitarian crisis. Other experts and I have called for a 5% increase in allocations for both the Centre and the states. How do we finance it and how will the centre support the effort?

Obviously, this cannot be down through tax mobilisation as tax collections are already down substantially. An increase in tax rates will have a disturbing effect and even a negative impact from a macro point of view. By the same token, the increase in expenditure will be a big fiscal stimulus in itself. There can be some reallocation of unwarranted subsidies and capital expenditure. But, none of this will be ultimately adequate enough for raising 5% of the GDP. Then the ways and means advances can be increased up to a point. But ultimately it will have to be a question of additional borrowing and it will have to be in the terms of reference of the 15th Finance Commission. The existing FRBM limits have to go and the escape clause is not enough for meeting the needs of the Centre and the states. Ultimately it is a question of additional borrowing.

Where do we borrow? Some have called for direct monetization. That will be my last point. Macroeconomically, it makes no difference if the Reserve Bank India picks up public debt in the primary market or the secondary market.

Technically, it is only direct primary market buying which is monetization. Politically, it makes a very big difference. That is why Rangarajan did not want direct buying of Government securities by the Reserve Bank of India. Now, Rangarajan is saying that it may not be avoidable. He said that he could be quoted. It is not the first best solution. Commercial banks need to first pick up debt to the maximum possible. But, they have to lend to corporates, SMEs and others. Ultimately, as a last resort, the Reserve Bank of India may have to come in as a buyer and pick up 1% or 2% of the GDP, but not the whole. Let me stop my initial remarks.

Govinda Rao

The biggest loser of the 15th Finance Commission has been Karnataka. That is why they got a special grant of Rs 1900 crore.

Now let us have Rajesh Kumar Singh

Rajesh Kumar Singh

From the administrative side as finance secretary, Kerala, I would like to touch upon some bottom-line issues. The pandemic has led to a fall in revenue and also led to an additional burden on the state in form of additional health expenditure, and expenditure on various social security measures. We had to ensure minimum cash payment and food supplies to strengthen social security measures and protect lives. The only way to sustain the social security net, was to ensure a minimum cash payment to vulnerable sections and free food supply. The only option was to front load our borrowings at a high cost to ourselves.

On the vertical and horizontal devolution, Kerala's perspective is as follows. The reduction of vertical devolution from 42% to 41% is perfectly understandable, given that Jammu and Kashmir has been taken off from the state list and listed as Union territory. The issue we have is that, the Government of India has been increasing additional excise duty on oil and road cess and pre-empting the states from getting the benefits of the fall in oil prices. We have

---

Rajesh Kumar Singh, is the Additional Chief Secretary (finance), Government of Kerala. He is a 1989 Kerala cadre Indian Administrative Service Officer. Before this, he worked as the Additional Secretary under the Ministry of Consumer Affairs, Food Public Distribution, Government of India. He has also worked as the Chief Vigilance Officer of Food Corporation of India in the same Ministry and as a Joint Secretary-level official in various ministries such as the Ministry of Agriculture Farmers Welfare, Petroleum Natural Gas and Information Broadcasting since 2012, returned to the parent cadre after completing the tenure. Mr Singh, a native of Bihar, had earlier served as the District Collector of Malappuram, Commissioner of Commercial Taxes, Special officer of NORKA, Secretary of Ports and Local Self Government Departments in Kerala and as the Additional Director of Kerala Tourism Department.

only a share of the basic excise duty. This reduces the room for manoeuvre to state governments.

We can't increase the VAT rate, as it will increase the oil retail prices and we will be blamed by the consumers. The international oil prices and the prices of India's oil import basket have fallen by 52%, and the Government passed only 5% to the consumer. The rest is pocketed by the Government. So, the 41% vertical division is not strictly true, but a bit of a myth. If the 15th Finance Commission creates a cess for defence expenditure as feared, our vertical division share will plummet further.

Regarding horizontal division, we have problems with the use of the 2011 population census data. We suggested that 2011 population be weighted at 30%, demographic performance at 30%, income distance 20%, area and environment 10% each. They went along with the trend in the previous Finance Commission recommendations, and weighted 45% for per capita income distance. Kerala, because of our reasonable per capita income growth, ended up with a 0.6% share which hit us most. That is why our share in the horizontal division has come down from 2.45% to only 1.94% at present. There is nothing we can do about it.

We recommend that the criteria be nuanced a bit, and the tax performance criteria dropped, as it is no longer relevant in the context of GST. We have requested that the population criteria be enhanced by factors like the age composition and urbanisation share, which are heavier burdens on the state governments. We have also suggested that demographic performance and forest cover weightage be increased.

Nothing can be done about the debt ceiling, with no revenues coming in. We have requested for raising the debt ceiling from 3% to 4% of the GDP. In March, the debt went above the FRBM ceiling. The Centre then sanctioned something extra, and allowed a deviation from the FRBM ceiling, primarily because they did not pass us the compensation funds on GST shortfalls. Unless the economy is quickly revived, we will remain dependent on debt. The Centre will have to exercise more flexibility on the debt ceiling side.

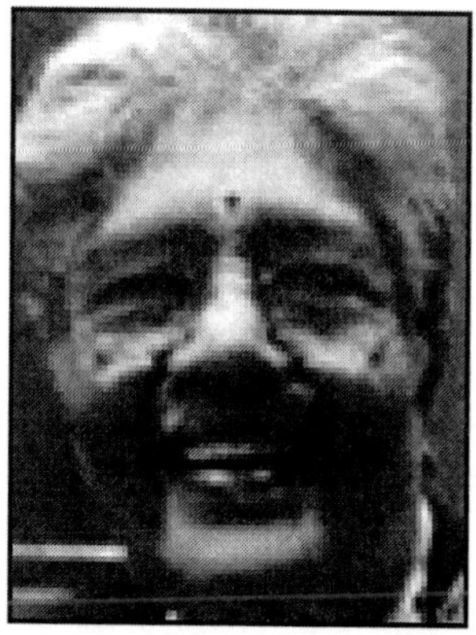

Geeta Gouri

I shall speak about a topic that I am comfortable with, namely the Regulatory Commissions, particularly in the electricity sector. I am not going to say something very specific to Kerala, but rather about redesigning the state's financial concerns. Considering what happened in the electricity sector, the 15th Finance Commission report had a huge section on electricity. In the electricity sector, the present model we follow is mainly focused on subsidy and cross-subsidy. The interesting thing is that the load curve has flattened. This is because a lot of industries have either left because of the lockdown, or because of captive generation of their own. The load curve has also flattened because of a new phenomenon or paradigm that has come in, namely decentralised energy.

This decentralised energy is something very important because almost every household will become a generating and consuming centre. Taking these two into account, I think we may have to start redesigning the entire model. So that

---

Geeta Gouri, has been Member (Commissioner), Competition Commission of India (2009 2014) prior to which she was Director (Tariffs), Andhra Pradesh Electricity Regulatory Commission (1999-2009). Her regulatory experience of 15 years in these two Commissions at their formative stages shaped her perceptive insights into regulatory activities. She has authored and edited several books on wide ranging subjects: Pricing for Welfare: Petroleum Products in India; Privatisation and Public Enterprises: The Asia-Pacific Experience; Efficiency through Competition in Public Utilities - Policies for Restructuring. Some of her recent papers have appeared in *Review of Industrial Organization* (June 2018); *The Criterion Journal of Innovation* (Vol 2, 2017); *Concurrence Review 2015*. Her book *A Commissioner's Primer to Economics of Competition Law in India*, published by Palgrave Macmillan's, Springer Nature, Singapore, is to be shortly released.

is what happens when we have decentralised energy and solar energy competing with thermal energy, especially power from coal. Maybe it is important to try and get back into the sector by saying we are going to cover only the fixed costs and need not include the variable cost. This could be a drastic situation. I am talking of the post-Covid scenario, because electricity also has a major role to play. We have to also pay attention to the decentralisation taking place in the agricultural sector, particularly in areas where there are plantations. For example, there could be more definite changes in fruit growing areas in Andhra Pradesh. Maharashtra has made important changes because they have transformers in each of the centres. Given the fact that we have very limited time and looking at the different paradigms that are coming to, perhaps the state sector must get more funding from the Centre, which is very unlikely. The three sectors namely health, electricity and education are all in the concurrent list. There has to be a redesign in terms of how they can manage on their own, and become more self-sufficient than relying on subsidies. We have so many of these UDAY schemes, and there has to be a rethink of Regulatory Commissions and their roles. We also have to think whether we can redesign and unbundle the power sector and thereby look at it differently. I will stop here.

R. Mohan

The first report of the 15th Finance Commission had come before the outbreak of the pandemic. So, the revenue and expenditure projections made by the states as well as the Centre were much before the pandemic situation. The panellists have stated that they have become irrelevant today.

Now the question that we are faced with is whether the 15th Finance Commission should get more time than October 2020, to submit its report. In all fairness, it is my personal opinion that the states and Centre should get an opportunity to reassess their revenue and expenditure pattern and so some more time should be given to the Finance Commission also, to look at the whole gamut of issues. Thereby, extra time given to the Finance Commission for submitting its report for the period 2021-22 to 2025-26 will be in order.

There is also a need to have a total relook at the FRBM fixation, which successive Finance Commissions since the 11th one have been having. The approach of the14th Finance Commission was a welcome change. States should not be compelled to adhere to FRBM targets like 3% of GSDP, which

---

R. Mohan is currently an Honorary Fellow in Gulati Institute of Finance and Taxation (GIFT), Visiting Fellow at the Centre for Development Studies (CDS) and an officer on special duty at the office of the Chief Minister, Government of Kerala. He is the former private secretary to Chief Minister of Kerala and was a member of the Kerala Public Expenditure Review Committee. Mohan took voluntary retirement from his position as Commissioner of Income Tax (Appeals) in 2016. He also had worked with the Reserve Bank of India before joining the Indian Revenue Service. He is the author of several research papers in the area of public finance.

is totally unrealistic in the post-pandemic situation. The whole philosophy behind the FRBM Act has come into question because the state withdrawal from social sectors has had a cataclysmic consequence in each and every country across the globe. This has to be factored in, and the framework of the FRBM review committee should no longer haunt the impending report of the Finance Commission.

This is the first and foremost plea. Now the demand and supply side deceptions have come in a big way. For a state like Kerala, the consequences are going to last much longer because Kerala is a remittance dependent state and almost 40-50% of its GSDP comes from remittances, mostly from the Gulf Cooperation Region Countries. Not only are those remittances going to ebb, but the state is going to face a huge financial obligation towards the reverse and return migration, which is going to be a reality from the month of May.

Another question that comes to my mind is that some people have pleaded for a revision of the first report of the 15th Finance Commission. I don't think that will be in order because the Finance Commission's first report has settled much of the dust and din that the terms of reference had raised. These terms of reference were haunting state finances, and there is much peace after the first report has come in. Some states have lost. Of course, there is no doubt that they need to be compensated, but the Finance Commission's attempt to compensate was throttled by the Union Government in the Action Taken Report, as a result of which Karnataka and some other states lost out.

Now there is a miscellaneous financial provision in the constitution under Article 282, which has been elaborately debated by Professor Rao and others in the 9th Finance Commission. My question is whether that should be used at this hour by the Central Government. Not in a whimsical or capricious way, but taking into confidence every state, discussing with them and forming an objective criterion for disbursing grants post-Covid. Of course, Central Finances are also not in a good shape. So, Article 282A, which is being used in routine manner, is an article, which has to be used in a situation like this. Can we use it objectively and in all fairness? That is another question that comes to my mind now. Thirdly, the issue of finance raised by the Government of Kerala, is a matter to be looked into. The surcharges and cesses have become a routine and they eat into the devolution granted by the Finance Commission. The 14th Finance Commission's increase of the tax share from 32% to 42% was a steep increase. I am not going into the arithmetics, but the surcharges and cesses have gone up to such an extent that it is in fact eating into the higher devolution recommended by the Finance Commission.

Petroleum prices have also arbitrarily been kept entirely for the Centre, because basic duties have been left untouched and only additional excise duties have been increased. Surcharges have become a way of revenue raising resources for the Centre. In the post-pandemic situation, the Centre should think of sharing this with the states through some mechanism at least for a year, because it is not currently permissible. The last point I want to make is that cooperative federalism in its form and content requires equal treatment given to Centre and states. Kerala has a CMDRF like every state. That is a liquidity cushion when our revenues dry up during natural calamities and pandemic situations like this or when our expenditure burden rise.

Now the Ministry of Corporate Affairs in their clarification, has said that it treats the PM Cares and PM National Relief Fund on a different plane than the CMs distress relief fund. The Chief Minister's fund is not eligible to be counted as part of the 2% CSR mandated by the Companies Act. This is not in the true spirit of cooperative federalism and it doesn't even confirm the basic tenet of federalism. These things should not come in the way at least in the post-pandemic situation. Thank you.

Pinaki Chakraborty

Thank you; I will just speak about some of the issues that the 15th Finance Commission may have to field, given the kind of revenue shortfall and expenditure increase happening. There is serious economic concern that has already emerged and needs immediate response. Economic responses have been quick to build on the initial advantage that India has gained, in the last 5 weeks in controlling the spread of the pandemic. These responses in my view should have three components for which we should go back to the Finance Commission.

I think we need to discuss immediate, short-term, medium and long-term responses. The immediate response should focus on the unprecedented hardships the lockdown has brought on the people in various sectors of the economy, especially informal sector workers, migrant workers, women and children.

Pinaki Chaktraborthy was formerly the Director of National Institute for Public Finance and Policy(NIPFP), New Delhi and currently Advisor to ADB. He served as chief economic adviser to the 14th Finance Commission of India from May 2013 to December 2014. He is also a research affiliate at the Levy Economics Institute of Bard College, New York. Chaktraborthy has worked with the United Nations Development Programme (UNDP) – Nigeria and UNDP–Kenya. He has more than 15 years of research experience in the areas of public finance. He has also served on the advisory committees of universities and as a member of research institutions in India and abroad. Chakraborty has held visiting faculty appointments at the University of Ottawa and University of Carleton, and at the Centre for Development Studies, the Indira Gandhi Institute for Development Research, Mumbai.

These responses should be based on three pillars namely livelihood, lives and mobility. Both Union and state governments should focus on strengthening these three pillars simultaneously. The short-term measures should try and bring back normalcy that predates the lockdown. The medium-term measures should include a comprehensive response package, to bring the economy back on track, while long-term measures should be taken for the revival of growth and a sustainable fiscal and monetary stability.

Look at the constitutional assignment and the fiscal resources. Health, as all of us know, is a State Government subject. Health expenditure is around 1.2% of the GDP and 90% of this is spent by the states. The states have to provide Covid-related health expenditure for a sustained period of time and they will certainly require additional resources for such expenditure. If such resources are not provided for, regular health sector priorities will suffer, resulting in a decline both in the quantity and quality of non-regular health services. In other words, the health budget at the state level has to increase significantly to deal with the pandemic and sustain the existing level of medical services. That debate is for the moment, unfortunately missing.

The second issue is providing a livelihood response. This requires significant front loading of expenditure as Kerala has done and increasing the existing level of social protection expenditure. In other words, what is budgeted for 2020-21 will require a significant step up that includes health expenditure. It was argued that a new budget should be presented by both Centre and states. I think a financial emergency is not something that we would like to have and we should not create panic. I think expenditure can always be incurred through supplementary demand for grants.

The third issue that I wish to highlight is that the Government at the Centre and the states together should provide a package for economic recovery, which the existing budget does not provide. The real question is about the number that one needs and the Finance Commission's role therein. We have been hearing about a 'V' shape recovery mentioned by former Reserve Bank of India governor Duvvari Subba Rao day before yesterday.

Rao said, India would bounce back in 2021-22 with a 7.4% growth. While we hope that happens, a meaningful socio-economic response will require fiscal resources. Let me give some macro numbers here and evaluate the Finance Commission estimates in this context. IMF has projected India's GDP growth rate at 1.9% for 2020-21. Some estimates done, as per informal EPW Research Foundation projections, we are heading for a negative growth.

That means nominal GDP may decline in absolute terms in 2020-21. Compare this with what the Finance Commission has assumed, which is 11% nominal GDP growth rate, based on all taxes that have been projected, and as Dr Rao mentioned in his initial remarks, the Government's budgeted revenue is much lower than what the Finance Commission has projected.

If we take 4% as the inflation target, the nominal growth in the year 2020-21, which IMF has projected, becomes 5.9%. Some quick estimates of just this reduction in growth, gets us an extra 2.5% increase in fiscal deficit for the Centre. In that case, it will make the Centre's deficit to 6% from 3.5% now. A similar estimate at the state level takes the total fiscal deficit to 11% of the GDP. This level of deficit is just to maintain the existing level of expenditure and not any additional expenditure for responding to Covid and recovery.

Estimates also show that in many states, GSDP will show negative growth rates. In other words, we are talking about a large fiscal gap. What is the solution and what then are the options before the Finance Commission? To start with, the Finance Commission needs to re-evaluate GDP growth and work on a mechanism to finance this large gap in resources. My suggestions are to focus on revenue expenditure and slow down new capital expenditure, to make existing resources available to fight Covid for the rest of the current fiscal year. It does not provide additional resources. It is thus necessary to prioritise from revenue to capital.

This has implications. The state can argue in that case for a framework that can accommodate this and they should not be penalised for having a larger revenue deficit or not having a revenue deficit as a norm. Allow states to borrow more. This has happened in the past during the global financial crisis, when FRBM limits of the states were raised to 4% of GSDP. So, states can argue for a higher level of deficit. I think the level should be an extra 2% of GSDP. The 42% share has become a meaningless number as the divisible pool has shrunk very significantly and will shrink more.

In a recession and in a depression, arguing for a certain percent of revenue, may not result in significant increase in resources for states. I would rather ask for specific grants for Covid response. A joint memorandum by the states in this regard may help.

The incidence of Covid is different in different states, so the socio-economic response also has to be different. It may be possible for the states to argue for the creation of a Covid response and recovery fund by the Centre, from which states can probably borrow over and above the FRBM limits with a longer maturity.

Borrowing can be approved by submitting specific plans for recovery. Management of fund can be worked out in consultation with state governments. Finally, an important point made by Isaac is that interstate migration and interstate quarantine is on the Union list. In other words, states are now providing the Central function. It is not the time to debate on this, but given the limited resources in the hands of the states, who have been trying their best to deal with the pandemic, additional resources will have to be made available to them for effective response, sustainability of finances, livelihood security and bringing the economy back on track.

Thank you very much.

Govinda Rao

I will make just four points. Number one, sometimes demarcating what belongs to the Central or state domain is confusing. Public health and public order are examples. The concurrent list basically means that the Centre has the power to intervene, as in the case of an infectious disease, which is contagious. That is one of the reasons why the states actually intervened using the Epidemic Disease Act, but the Centre came up with a more Draconian Disaster Management Act and actually took over and centralised the entire power.

On the 15th Finance Commission recommendations itself, if you look at the difference between the Finance Commission estimates of revenue for 2020-21 and budget estimates, it will be noticed that the difference in tax devolution in fact, is Rs 71,000 crore. If you say the growth of GDP in this year is zero in real terms and 4% in nominal terms and project devolution in the current scheme of things, it will be lower by something like Rs 2.2 lakh crore. This basically implies that 2021 figures will have to be revisited. The states will have to go to the Finance Commission and tell them that these estimates have gone completely awry.

It is ironic that the budget estimate and the Finance Commission estimates of revenue differ by Rs 71,000 crore for the same year. My article in the Mint, being published tomorrow, describes the extent to which the overall fiscal deficit can be surpassed. My estimate is about 10-12% of the GDP, for both Centre and states taken together. Given that the household sector's financial savings is about 7% of the GDP, there may not be anything left for the private sector and therefore, there has to be some monetization, maybe 2-3% of the GDP.

The states have a problem. The amount of money or the additional comfort they get from increasing ways and means, is just about Rs 55,000 crore now, as against Rs 37,000 crore earlier. There is a need for additional money, as they have much more expenditure to incur. So, it is imperative that FRBM targets must be revisited.

Taking the escape route is not going to help. This is something, which the Government of India should take up. The Finance Commission comes in much later. Even in 2008, it was the Government of India, which allowed the states to borrow additional money. There is always the option to borrow from the National Small Saving Fund, but the interest rate is a high 8.5%. That is a much more expensive way of borrowing. Unless and until monetization of the deficit is done, the yield curve will be much higher and the cost of borrowing will be much higher as Kerala found out. They had to pay something like 8.96% for the borrowing they had done.

The Pandemic has to be addressed both by the Centre and states concurrently. However, coordination has been completely lacking from day one. The Centre makes announcements and states have to bear the burden. The Prime Minister makes statements, but there is no supporting help from the Centre at all. Obviously, this cannot go on forever. There has to be much greater coordination.

In fact, in terms of the expenditure, the Central Government does not really have much of a burden due to the pandemic and the burden has to be borne by the states. Therefore, my plea is that state governments make a combined effort and ask for much larger grants, for the money they have lost, firstly, on account of the forecasting error, and also for the economic slowdown caused by the pandemic.

It will also be better if the Finance Commission's term is extended, so that there is a semblance of normalcy and order in the economy, before they make recommendations. Making projections during such a year and using it as a base year, is going to be dangerous. At the end of the day, it is disappointing that the Finance Ministry has not been coming out with any useful assistance to the states. Let me stop here.

Abhijit Sen

I think at the moment everything is focused around what the Centre does and clearly then, the Centre must take responsibility for climbing down from its pedestal and give importance to tackling the pandemic.

There is a huge scope for decentralising. I think it is important for the Finance Ministry if not for anything else, to delegate some of its thinking to the Finance Commission, by providing the sort of letter it requires for the Finance Commission to reopen all these issues. That has to be done immediately.

As far as the states are concerned, they need a forum. States should be saying, "Look here we are, taking necessary action and now we have been forced into a situation where we don't seem to have either the resources, or the authority to do what we want. Let us get that corrected in terms of an institutional structure, which already exists and if it needs some tweaking, let us talk about it."

I think the vacuum which we are getting sucked into as a result of non-action, is the worst of what can happen.

Sudipto Mundle

I shall just make some very specific comments on things that have been said by others. There was a suggestion that we should set a floor to the devolution amount. I don't think that is possible, as devolution is a share of taxes. So, setting a floor for devolution amount seems to be a contradiction in terms and that cannot be done.

If the Centre wants to extend additional financial support to the states, apart from room for borrowing and (somebody again mentioned Covid-19 grant as a special grant in the next Finance Commission report), then it should revisit all these questions for giving a Covid-19 grant of the scale that is required for financial support. Ultimately, it is not the Centre which is going to do everything.

A remark that I would like to make in response to Pinaki Chakraborty's statement, is that we should stop using the ludicrous estimate of the IMF. I don't know where they get these 'positive' growth numbers. It is in fact, a very negative shock. There is no way we can avoid a very significant recession. Various calculations will vary. Our own group at NCAER and NIPFP is looking at an annual decline in GDP, between 15-17%, because it is going to be a 31-33% decline in the first quarter and even if it improves after that, for the year as a whole, negative growth of 15-17% is likely.

D. Narayana

As regards fiscal architecture, it is still in the first report of the 15th Finance Commission. There is no guidance on how to handle a crisis. So, this entire issue has to be relooked in the light of the lockdown and sharp reduction in GDP growth. How do we fund the revival of the economy, especially when the financial sector is in dire straits? Here, we need to make a mention of FRBM. States should make a statement to the Finance Commission on how to go about it. That is my first point. I did not see the panellists making the point.

It is also necessary to mention the Disaster Management Authority and funds. Now, the funds are almost entirely for natural disasters. Allocation is based on past expenditure and the index with a score for cyclones, floods and droughts. Disaster means natural disaster for them, and epidemics do not appear anywhere in the Disaster Management Act 2005 or the annual reports of the authority or Finance Commissions reports.

D. Narayana is currently the Honorary Fellow of Gulati Institute of Finance and Taxation (GIFT). He worked in various capacities including the Director of GIFT (2012-2019), the RBI Chair professor at Centre for Development Studies (CDS) (1980-2012), Technical advisor to the State Planning Board (2013-16), Govt of Kerala, member of the Kerala Public Expenditure Review Committee, Chairman of the Committee on implementation of Karunya Arogya Suraksha Padhathi. He holds a Ph.D. from the Indian Statistical Institute (ISI), Kolkata. He was a Fulbright Fellow at Harvard Centre for Population and Development Studies, and a Visiting Professor at the Unit of International Health at University of Montreal.

Now the reality however, is that during the last two decades, India has lost more lives due to epidemics than floods, droughts, earthquakes and cyclones put together, yet there is no mention of epidemics at all in the Disaster Act. In fact, the states have also not raised this sort of an issue in their memorandums. I think it is time to take this up, because if you look at the last 10 or 15 years, states have faced many epidemics. Even our own experience in 2018 with the Nipah virus, had been such that we had to enforce a partial lockdown in some of the districts. So, there was a great loss as one of the mainstays of Kerala's economy is tourism, which took a big hit that year. So, I think it is time to have a relook at some of these issues.

Thank you.

Geeta Gouri

I shall add a little more to what has already been said. The sense I get from all other speakers is this undue Centralization that is taking place. We cannot afford to lose the entire federal structure we have and I don't think anybody disagrees. That is why I kept saying, that we have to redesign the structure somehow, in a manner that states do not get much too dependent on the Centre. My focus on the electricity sector was based on this consideration. This redesign will help make some states self-sufficient or be persuaded to collaborate.

I think of regional collaborations, say between Andhra, Telangana and Kerala or between Andhra, Telangana and Maharashtra. The reason why I reiterated about redesign of the electricity sector is because we are getting too dependent on the Centre. Regional cooperation would mean we could move ahead in terms of the power market.

I know it doesn't come within the gambit of fiscal policy of the 15th Finance Commission. I have been through the whole report. They have not considered this dimension. The design I am thinking of and the liberty I am taking on regional cooperation, for working out power markets is because you have a lot of solar power solutions happening and a lot of stranded thermal power stations that are falling part. The idea is to get them to work by making the tariff attractive, so that industry may make a comeback.

This has somehow not been thought of because the whole argument went into issues of subsidy and cross-subsidy. Also, the report of the 15th Finance Commission is very unimaginative in terms of sector redesign. It is true that states will go to the Centre, and ask for more assistance, which is exactly what the Central Government wants. The inter-ministerial group is also for that. They want to try and change the whole structure of the Union of States and get it more centralised. That is why the financial emergency that was discussed in the morning is upsetting for us. This is the point I wanted to make in redesigning the sector, which is in the state list.

Govinda Rao

There has to be coordination not only across states but between union and states. There is greater need for an institutional mechanism for coordination, which we do not have at this juncture.

Rajesh Kumar Singh

I don't see any ground for financial emergency, rather only smart tactics to reduce the divisible pool and preempt it for the Centre, so that state finances are choked. States will then get dependent on the Government of India's largesse. That is the way to look at it. Ultimately, the Centre will agree to raise the debt limits.

R Mohanan

I will make two short points. There is a general agreement that Covid-19 grants are to be given to the states. How can it be done? Should we wait for the President to give an additional ToR for the Finance Commission, and make an assessment or can the miscellaneous provision under Article 282 be requested by the states, with the caveat that it is distributed objectively and not as a gratis? Now any declaration of financial emergency will ensure that whatever little is left of the federal structure will be destroyed. So it should never be allowed.

Thomas Isaac

We should go for a Covid-19 grant but not from the Finance Ministry. Professor Sudipto suggested we seek it through the Finance Commission, through an additional ToR because of unexpected circumstances. Let the Finance Commission decide rather than the Finance Ministry.

Govinda Rao

Let me state that there are three important issues that this crisis has brought out. One, this crisis has brought out the tendency to centralise powers and there is a lot of apprehension that it creates. This centralization should lead to a lot more thinking on these issues and we need to bring checks and balances in the system. Today, there are not enough checks and balances in the system. That is one of the major issues we are facing.

The second thing is you have this basic problem of the errors in projection. I mean it starts with the errors in projection and then of course, the unforeseen circumstance that makes it worse. Since the Finance Commission is still in session, it is important that an additional term of reference should be given. The states will have to lobby with the Centre that it should give an additional Term of Reference. Failing this, the next alternative would be to go to the President and request an additional Term of Reference be given to the Finance Commissions to correct the mistakes they have made. They should also demand a Covid-19 grant and distribute it according to an objective formula by the Finance Commission, and not the Finance Ministry whose objectivity is suspect at this juncture.

Thirdly, this has brought out an important lacunae of the federal structure of the country. Today we don't have an institution to monitor Union-state coordination and interstate coordination, competition and conflict resolution. We have an institutional vacuum on this.

Thank you very much.

Thomas Isaac

The reason why the discussion focused on the threat of financial emergency in the morning is because the Central Government is allowing the situation to drift. What has been done in the last one month except for RBI making some feeble interventions?

Govinda Rao

The point I want to make is that when the Centre and the states have a concurrent jurisdiction on a particular subject, the Centre should look at the overall framework. It doesn't know what is really happening in the states. It should be up to the states to do the relaxation and decide its format. You can't sit in Delhi and decide these issues. They should know what their competencies are and confine themselves to it. Now everything has to be done with the concurrence of the Centre.

Thomas Isaac

I was referring to that. Are they deliberately allowing the situation to drift to such a state so that a financial emergency can be imposed? I don't understand how they allow the situation to aggravate.

Govinda Rao

They are clueless. They just don't know what is happening.

Sudipto Mundle

The kind of cautious thinking required to let it drift, so that they can have a financial emergency is not present. There is a deficit of ideas. It is not just the states. Financial markets are getting spooked after Franklin Templeton closed down some of their mutual funds. We are in a very risky situation and it is very important for the Centre to give signals that they are on top of the situation. The Inter-state Council, the constitutional institution that monitors Centre-state coordination should be utilised in such situations. This, unfortunately, is not being done presently.

Govinda Rao

The Inter-state Council cannot act as a referee between the Centre and states because it is a part of the Union Home Ministry. You can't have both a player and an umpire on the same institution.

Sudipto Mundle

I agree with you Govind. States should now lobby for a change in the architecture of the Inter-State Council.

Govinda Rao

At the moment there is no such institution with such an objective. The Inter-state Council cannot undertake the task at this particular moment of time. It was a recommendation by the Sarkaria Commission and was not supposed to be under the Home Ministry. But, it was put under the Home Ministry, thus completely ruining this institution.

At one point, the Planning Commission had a good role. They had the power to give some money to the states. But then, the point is there has to be a proper institution for inter-governmental coordination and conflict resolution. The Finance Ministry and Government of India do not have a clue of what is happening, and the capacity of the Finance Ministry has never been so low in the past.

Abhijit Sen

You have made a point that I will reiterate in a slightly different way. It is important to note that today, we face a situation in which we do not have a formal body in India to coordinate between health issues on one hand and financial issues on another. It is the sort of task that the Planning Commission could have easily undertaken.

Govinda Rao

I do not agree. If that was the case, the health sector would not have been in this condition today.

Abhijit Sen

You need something that works both across the Central government departments and also across states, without being an implementation unit. You probably might be having a dislike for the Planning Commission.

Govinda Rao

The point is simple. I don't dislike the Planning Commission. State governments ignored the health sector. The Centre came forward with its own schemes called National Rural Health Mission. The money is given under the budget head, but is poorly targeted. The total money spent is just 1.2% of the GDP in a country like ours. Historically, there have been so many people who have been saying this, but neither the Planning Commission nor states, ever bothered about the health sector.

Section 4

Covid-19 Pandemic and State of State Finances

Jayati Ghosh

Thank you very much and thanks to GIFT and Thomas Isaac for hosting this. It has been a fascinating set of discussions this morning and I am sure all of us who listened have learned a lot. I just want to reiterate what has already been said; we have been in a terrible situation even before the Covid-19 pandemic and the states have been faced with a stressed fiscal situation. Now these states are being asked to do all of the heavy lifting. The states have to handle the pandemic and also to confront the catastrophe economic fallout that is an obvious outcome of the pandemic. But the states have no money with which to do it as they are not given the resources including the special grants for the pandemic possibly through the Finance Commission or otherwise. Hence, the important issue is that we need to explore ways and means of accessing the needed finance for the

---

Jayati Ghosh, Jawaharlal Nehru University, has also been Professor of Economics since 2021 at the University of Massachusetts Amherst, USA. She taught economics at Jawaharlal Nehru University, New Delhi for nearly 35 years. She has advised governments in India and other countries, including as Chairperson of the Andhra Pradesh Commission on Farmers' Welfare in 2004, and Member of the National Knowledge Commission of India (2005-09). She was the Executive Secretary of International Development Economics Associates. She has been a consultant to international organisations including ILO, UNDP, UNCTAD & UN Women and is member of several international boards and commissions. She has authored and/or edited 20 books and more than 200 scholarly articles. In March 2022, she was appointed to the UN Secretary General's High-Level Advisory Board on Effective Multilateralism. She also writes regularly for popular media, including newspapers, journals and blogs. Jayati Gosh is a Distinguished Fellow of Gulati Institute of Finance and Taxation.

states right now. Many suggestions are being offered including special grants either mobilised by the Finance Commission or otherwise. While I completely agree with demands for grants I would also like to highlight the need to think through all the possible ways.

I would like to suggest that we should also look at the role of the central bank wherein the RBI buys up bonds of state governments at the lowest possible rates. This is being done in all other countries wherever there are federal systems. It is one of the ways in which the governments could ensure that their borrowing costs are kept under control especially when the states will have to incur substantial expenditure by way of providing the necessary health support, food or income transfers. I don't think that it is a Finance Commission matter. It is also recognised that the pandemic is playing out differently in different states and the states have different degrees of fiscal capacity. So there is the need for ensuring an equitable sharing even of the additional resources from the Centre for dealing with the health crisis on account of the pandemic and for the recovery. With these introductory points that I wanted to make, maybe now I can request Yamini to talk.

Yamini Aiyar

The Interstate Council which, as was rightly pointed out in the last session, has significant challenges especially because its home is the Home Ministry. But, either way let us not forget that the NDMA and NDRMF is also under the Home Ministry. I think for the moment, we shall have to put up with the failures of the current system and use it in the best possible way. We should be able to find a way of bringing the NDMA and NDRMA, which also shape the formulae for the state's Disaster Relief Management Fund, into a consultative and deliberative mechanism. That allows for much more agility in the formulae, so that one can be responsive to state specific needs as the pandemic unfolds, over the course of the next few months to a year.

The second issue I have wanted to highlight was that, we haven't spent enough time talking about the current mode of fiscal transfers that govern how

---

Yamini Aiyar is the President and Chief Executive of the Centre for Policy Research, New Delhi. She serves on a number of government and international policy committees as well as boards of nonprofits and think tanks. Her recent policy commitments include: Commissioner and Chair, Governance Working Group, Lancet Commission on Reimagining India's Health System; Member, Chief Minister's Rajasthan Economic Transformation Advisory Council; Member, United Nations Committee of the Experts on Public Administration; Council Member, United Nations University; and Member, Technical Advisory Group, National Data and Analytics Platform, NITI Aayog. Her research interests span the fields of public finance, social policy, state capacity, federalism, governance and the study of contemporary politics in India. She has published widely in academic publications and the popular press, and writes regularly on current affairs and policy matters in mainstream Indian newspapers. Yamini is an alumna of the London School of Economics, St. Edmunds College, Cambridge University and St. Stephen's College, Delhi University.

health infrastructure and social protection expenditure takes place at the state level. Those are the centrally sponsored schemes and Central sector schemes. As professor Govinda Rao said in the previous session, the National Health Mission has come to be the dominant form of non-wage-expenditure, in most states. Kerala is an exception, as it is almost all cases. Not only is it a dominant non-wage expenditure, we must also remember in many states, salaries and wages and liabilities occupy about 80% of state health budget. Over the course of the last 15 years, states have got quite used to drawing on NHM to substitute for the expenditure they should have added on to their health expenditures and so, NHM becomes extremely relevant in terms of providing the finances that are needed for states to build up a health infrastructure

Right now, the National Health Mission has 2000-line items, which makes flexibility in expenditures near impossible. Over the years, the actual process of spending under the National Health Mission has been overloaded with paperwork and red-tapism. In Uttar Pradesh, my colleague calculated that a single file for release of funds into the NHM societies and the district societies from the state treasury has to go through 22 desks before the fund release is cleared. This structure and architecture of how NHM is organized at the moment is such that, it makes speedy and effective expenditures extremely difficult. Added to it, is the problem that the scheme is shared 60:40 which puts a fairly large amount of pressure on state finances.

I think in the case of programs like NHM, we need to at least go back to its original design which had more flexible funds or flexible pools, which would allow states to spend the NHM funds they required and at the same time get away from this 2000 line item 22-25-35 desks of clearances, that need to be obtained to release expenditure. One also has to push for at least a 90:10 share ratio, if not a 100% share ratio for NHM, so that the states are able to spend more on healthcare, which is frankly the need of the hour.

Similarly, a case can be made for other Central sector schemes, many of which dominate the expenditure for social protection programs, and in particular, programs for food and provision of food security and cash security. The infrastructure, preparedness and ability of states to implement schemes is very varied and if there is anopportunity to bundle these schemes together it must be done at the first opportunity, so that states receive untied funds which can be used for the provision of food and cash security.

I think we will be making significant progress in complementing and supporting states rather than have states run around, as they are currently in the PMGKY schemes that are being implemented. The requirements of the Central

Government have, as we have seen over the last 40 days, caused significant stress on the ground. The ability to reach banks is extremely varied and in northern states in particular it is difficult. Therefore states should be in a position to be able to determine the most appropriate mechanism by which they can ensure that they are providing both food and cash security to their citizens.

A related issue that we do need to actually talk about is the issue of portability of food security and cash security for migrant workers. Again, this is a matter that requires deep interstate coordination, as well as Central support because of a significant spill over effect. We will not be able to bring workers back if we don't ensure that we can restore their dignity and their trust in our ability to offer protection. So a portable social security system is the need of the hour and we have to move in that direction urgently and quickly.

Jayati Ghosh

Those were some really important and interesting points.

Balveer Arora

Thank you. What I propose to do is to briefly touch upon some of the political and governance issues that were raised and also try to see what exactly seems to be the game plan of the Government, to the extent possible. I am going to speak about what is going on in terms of constitutional activities and governance activities, in the name of Covid.

The first point that we need to take into account, is the unprecedented centralization undertaken through often little-known acts, less talked about. Rao mentioned the Epidemics Act and the Disaster Management Act. Who would have thought that it would be the old colonial Epidemics Act that would be invoked. But, it is the Disaster Management Act 2005, which gives the Executive greater powers which was more extensively used. The reason is that it gave the Executive a free reign without accountability to Parliament. Making a declaration under the emergency provisions, would require some degree of accountability to Parliament, which I think Government is not very keen on.

Balveer Arora is Founder-Chairman, Centre for Multilevel Federalism (CMF) at the Institute of Social Sciences, New Delhi. He earlier taught Political Science at the Centre for Political Studies (1973-2010) at JNU. He was Rector and Pro-Vice Chancellor of the University from 2002 to 2005. Professor Arora obtained his Doctorate in Political Science from the University of Paris Pantheon-Sorbonne (1972). He was made a Knight in the Legion of Honour, the highest civilian honour of the French Republic (2011) and received as Officer in the Order of Academic Laurels (2003). Dr Arora has been a visiting professor at U Penn, Philadelphia, and Sciences Po Paris. He has written extensively on Indian Federalism. His major works includes *Multiple Identities in a Single State* (1995); *Diversity and Unity in the Indian Republic* (2010); *The New Party System: Federalised and Binodal* (2013) and *Yojana* (2013)

Another notable point is entry 29 of list 3, which is referred to as the concurrent list. In short, this means that the Government is being legally well advised in this, as well as other areas. Wherever it has legal acumen, it has chosen of path of least accountability and maximum executive latitude. That is one point I would like to stress on.

Haseeb Drabu talked about cannibalistic federalism. He did not elaborate. I think it may refer to something like slow erosion of the powers of the states or hollowing out of the substance of federalism, where you have states existing but gets transformed to the level of a municipality. Under the DMA we have seen that there is a parallel line of communication with the district administration and there is a direct activity in the form of these inter-ministerial teams. This is the big difference, which makes me think on the question of financial emergency. I agree that if the Government goes down that route, one should oppose it strongly. But my feeling is that it will get around the need to declare any such emergency. Another issue, which I would like to pick up, is the way in which the Government is turning to charity and civil service organisations to fulfil state functions. I think this is something to be noted. It is an abdication of state responsibility and all problems faced in public domain and any action taken to alleviate it, has to be by a public authority and not a charitable organisation.

I would like to make two points on charity. All state and Central funds should uniformly be eligible for CSR funding and receiving foreign donations, exactly like the PM Cares Fund, which should distribute it to the states using the formulae of the Finance Commission. That would probably be less controversial.

Now let us look at the impact on the federal system. Micro management of governance has crept in as this whole episode unfolded. States with crippled finances face an epidemic which has directly impacted state revenues. The whole idea is that the federal system needs to be given more oxygen. Local primary health care centres, the 'Ashas' and other auxiliary medical personnel are all in need of support and funding. However, this is not happening because of emasculated state governments.

As far as the Prime Minister's video conference with chief ministers is concerned, for a moment I thought the Centre felt the need to consult the states, because it saw the states moving ahead with their measures and therefore thought it better to lead them than to ignore them. What seems to be happening is that, despite the growing frequency of these conferences, (we had the fourth one today), I am told that only those who were not able to speak will be allowed to speak. It is a curious procedure. It keeps up the façade of consultation. We need to look at it a little more closely and find out whether there is any substance to it, which gives it some significance in federal terms.

The last point I would like to make is an open-ended question. While trying to incorporate this exceptional accumulation of powers as the new normal after the pandemic, will the Centre use what I call "conditionality," to bail out state finances? All these are worries that I am articulating. But when finance or powers are accumulated or concentrated, shedding them is even more difficult than undoing the lockdown or deconfinement.

The second major point I have to dwell upon is the impact on democracy. I think there has been no pause in the wider agenda of the Central Government. The relentless pursuit of other aspects of the anti-democratic agenda continues, whether it means accentuating social fractures, or curbing of democratic dissent, right to protest or freedom of expression. The second consequence for democracy is that, we have the largest fund in the history of Indian democracy in the hands of the BJP. These are the electoral bonds and also the PM Cares Funds. This is a major concern for the polity because it is unregulated money, which is available for all kinds of purposes. Against the background of weakened counter-powers like the judiciary and the media, it is little worrying at the moment. I am concluding the concern here. There will be others who take this up. I think we should make sure two things are taken forward. One is the emphasis on the health care system which has suddenly come to the foreground, with the pre-condition of a functional multi-level system. Kerala has shown the way. The other is the third tier of federalism. Yamini had also spoken about it. Focus on these institutions, which are in the frontline, can make a difference once the spotlight is on them. We should try and see it is not shifted away.

The last point I would make is about migrant labour or guest workers, as they are called in some countries, and the questions of citizenship. As we pursue the path of development, in which there are many other issues to be raised, who is responsible for feeding them and looking after them and who is responsible for seeing them safely home? These are all major concerns.

Jayati Ghosh

These are very sobering reflections I have to say. It is very telling that only 7 chief ministers were allowed to speak. We are in challenging times. Nobody knows it better than the Kerala government, which is in front of the firing line.

Praveen Jha

Extremely important foundational issues have been raised. Structural, long term, institutional etc., all of which are extremely important. While endorsing that, let me just come to some of the basic concerns of the session. The first is the question of state of state finances. In the current context, we know that resource mobilization in general, is almost in the 'intensive care unit.' Trends till February 2020, show that even the revised estimates of the Gross Tax Revenues in the last budget will not be met. Already it is some Rs 3 lakh crore less than budgeted initially. From that we are looking at figures, which are some Rs 1 lakh crore less than what was to be shared with states as per the revised estimates. Out of revised estimate of Rs 6.56 lakh crore, it appears that only Rs 5.06 lakh crore have been shared with the states as yet. We already know that there is a huge crisis there. The way things have panned out subsequently, it can only become worse.

Praveen Jha, Professor of Economics at the Centre for Economic Studies and Planning (CESP) and Adjunct Professor at the Centre for Informal Sector and Labour Studies (CISLS), is with the School of Social Sciences, Jawaharlal Nehru University (JNU), India. Prior to JNU, he taught at St. Stephen's College, Delhi and at Lal Bahadur Shastri National Academy of Administration, Mussoorie. He has been a Visiting Fellow to several Institutions/Universities, including University of Bremen (Germany), Tianjin University of Finance and Economics (China), Rhodes University (South Africa), Sam Moyo African Institute for Agrarian Studies (SMAIAS), (Zimbabwe), and Kassel University (Germany). He has also been associated with several research studies with UN institutions such as the ILO, the UNICEF, the UNDP, FAO etc. He is one of the editors of the Journal, Agrarian South: Journal of Political Economy.

In my opinion, the shortfall in the current fiscal year, will be 25-50% of what has actually been shown in the budget. That is the basic backdrop. So, what can states do in terms of issues, which are of the 'here and now variety?' First, I think states must demand what has been collected by the Centre through cess and surcharges. A part of that must be shared with states at least as an emergency provision. There is just no other way. Where are the states going to get resources from? That is something which should be discussed very seriously by the finance ministers of states.

Of course, as the Chair mentioned, provision with respect to financial easing vis-a-vis the Central bank, to support the states, should certainly be taken into account. States should be allowed to borrow beyond the set limit. FRBM must be relaxed at least for the time being. Fresh loans, advances etc. should be permitted.

If there is a relaxation of 0.5% GDP as fresh loan etc., the fiscal deficit will increase to 4%. That alone will fetch Rs 1.12 lakh crore or so. Apart from these, there are a couple of other small issues which are linked to the Finance Commission recommendations. One, there was a special provision that the Union Government has accepted, to meet revenue gaps of some states. I think it should be applicable to all states instead of only a handful of states, in this kind of an emergency. This also applies to the entire loan repayment and extended moratorium on it.

We of course have a very frequently discussed issue, which I think must be considered. Several people have raised it in today's conversation and that is, the Union Budget's provision for capital expenditure. That should be simply passed on to the states right now. Apart from that, a lot of expenditure has been marked for things that do not make sense at all in the current context, like the Central Vista project and so on. That money should certainly be used to support states.

Finally, again with reference to what the Finance Commission has mentioned, at least 50% of the money that was supposed to be transferred to local bodies without any further delay through the state exchequers, should be transferred. Such provisions do not require a very significant change in fiscal architecture. These are things that can be done and provided there is sufficient pressure from the states on the Union Government, it can succeed without any major hassles. Let me stop there.

S.M. Vijayanand

The first point I want to make is that in the changed scenario, we need a new memorandum of the state for the whole year. Since we have to take care of the new spending needs, which are similar for most parts of India, we need to highlight it from a survival angle. This includes food needs and social security needs, which are all new. Another important point is of course migrant needs which have not been considered by any Finance Commission. These are new realities, which are to be assessed by the Finance Commission.

D. Narayana earlier made a point regarding the need for a new conceptualization of NDRF and SDRF, to include such pandemics in its agenda. As regards additional resource mobilisation, I fully agree that it can come only through what Dr. Isaac suggested, as some kind of pandemic bond which the Reserve Bank of India has to buy, a little increase in the borrowing limit and of course taxing the super-rich.

Coming to state finances, which is the topic of the day, obviously, you can only get funds by realigning and changing the plan. But then, we have to really

---

S.M. Vijayanand is Former Chief Secretary to the Government of Kerala and currently the Chairman of the 6th State Finance Commission, Kerala. In the past, he has served as the Secretary, Ministry of Panchayati Raj, Government of India; Additional Secretary, Ministry of Rural Development, Government of India; among other positions, and spearheaded Rajiv Gandhi Drinking Water Mission, Ministry of Sanitation, Government of India (1992-1996). As the chairman of the Kerala Institute of Local Administration (KILA), he played a major role in the efforts at decentralisation of power in the State through the Panchayat Raj system. He has also conceptualised and operationalised 'Kudumbashree', a women's self-help group movement in the state of Kerala.

identify the parts which can be excluded, and assess whether they are the non-welfare, non-labour absorption types. So agriculture, MSMEs and construction will get priority in this order.

Earlier a lot of people spoke about bringing down capital expenditure. But what kind of capital expenditure? I understand in India, maybe not in Kerala, next to agriculture, construction absorbs more ordinary labour? So, let us be nuanced. In Kerala I would bring in the idea of efficiency of expenditure. An increase in public expenditure efficiency can bring down cost by 10-20%, which is a gain and quite possible. New taxes at this time may not be very viable, but the possibility of exercise cannot be ruled out.

If the Government of India relaxes the ceiling on borrowing, we would now be an attractive proposition for multilateral and bilateral finance, because of the Kerala model. So, I think we should use the advantage and push for it.

Then there is something not very popular in Kerala and that is user charges. There need not be an increase in user charges, but some kind of a cess like during the Bangladesh liberation. People know it is for this purpose.

Now I will touch up on my main area of understanding, local government finance. The big point I want to make is that local government finance is very critical at this point of time. Since Kerala is tied to the state plan and given the state's own source of revenue, it is obvious that local government revenues will shrink. Nevertheless, I need to emphasise that local economic stimulus is not something we have understood. Just consider what happens at remote places like Attapadi in Wayanad and Vattavada in Idukki, and places in northern Kasaragod. Local government action is not much understood even in Kerala. We have to be very careful about that.

Local government finance offers us something which we all need and is commonly called in Kerala as the 'escape tax.' There are a lot of people who actually need to be taxed, but are not taxed. This is so in the case of property and profession tax too. A totally impressionistic estimate, as per my understanding, is that it is almost 40-60%. We can resort to a tax mapping and organise a rigorous collection drive to the same extent.

I would personally suggest that some sort of authority overlooks this effort. Officers from the commercial taxes department can be used to find out whether assessment has been done as per the local government decision. If not, we need to find out if some kind of a concurrent audit or tax audit is required if collection is extremely poor.

Another easy thing that the local government in Kerala, particularly gram panchayats, can do is try out MGNREGA. I am sure MGNREGA will not be cut for a few years. Efficiency of MGNREGA expenditure, can substitute much of agriculture investment and can be easily done.

The second state Finance Commission headed by Prabhat Patnaik, has suggested automatically grading many local government user charges and taxes, to the money value. Though there was a general consensus, it could not be legislated. It will of course be challenged in the courts, but it may stand in good stead because many local taxes like user charges, rents and others have not been revised for approximately over two decades. Then, there are unutilized taxes like advertisement tax and a tax which was wrongly named at that point of time, called service tax, which is only a betterment tax as a percentage of property tax. This is the right time, as people know there are no resources and will be in order.

I have a special request to the finance minister. There is lot of confusion on entertainment tax. The local government taxes were excluded and in Kerala, entertainment is a local government tax. Unfortunately, it has come down very sharply and now it is just 8%. The local government has lost heavily to the tune of Rs 100 crore in two years, on this account. So, we need to look at it and probably restore it. It requires legal intervention.

We should also create a local government development fund, legislated by the Left Democratic Front government, not exactly like KIFBI, but to issue infrastructure bonds for the local government. It can raise revenue through projects or escrow of local government revenue or government standing annuity, so that its current capital expenditure needs can be met, which can be repaid in the future.

The point that I want to raise next is that the government and panchayats in Kerala spend a lot of money particularly in agriculture and allied sectors as well as social sectors. It will be useful if we prepare a single plan at the local government level, not by the state government, but by the local government. It will be a single plan that will boost up efficiency to a great extent. Just by efficiency enhancement, we can save 15% to 20%. Presently local governments spend about Rs 15,000 crore in all and they can certainly do this.

Under Centrally sponsored schemes, we have to particularly concentrate on pruning funds in projects, like the smart city. They will all undergo a crunch but we have to do that. The last is a general point not only for local governments, but for all others too. Greater transparency and accountability of the money collected for Covid, or any other purpose as claimed, will elicit a much better response.

Jayati Ghosh

Those were a lot of very useful and practical suggestions.

Sushil Khanna

I will highlight one or two things. We are saying that, we as a country or state did not spend enough on health and maybe we need a big booster dose. Kerala is an exceptional outlier. I think the way the whole thing has been handled, it has now become an economic issue far more than a health issue. A lot of this is because of falling governance. A comparison shows that other countries have done it very differently. Here people have just abandoned trucks on highways, some companies are searching for some 190 trucks. All this because you had a sudden lockdown.

This did not happen overnight. In South Africa, where there are a large number of migrant workers, they were given three days to go back to their homes. By giving a sudden order and changing it every day, people panicked into making hasty decisions. Now there is a sharp fall in consumption levels of people. Some people talk of a 40% fall in consumption. This means there is going to be widespread hunger now.

Sushil Khanna, a retired professor of Economics and Strategy Management at IIM Calcutta, has also taught in several universities abroad, including, Katholieke University, Leuven and Copenhagen Business School. He held, the ICCR Chair on Corporate Responsibility and Governance at Leipzig Graduate School of Business, Germany. He has a regular teaching assignment at University of Washington at Seattle. His research interests include issues of development economics, industrial policy and technology transfer, and public sector. Prof. Khanna has served as member of Board for Restructuring of Public Sector Enterprises, Government of India. He was associated with Kerala government as the chairman of Kerala Financial Corporation and as a head of the committee tasked by the government to prepare the "crisis and turnaround strategy" for Kerala State Road Transport Corporation (KSRTC).

As Sudipto Mundle said, there is a 20% to 50% contraction in the economy. We are looking at a very large economic disaster, the worst of which is to be confronted by states. The state will have to provide bailouts, with people thrown out of jobs and small industries decimated. This is even worse than demonetization. The collapse of revenues that Isaac mentioned, is proved by the fact that he got only 10% of the expected amount. The Delhi finance minister mentioned a similar ratio. The state governments are looking at 90% collapse in the short-term revenues.

Praveen's estimates are very optimistic. We are going to see a sharp fall in Central Government revenues also. They also lost 90% of their revenue. This obviously means that we have to move to financial markets and borrow. Jayati began by saying that the role of the Central bank is crucial to the whole thing. Propping up of the market is crucial. India has a narrow bond market. It faced a collapse last because of the Franklin Templeton mutual fund.

Today, the Reserve Bank of India has pumped in Rs. 50,000 crore to bail out mutual funds. While States need a bail out of some Rs. 500,000 crore at this point of time, they have not been given even Rs. 50,000 crore. This is what I want to emphasise on. Day before yesterday there was a piece in the *Wall Street Journal* on how the banks in the United States have not been helping the Federal Reserve. So, the United States Federal Reserve is now buying the bonds of the state governments and also corporate bonds because their banks are not buying it. The Central bank is buying it directly.

In our case, the Central bank says that they are getting back the money they give out to banks. That is why the reverse repo rate was cut to eliminate lazy banking. That is also a governance issue. The way the government has frightened bankers out of their wits, they now tend to walk away from even genuine lending risks. Today to many people, the failure of any company means some banker has helped somebody to syphon off money. That seems to be the core issue. You have made the whole financial sector very fragile. Our ability to borrow is also under pressure.

Interest rates may come down only if the Central bank actually intervenes to put money to support the bonds being floated by the states. So, we are looking at very new needs of the state government, not Covid or health. It is taken for granted that they will be there and even if they lend, states will need 10% to 20% of the GDP in the social sector to prevent widespread hunger and also prevent decimation of small industries.

States have very little leeway in the financial market. It is entirely a Central prerogative. They control the banks and they can do what they like. They can ask the banks to lend on their behalf as the finance minister was doing some days ago. But since the states have no leeway at all, they cannot help the small industries. State financial corporations have all been decimated. They are almost finished. Kerala is again an exception but by and large, it is all gone. Their size is very small. Due to inadequate funding, these institutions cannot borrow from depositors. Hence, their ability to help small industry is limited. For a long time, the new liberal policies rolled out since the nineties ensured that states withdraw from such activities and private banks step in to do the job.

We may even see a 5-7% contraction in GDP. A similar contraction of revenues of both Central and state governments, will mean that there is no other option but to monetize the deficit and let the banks pick up a part of the bonds that the states will have to list. This is going to be unprecedentedly tricky. I don't think you have to worry about inflation because there is a collapse of capacity utilisation. It was already at a low 60% to 70% and it has now gone down by another 30%. So, except for farmers, Limited companies and a few others, most are not able to produce. Shop shelves have been going empty because goods are not arriving as those companies are unable to produce and sell goods.

This has not happened in some other places. I am currently teaching a course in the University of Washington, Seattle. Some of my staff are engaged, many are working from home. Even in companies like Boeing, production is on, but they are not selling any planes. But, people who have to produce important strategic goods are allowed to go to work on the shop floor.

If you think of mindless shutting down and not allowing any leverage for state governments to manage it, we will soon be going into a severe economic crisis. I would like to argue that what began as a health crisis, has now become a full-blown economic crisis, particularly since the Home Ministry interfered and was giving orders. As Rao said the Finance Ministry seems to be shut down. The Finance ministry does not have any ideas. They talk of giving Rs 500 to somebody. That is what the finance minister says. So, I think we are in it for the long haul. Unless the states combine together to ask for a package, we are going to see lasting hunger, something we have not seen from the mid-sixties. This is my assessment.

Jayati Ghosh

Very depressing but also very insightful. We shall now go for a quick second round. Everyone is alluding to the enormity of what is happening. I think we have to remember this. Sushil also alluded to this. Sudipto gave very horrific numbers and he spoke of a 30% decline in this quarter and 17% overall fall for the year.

We are talking about a very dramatic collapse which requires a very huge intervention. So, there is no option but to monetize the deficit, whatever you say and whichever way you look at it. Yes, you can raise some taxes like wealth tax and so on. The Indian Revenue Service people have also suggested various taxes. This is not going to be enough. We are really talking about the need for a fiscal stimulus of a minimum of 7% to 10% of the GDP, which is not even the average of what is happening in the rest of the world.

Across the world, from developing to developed countries, the size of the fiscal stimulus package that has been given, is between 5-20% of the GDP. So at least 5% or better still, 7% of the GDP is the kind of expansion we need of which, let us assume, around 5% will have to happen immediately.

A gathering like this is perhaps a good idea. It has allowed us to ponder together about possible solutions and how we could make it a reality, in a way that ensures states also get a decent share of it. Yamini has some good ideas like the use of the existing schemes to multiply the amount that is being given. But it is not about small amounts. We are talking about quadrupling the increase in spending on many of these things. Whether it is food security or MGNREGA or any of the things we have to use those available schemes, which always spread a lot of the money out in equitable ways.

Second of course is that we basically have to get the Reserve Bank of India to buy up all state government bonds completely and a big portion of all the other debt as well. There is a strong precedent for it. The United States Federal Reserve has already brought up every available debt in the last few months. It can be done, if we too think on similar lines.

Let us list some proposals that could be done along these lines for executing very large increases. There is no point asking for small change. I think Sushil Khanna also mentioned this. You really need very large increases to confront the kind of risk and the scale of the challenge we face today. So, would anybody like to make a point on that?

Sushil Khanna

I am against putting any more money in centrally sponsored schemes. You have to give money directly to states and let them handle the crisis. This is because the extent of the crisis and its nature varies across states. Some of the people at the margins are returning in some states. There are other states which face entirely different kinds of problems. If we incorporate such a huge amount into mutual funds, we can look at a minimum of Rs 5 lakh crore for the states. That is not a big amount but rather just a head start.

The banks are not buying bonds though the Central bank has given them money. They are not funding. Nobody wants to touch anybody else, because debts can put them on the scrutiny list of vigilance officials. They want the Central bank to directly buy it, because banks feel they already carry enough government paper. Unless the Reserve Bank of India forces them to, or the Reserve Bank of India directly holds it, they are not going to buy bonds. Many have exhausted their limits. So, at this point of time I don't think this is appropriate to add a little bit here and there. As far as certain taxes are concerned, I have no problem with some cess occasionally for local governments.

But that will not solve the problems. We, especially the state finance ministers, are looking at a very large leeway. Now that production has collapsed and people are without jobs, they need aid at this point of time. Isaac was getting Rs 2500 crore per month and it was enough to pay salaries and for a little capital expenditure. We are in fact, looking at much larger numbers now.

I am not in favour of centrally sponsored schemes being multiplied. I am thinking of direct funding to states. State governments have to come forward with this demand. I am only disappointed that of the many finance ministers, only a few came despite the efforts made by Thomas Isaac to make them join in this effort. Coming together to boost state finances is a very important part. Arora has already mentioned how autonomy of states have been undermined. We have to fight back. That is all.

Jayati Ghosh

We definitely want to see a lot of money going to states, as well as guarantee of employment. These are centrally sponsored schemes. I don't think the two are contradictory.

Yamini Aiyar

We have to think of this in terms of the kind of systems that already exist, what systems are working well and can be enhanced, as we are in an emergency situation. We need to consider what systems need to be put in place, in order to ensure the response is suited to state specific contexts. It is in this context, which I think MGNREGA and the National Food Security Act could help, as these already have a very robust well-functioning mechanism. No doubt, there are a lot of challenges but they relatively do have a well-functioning architecture. That architecture needs to be fully supported and enhanced significantly, in order to ensure that we are dealing with the current crisis of hunger.

At this point, adding anything new is not going to be helpful. However, having said that, I also agree that a centrally sponsored scheme or a sort of centralised mechanism is not the most appropriate. I am for bundling up the existing schemes, which are over 600 to 700 in number into untied grants that states can then use. Even if you exclude MGNREGA and PDS, you still have a substantive amount of centrally sponsored schemes in existing budgets, that can be repurposed in order to be able to enhance transfers to states and provide appropriate social security to people who are in need.

I am certainly not arguing for more centralization. I am arguing for a deeply federal architecture, for the provision of social protection, by sticking to the key pillars that states have effectively utilised, to be able to provide basic social protection to their people. I completely understand the importance of responding. However, if we enhance financing, it has to be according to the nature of the pandemic and the nature of economic consequences, which are going to vary in different states.

That is why we need an interstate council arrangement to have a serious deliberation, to arrive at a consensus formula that is responsive and agile enough to change, as the nature of the outbreak itself changes. I would like to take the opportunity to add one more point on local government which hasn't been brought up. As Vijayanand and many others have articulated the centrality of local government in responding to Covid-19, will hopefully ensure the re-emergence of local government in the debate on fiscal federalism.

But if you look at the first report of the 15th Finance Commission, it has broken up the financing given to rural local bodies, as well as urban local bodies into a basic grant, and 50% into a tied grant, which is connected to water, sanitation, open defecation free etc. Although these might be important goals, this might not be the time to tie down local government funding. I would urge that the 15th Finance Commission redeliberate on this and also look at converting these tied funds into untied funds, so that local governments are in the position to draw on finances that they need, to be able to provide the kind of localised response that is necessary to deal with both the economic and health crisis. Thank you.

Jayati Ghosh

The biggest issue that arises is the political viability of all these suggestions and as per Praveen's statement, it is just not viable at the moment. In other words, the political economy of India today, is one where you have a very centralizing government, which is doing everything that it legally and otherwise can, to further entrench its power. So, in a sense what I am asking you Professor Arora is, what are the chances for state governments, which are trying to develop a federalist cooperative structure? What are the ways in which this could be attempted?

Balveer Arora

I didn't mean to say all is lost. One can definitely fight back. The purpose was to point out difficulties associated with all this. We must also understand that one must not underestimate one's opponent. Nevertheless, I am fully in agreement with much of what was said regarding the mobilisation of support and increasing testing, as the WHO wants. Yamini made some excellent points. Regarding the interim Finance Commission report, if we are able to press for a review on many points and then try to work through that, it would at least have a parliamentary legitimacy. Otherwise, my fear is that things can be kept outside the constitution, outside parliament, outside accountability channels. I have noticed the tendency is to go in that direction. The second thing is that we have to be prepared for some amount of political distancing. They will try to distance themselves from things that do not show them in good light. This political distancing as an attempt to wield power, and not responsibility is the second thing. Now Jayati, it is important to understand the type of people who are wielding power and I still hold that finance ministers of states should get together and continue to press their demands. However, it is a long haul.

Jayati Ghosh

As depressing as the first one.

John Samuel

I tend to agree with most of the points raised here. I am particularly in agreement with what Praveen Jha and Vijayanand said. I see it from three points. Firstly, when you look at it from a political point of view, we are clueless as to what the Union Government is set to do and that really is a big issue. It is very surprising, because almost all the states are facing a serious financial crisis and yet we have got nothing from the federal government.

As far as states are concerned, the situation is different in different states. Let me take the case of Kerala. Kerala has a triple problem. One is, we know our service sector is one of the biggest sectors that is going to be affected because remittance is going to reduce. A very significant reduction in remittance puts us back in many ways. This is true for real estate and almost every sector. That will also have an implication on the lives and livelihood of the people apart from the government.

John Samuel, CEO Tran Civic International, Bangkok, is an international development practitioner, with more than thirty years of experience in organisational leadership, humanitarian action, sustainable development, public policy and advocacy. He is the founder and Chief Mentor of the Institute of Sustainable Development and Governance, and Bodhigram Foundation. He served as the Head of the Global programme on governance assessments and Global Democratic Governance Advisor at UNDP, as the International Director of Actionaid International, and as the CEO of Asian Forum for Human Rights and Development. He served as the CEO of the National Centre for Advocacy Studies in India. He was a visiting fellow at the Institute of Development Studies, University of Sussex and at the Advocacy Institute, Washington. He has published extensively on issues related to public policy, sustainable development people-centred advocacy, and democratic governance.

It is very different in other states and the approach thereby, should be different. One is that, all state finance ministers, as Isaac has done today, need to be brought together because we are in a catch 22 situation. We do not know what the Central government is going to do. Hence all the non-BJP state governments will have to come together and pressurise the Central government for a fiscal package. It also means lifting FRMBM limits and getting Reserve Bank permission for bonds. This needs to be done with utmost advocacy.

Secondly, how do we liberate our own resources? By this I mean, whatever resources we have. I agree with Vijayanand that there is a lot of scope for financial efficiency. We need to really work on managing the deficit. That is the primary thing, this deficit management. None of the states can in the present context manage it, unless there is support from the Union Government.

Next is the refinancing strategy, which will have to be done entirely by the Union Government. But each of the state governments should also have a strategy. It is very necessary to have an expenditure management and a financing strategy. As Isaac may also know, the NRIs are in a paradox. There is a very significant amount of money in the banks, for which we get very little interest rates. As a NRI, I get hardly 4% or less. Our treasury gives an 8% interest rate to employees. Even if we have a special permission within Kerala, we can have a special bond for 3-5 years. I think one of the strategies for Kerala would be to raise a substantial amount of money from NRIs. One way to fund the public finance and deficit to some extent, is to also have a very strategic investment plan. Both these two things are important for Kerala.

As far as the Finance Commission is concerned, we need to see it from two angles. The ideal thing is to get the terms of reference redefined. The Finance Commission will have to be responsible for the division of resources. My sense is that the BJP government at the Centre will use this financial crisis as a means to extend a sort of financial emergency, which will be a proxy political emergency. That is my biggest fear. I don't think that they don't have a clue. Actually, they have a game plan. They are actually making a political point. We need to be very careful. Balveer Arora spoke about it. I think we are moving into a 'police raj', like what happened in Thailand and in many other places. There could be restrictions on the media. So, one has to be extremely careful about the democratic deficit, which may happen.

Even the Kerala government, which is far better in terms of financial transparency and accountability and also local government finance, could set an example. How about a white paper taking everybody into confidence and laying out a collective strategy? Once that is done we have to very clearly demand from the Centre whatever needs to be done, and it can be also used to mobilise at least some state governments because unless we do it, I don't think the finance ministry of the Union Government will do any wonders in the present conditions. They are sitting on the fence. I also think the strategy is being planned elsewhere, rather than in the finance ministry. That is a very serious concern which I have.

I am largely in agreement with almost all the points which were said. But I also feel that while every state government will have to have their own separate strategy, they also need to have a joint strategy. That joint strategy is a must and that has to be both a political and policy strategy because unless we do that, the Central Government may take any state including, the Kerala government, for a ride.

Actually, politically they have very good strategic team with crony capitalism stuck to their agenda to delegitimize opposition parties. Hence opposition parties will have to come together.

Thank you.

Jayati Ghosh

We have gone beyond our time. Maybe I can call for closing comments from all participants.

Praveen Jha

Given the scale of the problem, a big crisis like this needs a big bang kind of response. There is this huge resistance to the big bang approach from the Central Government. Hence it is important to mobilise almost everything which can be done under the circumstances without losing the hope for the big bang. Monetization of debt is absolutely necessary with the Central Bank supporting the states.

In a situation of this kind, all hands have to be on the deck, whatever be the small measures that they take. For instance, the possibility of a surcharge is within the domain of the states. Whatever power the states have should be utilised. For example, all taxes which can give resources to the states right now. Such transactions should be eased. Alcohol for instance.

Finally, apart from a lot of things that happened, like money flowing through the state exchequer from the Centre and so on, I think given the economic vulnerability of special category groups, special programs etc. have to be prioritised. I don't say how, but that can be very much on the front burner.

S.M. Vijayanand

Just one clarification. Kerala local governments have their own revenue of Rs 2000 crore now. With some efficiency, it can raise it to Rs 3000 crore, though not immediately, but in the next four five months because they are going for elections. Two other points not related to this. All of you very influential friends should try to bring primary health care on the agenda. Then I am sure funds will flow. They all want votes. They know the importance of primary health care, not only in urban India but even in rural parts.

The second important point is that for the first time ever, the migrant issue has come to the fore. Politicians have realized this and so also the panchayats. They all know the importance. We have an old Act called the Interstate Migrant Workmen Act of 1979. This is now being subsumed in the labour court. This is the time to focus on the rights of migrants, and we have had a lot of experience over the last few years on legislation, whether it be for people with disabilities, mental health care, juveniles etc. With that experience we should all try to get some justice for the migrants on a sustainable long-term basis.

Thank you.

Sushil Khanna

S.M. Vijayanand made a very important point, which he did not include in his summary. We have to give a new memorandum to the Finance Commission. It is easier to talk to people who are professionals, even though they are appointed by the Government. All state governments should ask for this, as the situation has changed. Ask for a total change in priorities. Basically, increasing our borrowing and stuff like that. This is a strategy the Interstate Council can take up.

Jayati Ghosh

That is a very important point.

Balveer Arora

Of all the sciences we know of, futurology is a causality. Not able to clearly see 2020. So, I think we have to be a little modest and Jayati and Khanna also said that we are going through historic times and it is difficult to take measure of all that can happen. However, one should try to ward off the worst.

Thomas Isaac

The most important take from our deliberations today, has been about the enormity of economic collapse. The most pessimistic estimate so far on India by UN, IMF or all the different financial agencies has not gone to minus. They halted at Zero. Then comes Sudipto Mundle who says it will be 30% minus in this quarter, which is comparable to the trends in US, Britain and most other countries. This therefore, should not surprise us. For the whole year it will be minus 10-15%. So, it is a virtual economic collapse. I think the policy-makers of the country do not understand the gravity of the situation.

Two, I think there was a near unanimity that this crisis can be resolved only by large-scale monetization of debt. Professor Jayati said it has to be 5% of the GDP, give or take one or two percent. That is the scale of operation.

Three, there is definite unanimity that more has to be passed on to states. States should operate not just through the Centre or centrally sponsored schemes. The state governments, at the finance ministers meeting said that their own revenue was less than 25% of the budget and Centre's devolution too was coming down. The Centre is also refusing to budge on GST compensation. There is just no money. I don't think ever in our financial history has any government faced this situation. There is nothing to work on, except to give cheques on what has been borrowed.

Regarding the package to state governments. One suggestion is that FRBM limits should be raised. 5% is what most people have suggested. Fourth, Central devolution is coming down and therefore the idea that is being floated is that, rather than the Finance Ministry deciding what to give, the Finance Commission should be given an additional term of reference, in the background of Covid on the additional grant and what should be the size of the special Covid grant to be given to the states.

The situation has changed so much that even for the current year they can very well make new recommendations. So, we would like to go by the Finance Commission's route.

Fifth, GST compensation must be paid. It is a solemn promise ingrained in the constitution. If they refuse to do it, I think we will have no choice, but to go to the Supreme Court. I hope other states will join Kerala.

Finally, I am not writing off all centrally sponsored schemes. The MGNREGA must be expanded to 150 days of employment, wages increased by another Rs 50 and all workers should be given half the last year's earnings as advance. You can recoup it during the course of the year. So this would mean that the neediest people will be getting something like Rs 3000 to Rs 4000 per person on the income front.

This is the time to introduce universal pension. It is now a paltry Rs 200. Make it respectable. Kerala gives Rs 1300 and so also the National Health Mission. But NHM, which has this silly way of having 2000 budget heads, as Yamini said, is crazy. Look at the idiocy of the Centre coming to Kerala and telling us how to handle our health sector and what should be spent on each item and so on. They should have some sense of proportion. Before they thought of the National Health Program, we were spending so much more on health. Give us some credit for it and freedom for action. Remove these ties and give us triple or four times the amount. Money has to go into health. This is the priority.

Then there was discussion of income transfer, grants to small scale industries and farmers, John's statement on what is to be done and a white paper on what is happening in Kerala. One does not know what the emerging situation in Kerala is. The Kerala State Planning Board will look at the impact of Covid on the economy.

Kerala's situation is going to be tougher. As much as 33% of our state income comes from remittance and already estimates are that 5 lakh people will return. There may be a 25% shortfall in remittance and with its reverse multiplier impact, the shock will be much bigger. There is a committee studying it. GIFT has been given the task of looking at the impact on tax revenue. We will then see what is to be done.

There is a challenge I am proposing to you. Today morning brought out a sudden fear. There is a calamity taking place. Why is the federal government not doing anything at all? They have given Rs 15,000 crore as a health package, only half of which is to be distributed this year and the rest over the next three years. So is there something more than that needs to be done? That was the issue that suddenly cropped up in the morning discussions. Is somebody deliberately pushing towards declaring a financial emergency? Given the Covid pandemic etc. no political opposition can crop up. People will be more worried about other things than your democratic rights and so on.

So, it is important that a platform emerges in India which lays out what has to be done. In these few hours of discussion, certain contours of a program did emerge for the state package, MSME package, farmer's package, income transfer package and so on. It could be a 50 or 100-point program. It can be finalised by continuing these discussions in other ways so that there is a platform on which we can rally any number of thinking economists and social scientists in India. Every concerned intellectual is to be signing it saying this is the way out.

In the morning there was the important discussion with Sitaram Yechuri, Jairam Ramesh and D. Raja, and it was agreed that important political parties and states draw up a program failing which, you end up accepting whatever 'bhashan' or package the Prime Minister gives on every occasion.

We will have a program on what is to be done. Every finance minister in India has independently written almost the same thing. Day before yesterday, we also got a copy of the letter that the Punjab finance minister sent to the Prime Minister. We have sent a similar letter and endorsed it. So, every finance minister and every chief minister is writing. But, why is it difficult to come together on platforms stating the same thing? Nothing additional is required. It is not a fundamental alternative for India but only a way to handle this pandemic.

So, I think a take home from our discussion would be to evolve a kind broad program or platform where every thinking concerned Indian who believes things should not be allowed to drift to a disaster, can join in. I do not know where this is going to end up. I hope the political leaders here will follow up and I know that as Sushil said, more people should join in. I do not want to spoil the chances of a future broad platform by opening up my frustrations. That is okay. In politics things happen like that. I think a good beginning has been made.

Just two more points. Vijayanand I thought would elaborate on the role of local governments in Kerala, especially the magnificent show they are putting up. It is a multilevel planning that is taking place. Daily briefings and briefing at the top level, and then you also have them at panchayats and municipalities. They are in charge of organising kitchens, monitoring migrant workers and also going to implement reverse quarantine in Kerala.

They are also very innovative. They are not just taking down what is said from above. I went to a panchayat where they have a hot spot that is now opening up. Now the panchayat has decreed that everyone can only walk with an umbrella night or day. If you hold two umbrellas together you will be one metre away from each other. Monsoon is on its way. Everybody would have to buy an umbrella. The Panchayat says, buy a big umbrella and nobody should go out without one. It shows the involvement, the sense of ownership of what is being done below.

There are moments when you think that the People`s Planning Campaign, 25 years back was a breakthrough. We have wondered whether it was a visionary dream. So many people think it has rusted. But something which we never discussed in People`s Planning in Kerala was disaster management. Suddenly Kerala realizes this is very important and now every panchayat is preparing a disaster management plan. It was while this plan was being prepared, that the pandemic broke out.

All over India there was a demand that the Finance Commission at least remove distinction between the basic and conditional grants. Give it to the local bodies. Let them do what they want with that the grant. Panchayats will be forced to follow real priorities as they are closer to the people and they have to face the people on a daily basis. They will respond to Covid and they will respond to hunger much better than the state machinery. Therefore, just give them untied grants. That is one point that came up.

Look at the states who are performing better. Kerala, Tamil Nadu, Rajasthan which have a better public health system. That is the common denominator for these states, which are performing better.

We are very grateful that you have spared the time for being here. The impact of this conference will be much larger than dialogue between us. A lot of people are coming in, watching and sending messages. I want to thank each one of you. It was a very good conversation and I hope you will continue.

Jayati Ghosh

Very useful and fascinating day.

Section 5

Covid Pandemic and the Future of the FRBM Act

Prabhat Patnaik

The FRBM act in my mind, is the most mindless piece of legislation that has been enacted. It has absolutely no theoretic base. It represents the domination of finance on our political processes. We don't have a legislation that tells us that at least 3% of our GDP should be spent on health or that at least 6% should be spent on education, but, we have a legislation that tells us that the fiscal deficit cannot exceed 3% of the GDP at the Centre and 3% of the GSDP in the states.

A consequence is that this makes fiscal interventions more cyclical as opposed to anti-cyclical. The Government actually would have to reduce its expenditure in a period of recession, instead of increasing it. It takes us back to the colonial period, the great depression for instance, during which there was actually a cut back in expenditure that worsened the impact of the depression, because of the fact that under that regime, the government was supposed to balance its budget.

Prabhat Patnaik, Professor JNU, is an Indian Marxist economist and political commentator. He taught at the Centre for Economic Studies and Planning in the School of Social Sciences at Jawaharlal Nehru University in New Delhi from 1974 until his retirement in 2010. He was the vice-chairman of Kerala State Planning Board from June 2006 to May 2011. After the financial crisis in 2008 Professor Patnaik was appointed to an interactive panel by the President of the UN General Assembly with the task of discussing the crisis and recommending reforms of the global financial system. Professor Patnaik has written many books including *Time, Inflation and Growth* (1988), *Macroeconomics* (ed.1995), and *Re-envisioning Socialism* (2011). He has been honoured by various academic associations holding several visiting professorships and currently edits the monthly journal *Social Scientist.*

Now instead of balancing the budget you are allowed only 3% of the GDP as a deficit. And also, it is something which expresses contempt for the political process. Political process assumes that elected political leadership is actually in a position to take decisions for the benefit of the community as a whole. In any case its decision, whether they are right or wrong, must be subject to scrutiny. But, if you tie their hands by actually saying you can't do A, B, C, by legislation before them, you are actually showing a kind of contempt for the political process. In fact, this entire legislation, which is not just in India but all over the world, with the exception of the United States, is something that privileges finance over the democratic process.

It privileges predilections and whims and caprices of local finance over democratic institutions. The purpose of the specific legislation becomes particularly clear specifically at the time of the pandemic. Obviously at this moment, the idea is to spend as much as possible to help people who are caught up in this lockdown.

Yesterday for instance, we talked about enlarging the borrowing limits of the states which basically means that they can engage in a fiscal deficit. Many have argued that likewise the Government has to transfer huge amounts of funds to the distressed people generally. Suggestions have been made that there should be a universal transfer of about Rs 7000 per month, per household to every household other than those who opt out of it over the next few months.

In fact, in the United States now, an amount of $ 1200 has been handed over to everybody. As a matter of fact, all over Europe and the United States, the fiscal deficits are being hugely widened. But in India, the Central Government does not even make a promise. Not only should the Central government enlarge the borrowing limits at this time, but I would suggest even doubling every state's borrowing limits.

A point that Professor Chandrasekhar has made is that they must be allowed to borrow from the Reserve Bank of India at the repo rates. In other words, they would not have to go to the market but will be able to borrow from the Reserve Bank of India, at the repo rate at which banks borrow from the Reserve Bank of India.

I think that is a very good suggestion and that is something which should be implemented at this particular time. Not only at this time, but also even after the impact of the pandemic subsides, as the economy is going to be disrupted. And this disruption would require a huge Government expenditure financed with a fiscal deficit at least to start with. Later on, one can have taxes and other things to raise revenue. To start with, you have to enhance expenditure by borrowing from the Reserve Bank of India, through not just a fiscal deficit but by a monetized deficit.

Now if that is to happen, the FRBM must be kept in abeyance for quite some time, whether through legislation or otherwise. But the point that it has to be kept in abeyance is something which is absolutely without any doubt. It should not have been there in the first place. But given the fact it has been there as a fetter and this fetter should be removed especially at this particular time.

I would now like to call the panellists to speak for 10 minutes each.

C.P. Chandrasekhar

Besides the sort of absurd conceptual basis of the FRBM Act which Prabhat has referred to in his introductory remarks, I think we also need to emphasise the fact that there is a difference between what the FRBM is supposed to be and what usually is in practice at the Central level. Particularly, there is considerable difference in the way in which the FRBM works at the Central level and the state level. At the Central level, we know now that you push off the budget a whole set of expenditures, you window dress your figures so that the so-called deficit is actually not a true deficit.

The finance minister in September last year decided to provide a huge tax concession exploiting the little fiscal space it created for itself. It wasn't any game changer as people make it out to be, but a completely ill-advised move, as the shift to the GST regime.

What we had was a situation in which the Government had attempted in some sense to try and manage its effort, to use whatever little space it has expanded, by slashing social sector expenditure, expenditure on the rural employment program, food subsidy etc. And the aim is to try and deprive in

---

C.P. Chandrasekhar was a Professor at the Centre for Economic Studies and Planning, Jawaharlal Nehru University, New Delhi. His areas of interest include the role of finance and industry in development and fiscal, financial and industrial policy reform in developing countries. He is also a columnist for leading Indian magazines and newspapers. He has published widely in academic journals and is the co-author of Crisis as Conquest: Learning from East Asia (Orient Longman), *The Market that Failed: Neo-Liberal Economic Reforms in India* (Leftword Books) and *Promoting ICT for Human Development: India* (Elsevier).

multiple ways, including user cesses and non-payment of huge GST revenues in compensation and actually try and limit the extent of transfer to the states, so as to keep for itself a certain amount of resources. These will reflect the fact that despite its effort in some sense to side step its own rational FRBM Act, it has gone to a situation in which the only way it can even maintain its minimal expenditure, aimed at pursuing an engineered redistribution of income of corporates and upper income groups, has essentially been to deprive the social sector of the state governments.

Compare this with the FRBM Act, as it applies to the state governments. The restrictions on the state government are much more severe, because of the possibility of actually making such adjustments and borrowing by the very limited means provided by the ways and means advances.

Of course, the borrowing limits set for the states is extremely low and therefore, the degree to which the states have been tied down by the FRBM Act is far greater than what has been normally presented to be. Actually, looking at it from the point of view of the federal polity, the FRBM Act is one which intensifies the Centralization in terms of increasing the fiscal flexibility within a neo- liberal framework of the Centre and limiting the fiscal flexibility of the states. This obviously, in a context like this, where we have a crisis and states need expenditure to address the pandemic itself.

We need a huge increase in expenditure on a large part of the population which has been affected by the sudden stop in economic activities. Resources to actually keep in place the possibility of those undertaking economic activities, and to be able to revive as and when the pandemic goes away to the extent that it does.

We are actually in a situation where we are talking about the requirement of a huge increase in expenditures and the complexity actually lies in the fact that if you don't undertake these expenditures, the collapse in economic activities is going to affect the revenues that we generate. We are talking about revenues in April which are one-tenth of the revenues in many states for example.

We end up in a situation where we have to step up expenditures to generate revenues and then using the fiscal responsibility and budget management act, we are saying "you better be careful." "Don't go around spending" several people including ex governors of the Central bank have made statements in the media. They say that you should be very careful of inflation if you undertake such activities, knowing fully well, we are sitting on food stocks, large unutilized capacities and very limited supply side constraints. The supply side constraints come, because you are not spending and separating economic activities from the pandemic, such that it actually can provide access to basic foods and services.

Thus, the real issue then is that unless you spend, there is no way out of this trap and in some sense it is very clear that this crisis is more serious than the past experiences, which tell us that this FRBM is not only absurd, but something that the Centre is going to exploit by transferring the burden of making the expenditure to deal with the pandemic, to the states. When states like Kerala decide to go to the market and borrow large sums to front load their borrowings, you end up with paying interest rates so high that the burden of interest payments will only accentuate the problem.

So as far as the states are concerned it should be very clear that all states (and it doesn't matter which), should demand an end to this regime. The point is that I don't want to get into the argument that has been much discussed in the past, on the inflationary aspects, etc. The only reason why there can be supply side constraints at some points is that they come as a result of the sudden shock and the only way you can relax this sudden shock is by relaxing expenditures, for which you need to borrow.

Now the point is, one, we need to borrow and two, you need to borrow at rates which are reasonable and that means you cannot borrow on the basis of growing interest rates which are completely unaffordable, generally in the current situation.

The other argument that has come up is that, if the states confront the situation and begin to demand things like larger transfers, immediate compensation, allowing them to borrow not from the markets but to issue bonds, the Central Bank must be required to actually take these on. You actually have a situation now, where the Central Bank is ready to create liquidity in the banking system to provide credit to companies like Reliance and HDFC in the first round of the targeted long-term repo operations.

In the second round, when they wanted to get to more risky ventures, obviously the banks were unwilling. The second round was not successful at all. Basically, you need to allow them to borrow. That is the Central Bank, which may decide suddenly like the Federal Reserve, to go and pick up corporate paper from the market directly, rather than mediate through the banks. It should be willing to pick up bonds of the state governments at the repo rate. I would even say the 4.47% repo rate is still high and there must be a partial subvention that they reduce the repo rate of the states, given the large amount of expenditure they have to finance.

Limits must be hugely relaxed. In fact, they must be flexible, depending on what the situation demands. The second argument that demanding these things, will only encourage the Centre to resort to a financial emergency, is saying that things are getting out of hand on the financial front because of the indiscipline of the states. This is meaningless.

If this Government wants to enforce a financial emergency, it is going to do so on its own. It is so centralised that it is already in a position to outsource handling the pandemic to the states. All it actually does is monitor without giving the states the resources to handle it. So, let us keep threats of that kind aside. If there is going to be a financial emergency that has to be fought, it will come independent of what the states do, so that dealing with the crisis is successful.

I think therefore, the main effort should be to try to bring as many states as possible together. To start with, the Congress ruled states and hopefully other opposition party ruled states, will also come together. Subsequently maybe, they could even force the BJP ruled states, given the intensity of the crisis and demand, because if they do not, the crisis is going to stay with us at a far more intense level, for a longer period. I think I will stop.

C. Rammanohar Reddy

We had a fascinating discussion yesterday, though fascinating is not the word to be used in the circumstances. Disturbing would be more apt. With Prof. Prabhat Patnaik's permission I will focus on the fiscal side itself and look at the short term and long term separately.

Now, in the short term, as Dr. Pinaki Chakraborty, I think, said yesterday, with the 2020-21 GDP likely to contract or grow by just 1 or 2 percent, the fiscal deficit will go up to 5, 6 or 8 percent of GDP. The aim to abide with the FRBM targets would just not happen. The GDP is expected to go up slowly or contract, your expenditures are going to shoot up and your revenue is going to take a hit. That is going to happen.

I think what we are now talking about is not of the breach in FRBM, but about what freedom the Centre and the states should have to borrow more and spend more, during the time of the pandemic, on health and the overall economy, given the state of the economy following the extended lockdown. As we heard yesterday, it is especially important for the states to have the freedom to spend. And they don't have it now.

We did have a lot of discussion on this yesterday. Here I would like to put it a bit strongly. This idea of cooperative federalism, which the Centre keeps mouthing and sometimes even the states also do mention, just does not exist

---

C. Rammanohar Reddy, is currently the Editor-in-Chief of *The India Forum*. From 1988 onwards, he has been in the media. He was earlier with *Deccan Herald* (Bengaluru) and *The Hindu* before becoming Editor of *Economic and Political Weekly*, Mumbai in 2004, a post he held forover 11 years. He pursued an MPhil in Applied Economics, PhD in Economics, at the Centre for Development Studies (CDS), Thiruvananthapuram.

at this point. We have reached a point now where increasingly over time, the Centre has kept centralising its powers and it looks like it is too interested in controlling the states.

How else would you explain that even at this time of the pandemic, it is simply not responding to the states' concerns or giving them more powers in any sense? You can list so many instances. GST dues is one.

Second, the Centre is not responding to the state's demand for a financial package. Just yesterday the Chief Minister of Pondicherry said that in his interaction with the Prime Minister, he mentioned the state's needs for an economic package and there was just no response. Similarly, the Kerala Finance Minister, Thomas Isaac, was pointing out yesterday to the so-called Rs 15,000 crore allocated for health. Half of it is to be distributed now to all states and the remaining Rs 7500 crore is to be given over the next three years.

Everything to me looks inexplicable. How can the Centre use this situation to increasingly centralize more powers and take away powers from the states? I mean it reduces their flexibility and does not respond to their demands. As somebody pointed out, all the Centre has done in the past 6 weeks was a complete failure. Take Kerala, for example. If I am not mistaken the state had to borrow at 8-9%, but Reliance used the opportunity to issue non-convertible debentures to raise Rs 7,500 crore to retire its high cost debt at 7.4%.

The results of the central policies are that the corporates are taking advantage of it to reduce their debt burden, while the states are finding it increasingly difficult to borrow from the market whenever they are allowed to. What do the states do? To reiterate what Chandrasekhar said earlier and Isaac was saying yesterday, the best they can do is for the state chief ministers and finance ministers to continue to raise the issue publicly. Writing letters seems to be such an innocuous act. Actually, it could well have an effect if the Congress-ruled states and the other opposition-ruled states get together and keep pushing in the first instance to monetize the fiscal deficit, with the Reserve Bank of India picking up the borrowing, which I think is already happening.

Last year I think 75% of the Centre's borrowings were picked up by the Reserve Bank of India. There is no reason why it can't take up for example Chandrasekhar's proposal of the Reserve Bank lending to the states, directly rather than asking them to go and borrow from the market at 8-9%.

Over the past six weeks the states have, at different forums, raised these issues. They are in the frontline dealing with a pandemic, but there is very little help coming from the Centre other than creating more obstacles. It looks like you have to keep pressing for more resources and more flexibility and less monitoring. Monitoring is doing more harm than facilitating dealing with the Covid.

Looking at the long term, the first thing is that, as Chandrasekhar pointed out earlier, for the Centre the FRBM is just a label, because it is increasingly over the years, finding other ways of using extra budget accounting, so much so that the Central fiscal deficit is probably 5% or more, and not under 4% and nowhere near 3.5%, as claimed. The markets surely know that.

For the Centre there are so many deviations, and it is using whatever skulduggery possible. The difficulty is more for the states. In the N K Singh committee report, I think there is a built-in deviation to accommodate 0.5% for the Centre, but not for the states. If I am not mistaken the states had that flexibility during the 2007-2008 financial crisis, but they don't have the flexibility right now.

I could still be corrected, but I think it is still a rigid 3% limit and as we all know it is the states which have been forced to adhere to it over the past few years. Now the question that haunts us is, how can you have fiscal flexibility for the Centre and the states? What we should discuss is how to introduce such flexibility, while showing the financial markets that it is not reckless, which is what they are looking for.

Now after all, the borrowings are facilitated by financial markets, so somewhere you have to signal to the financial markets that it may not be adhering to some straight jacket limits, but yet you are aware of your spending needs and the revenues that you can raise. This can happen only if we overhaul the legislation.

How does one overhaul the legislation? The political situation is such that fiscal responsibility rules are still inflexible, when governments all over the world have been taking recourse to flexibility. This will then come down essentially to (a) political struggle and (b) for the state governments to keep raising these issues at various fora. However, in the long term FRBM has to be overhauled, while retaining, but at the same time signalling to financial markets that you will use that flexibility, even while looking at revenue and expenditure together. These are my brief comments about deficits both in the short term and long term.

R. Nagaraj

I think the Covid-19 crisis and the lockdown that followed, is to be seen as the biggest humanitarian crisis causing loss of lives, jobs and livelihoods. We have discussed the fiscal deficit and the FRBM Act. There can be theoretical arguments for and against and we have empirical evidence, for and against the FRBM act. I think at the moment, what we are facing is a humanitarian crisis globally. In such situations, historically, all rulers have taken a very liberal view of the problem.

If the present government at the Centre believes in ancient India of India, it can be seen that whenever there was a crisis, the kings used to open up their treasury for public employment generation. You will find huge public works programs were taken up, whenever there was a crisis. One example that comes to my mind is the huge lakes in Bikaner in Rajasthan. They were dug and re-dug to create employment as a source of livelihood for the people. It was there even in the pre-modern times. So, I think, regardless of the political system we have, in situations of crisis, the issue is humanitarian, not simple economics. That is something which somehow, I think, has missed out in the current discussion with the Central government.

R. Nagaraj, Visiting Professor at the Centre for Development Studies (CDS), Trivandrum. Prior to joining CDS, Nagaraj was a Professor of Economics at the Indira Gandhi Institute of Development Research (IGIDR), Mumbai till his retirement. He holds a Ph.D. in Economics from Jawaharlal Nehru University. His areas of research include aspects of India's industrialisation, applied macroeconomics, public sector performance, the labour market in India, and official economic statistics. His forthcoming edited book titled *Industrialisation for Employment and Growth in India: Lessons from Small Firm Clusters and Beyond* is being published by Cambridge University Press.

So, it is beside ideology. I think this is what is being noticed from experiences all over the world. I have been following the British budget discussion and surprisingly the new conservative government has said that they have allowed unlimited ways and means advances by the treasury for tackling the pandemic. I think it is unlimited; absolutely no questions asked. Similarly, the British finance minister Rishi Sunak has gone on record saying that supporting small enterprises, what it calls micro enterprises, is a commitment. He is willing to put in up to one trillion-pound sterling to support them. This is the kind of support offered by a conservative government and not by any left liberal government. So, I think there is something to be learned from these examples. Keeping this in mind one doesn't understand what is stopping our government from stepping up expenditure to support income and employment for those suffering from the Pandemic. It seems to be just fiscal conservatism. It is just ideology which is coming in the way. What is the political basis of this ideology? Is there a fear that things will go out of hand? Will inflation go out of hand? Will the financial markets be punished as former governors of the RBI mentioned a few days ago?

So, I think this seems to be a big fear. I think we need to explain the need for public expenditure, as many of us have done today. But I think we need to do more of it. As long as the debt is in your own currency there is no fear of you having a debt crisis. A sovereign government can always print money to repay the maturing debt. The only fear one can think of is runaway inflation. But today, we are not in that situation. We have short term glitches or say frictions in supplies which are causing inflation. This is in certain sectors.

My colleagues put out a paper yesterday, which shows that food prices have gone up in urban areas, especially in small cities. That is because of the lockdown. However, we have no shortage of supplies of any kind. All of us know that India is essentially constrained by food and foreign exchange. On both counts there is abundance at the moment. Given that, the fear that we will not be able to repay the debt is simply not there. When it comes to states, I agree that they are far more constrained as other speakers have said. But how can we overcome it? Can we think of a tangible rule that we can bring forward to suggest to the Centre? Primarily, we should first define a humanitarian crisis, consider all the expenditures under that and assert that all such expenditures should be outside the fiscal budget constraint of the states, until the pandemic crisis is over.

I think this can be done. This can be quantified. What does it take to say we are in a crisis? Today we are facing three of them, the health crisis, fall in wages and the debt of the small enterprises. So, one can have two or three items and estimate what it will take to keep the humanitarian crisis out of regular budgetary calculation. We can estimate and check all the expenditure by the states and it should be put outside of their Fiscal Responsibility Act.

Maybe like what Chandrasekhar said, the states should be able to borrow directly from the Reserve Bank to meet such humanitarian expenditure. I think if we can come up with tangible and workable propositions of this kind with some numbers thrown into it we will have a better basis to take the agenda forward. I will stop here. Thank you.

Venkatesh B. Athreya

Although Prof R. Nagaraj was saying that under a certain set of circumstances one can find a relationship between inflation and deficits, I am not convinced. Basically, one additional idea that has come in is that you can take a position that we don't worry about the fiscal deficit. Of course, at the moment we are sitting on large forex resources.

As Prof Nagaraj said, we have more foodgrain stocks and currently that is the problem. The farmers are bringing their crops to the mandis and are finding it difficult to sell them. The Government of India is not willing to buy up the produce quickly. That means there will be serious problems for farmers in the next six to seven months. So, just as wage earners and MSMEs require support, so do farmers.

The agriculture sector needs financial support as well and obviously the Centre has generally taken a position that it cannot help. Let us face it, we are not

---

Venkatesh B Athreya, a chemical engineer-turned-development economist, served as professor of economics at Bharathidasan University, Tamil Nadu, for nearly three decades. After completing his B. Tech degree in Chemical Engineering from IIT Madras, he went on to obtain MS and Ph.D. degrees in Economics from the University of Wisconsin, Madison, USA. He has written extensively on issues of agrarian change, literacy, gender, infanticide, food security, human development and political economy. Professor Athreya has held faculty positions/Fellowships/Visiting Scholarships in a number of reputed academic institutions in India and abroad. He has authored/co-authored several books. He was the lead author of *The Report on the State of Food Insecurity in Rural India* (2008) and *The Report on the State of Food Insecurity in Urban India* (2010), both published by the M. S. Swaminathan Research Foundation and the World Food Programme.

talking of some ideal world. We are talking of the real world. A striking feature of the Centre's response to the crisis has been callousness. Utter callousness in respect of migrant workers and daily wage earners across the country.

Likewise, utter indifference to the financial crises of state governments, much of which is a consequence of the Centre's fiscal policies. A measure of how desperate the states are, can be seen in Tamil Nadu. Though the ruling party supports the Centre, the Tamil Nadu government has written a desperate letter yesterday, requesting the freedom to raise their fiscal deficit to 4.5% of the GSDP.

So, I think all sectors have been badly affected and the Centre is following a policy of positive obstructionism. They are preventing state governments from doing what they were trying to do. Every single move of state governments to do something has been stymied by the Centre's mindless intervention and micro management. We are dealing with a much larger issue. I think that Ram Reddy talked about Centralization. He was, of course, right. But it is not just about financial Centralization.

Remember the extreme act of demonetization. Forget that. Forget even the ham handed design and implementation of GST. Look at what is happening to education. The State List is being whittled down, the Concurrent List is on the way to becoming a Union List. The regime at the Centre has launched an all-out attack on the federal character of the country.

All along the line, this Government at the Centre, has basically abdicated its responsibility in dealing with the pandemic. Its line is that, we have to accept the pandemic. Just consider the last 18 months!

The Centre's policies have been blatantly pro-corporate. From the time of the absolutely meaningless 2019 July budget, what I call a non-budget, followed by the September-October 2019 events, where corporate honchos came forward to say they could not even sell five rupee biscuit packets let alone automobiles, we had the series of concessions doled out by the Centre to the corporate sector: Rs 1.45 lakh crore for corporates via the reduction in the corporate tax rate to a flat 22% regardless of turnover, Rs 50,000 crore for additional export subsidies, another 20,000 crore for real estate and housing, totally amounting to Rs 2.15 lakh crore.

Then you had 65,000 crore rupees worth of direct tax concessions in the Union budget of February 2020. The other serious issue is the (lack of) credibility of the numbers put out by some of the Union government's official sources. All the numbers have become meaningless. In a sense, it is a problem talking about numbers. We just don't know what the numbers really mean.

Globally you are in a downturn. There is hardly any prospect of across the board inflation as of now. As Nagaraj said, there is some price increase in selective sectors because of temporary bottlenecks. We can have some temporary increase in prices, but not a general rise. Speaking of the general trend, oil prices are also falling. Only this Government has the unique distinction of never passing on the gains from the oil price decline to the people. It keeps on raising excise duty to increase revenues.

This has been the behaviour of the Government in the last six- seven years and I do not expect that mindset to change. One does not know who is advising them. Basically, the logic is of centralising power in all respects, not just economic but across, education, healthcare, day to day micromanagement. I think we also need to recognize that we have to make efforts beyond the state governments to reach the general public in a massive campaign on fiscal relations and broader democratic changes in Centre-state relations in the direction of true federalism.

We need to bring political parties on board for the purpose. Unfortunately, most political parties in this country do not have a record of taking a good stand on Centre-state relations. Of course, the regional parties will play a political role. One has to think of how to bring them all on board in this fight. Congress, at the moment may join but it is always uncertain. They may for the time being.

Yesterday, when Jairam Ramesh spoke, he was very careful to differentiate between neo liberals and Congress. But the track record of the Congress suggests a strong ideological commitment to neoliberalism. I think I can't really add more to what has been said by others here. I endorse pretty much all of what has been said.

We must demand white papers in the Parliament and the Assembly, of what were the presumed benefits of fiscal largesse towards the corporate sector over the years and what has actually transpired on the ground in terms of investments and jobs and people's incomes. So, we must make the governments accountable, on the claims made in favour of very generous tax concessions to the corporate sector in the name of promoting investment and growth.

At the very minimum, we should ask whether we can defer the concessions to the corporate sector for a few years. Why should we implement them immediately? The flip side of this generosity to the corporate is mindless selling off of PSU assets to limit deficits.

The other important thing we should demand is much more non-discretionary transfer to the states from the Centre.

Lekha Chakraborty

Let me flag a few points that I want to focus on.

First, I want to flag the "role of institutions" like Fiscal Councils in re-interpreting FRBM. Yesterday, I had a conversation with Bloomberg regarding the emergence of a new economic consensus at the state level, towards the formation of state fiscal/economic councils with the domain experts. I think we must explore this.

For instance Rajasthan and Madhya Pradesh have recently constituted state level economic advisory councils. Similarly, I think the states should take a lead in constituting state-specific fiscal councils. Otherwise, there can be a fallacy of aggregation if the (potential) fiscal council is just for Centre alone, and is going to be a homogenous entity analysing both Centre and state finances. So, I would like the honourable finance minister Dr Thomas Isaac to explore the importance of the subnational fiscal council to examine the issues of fiscal rules

---

Lekha S. Chakraborty is a Professor at NIPFP and elected Member of the Governing Board of Management, International Institute of Public Finance (IIPF) Munich—the world association of public finance economists. She is a pioneer economist in institutionalising Gender Budgeting in India, with Chief Economic Advisor, Ministry of Finance, Govt of India in 2004. She is also a research affiliate at the Levy Economics Institute of Bard College, New York. She has worked for the IMF, World Bank, the UNESCAP, the UNDP, the UN Women, and the Commonwealth Secretariat. She was visiting Professor at American University (US), Uppsala University (Sweden), Carleton University (Canada), and University of Utah (US). She is the author of "Fiscal Consolidation, Budget Deficits and Macroeconomy" and has papers in many national and international journals. She is also a columnist in almost all newspapers.

and budget management. This can also analyse issues related to fiscal forecasting errors and budget credibility.

Second, when we articulate about a new FRBM, we have to grapple with new levels of deficit and in yesterday's panel discussions, it was pointed out that the new threshold fiscal deficit could be "5% of the GDP." But again, we are getting into another numerical limit. We have to be extremely cautious whether this new threshold – suggested 5%, will be helpful.

Third, whenever we talked about the fiscal rules, our ultimate goal was to enhance economic growth. But now we are primarily facing a human tragedy. So, this crisis may turn into an opportunity with which we can try for a paradigm shift with the new FRBM framework integrating the "economic growth plus" or "GDP-plus" analytics.

We cannot just work out exclusively with growth parameters and arrive at the new number which is 5-6%, excluding the sustainable development perspectives. It has to be "growth plus," to address the humanitarian crisis which we need to tackle.

What then could be the new numerical limit for the deficit to do this "economic firefighting," if you insist on a numeric limit for deficit-GDP? This is what we need to think about the moment we talk about the macro-fiscal framework.

The fourth question is about which deficit we need to focus on as an operational parameter. This is also something we are grappling with, because we have started with the budget deficit (deficit financing requirements based on seigniorage, and expanded to the monetized part of deficit incorporating the ad hoc Treasury Bills financing) a long-time back, then moved towards the fiscal deficit (the entire net borrowing requirement of the Government) later.

Right now, the significance of the monetized deficit is being debated. So which deficit do we have to articulate as the operational parameter in the new FRBM framework? I remember the controversy—the dissent note by Arvind Subramanian, former Chief Economic Advisor - in the FRBM committee report, highlighting the significance of primary deficit (fiscal deficit devoid of interest payments), to capture the current fiscal policy stance of a government. The ideal measure of deficit is Public Sector Borrowing Requirements (PSBR), but paucity of data thwarted constructing this measure.

Fifth, with the re-emergence of debates on the efficacy of the monetized deficit, it is not only levels, but the financing pattern of deficit, that is an equal concern. Professor Sudipto Mundle had mentioned yesterday that the financing part of the deficit is immaterial, whether it is bond financing or not, from a macroeconomic perspective, but rather, it is only significant from a political economy perspective.

I think it is quite relevant both from the political economy perspective and the macroeconomic perspective, because any excessive mode of financing the deficit has its own specific macroeconomic consequences. It is quite distinct, just like bond financing, which may or may not trigger a financial crowding out, or a seigniorage financing, which may or may not be inflationary. So I think, the choice over the financing pattern of deficit has both political economy imperatives, as well as macroeconomic consequences.

My seventh point is about the debt sustainability clauses in FRBM. I attended the American Economic Association conference last year, in Atlanta. In the AEA presidential lecture by Oliver Blanchard, he highlighted that public debt is not catastrophic if more debt can be justified by clear benefits, like public investment or output gap reduction. He also highlighted that public debt has no fiscal costs, if the real rate of interest is not greater than the real rate of growth of the economy.

This was pointed out in yesterday's discussions, by the honourable Finance Minister Dr Thomas Isaac. If our *r* is going to be greater than *g*, it is obviously an unsustainable debt situation and invoking the "escape clause" will not help us either.

My eighth point is on "escape clause". There is quite a bit of ambiguity in the FRBM report on whether any escape clause exists for the sub-national-levels of government. We have two FRBMs in India. The new FRBM has done away with the 'golden rule' of fiscal rules, that is, the clause which relates to the "revenue deficit/surplus".

My ninth point is about "Excessive Deficit procedure". Against the backdrop of the pandemic, if we are thinking of an FRBM amendment to higher upper bound of deficit threshold ratios, we should also think about an "excessive deficit procedure" to avoid fiscal profligacy in the long run. In other words, allow the states to go beyond the numerical limit, but with a clear road map or an excess deficit procedure map, in which there is a clear articulation or plan saying that we will get back to the threshold position over a definite period of time. That is important, from the perspective of fiscal prudence in the long run.

These are the things that came up in my mind. Then when we talk about the debt and deficit we can also alter the maturity structure of the debt.

My tenth point therefore, is about the "elongation of maturity pattern of debt". The operational twist tool, recently introduced by the Reserve Bank of India by simultaneous selling of short term bonds and buying of long term bonds, was aimed at altering the structure of maturity pattern and enhancing liquidity in the system. At subnational levels, we may work with the maturity pattern of debt towards long-term bonds to pre-empt refinancing strategies, or the risks in the short run. For instance, Telangana has focussed on the elongation of maturity pattern of the debt.

To wind up, if the FRBM targets are achieved through expenditure compression, rather than enhanced tax buoyancy, it will affect the quality of consolidation, as it will have adverse consequences on economic growth in the long run.

There is a narrative behind FRBM that the fiscal discipline is growth enhancing. However, empirical evidence has proved that over adjusting to fiscal rules (especially through capital expenditure compression), has adversely affected economic growth.

This is a question of "life versus livelihood" we have to deal with. Of human tragedy. And of economic disruptions. I think we need to explore innovative modes of financing the deficit. We may go for limited seigniorage financing. I am not fully for the new monetary policy tools in the form of "helicopter money," articulated by the former Federal Chair Ben Bernanke. Otherwise if we pitch our expenditure decisions on stability of revenue, we may not be able to design the economic firefighting packages required to deal with the pandemic.

Globally there is a conversation about exploring the importance of a change in high powered money to GDP and we should have a threshold of seigniorage in mind, but not like a seigniorage forever. The seigniorage Laffer Curve, can give us a threshold regarding how much we can finance through the seigniorage. It is healthy to have a shift in the financing pattern of deficit from bond financing to limited internal monetized financing of debt. Exploring the external financial oligarchy to finance the deficit, by engaging in external borrowing, may have adverse consequences.

Thanks!

Thomas Isaac

Let us start the discussion. We can have the second round of panellists and then we will take some questions from the floor. Lekha you spoke about a Fiscal Council, but after the experience of the GST Council, I am wary of all councils to put it very frankly.

Now the council has been suggested in the same spirit as the 14th Finance Commission. The Centre has to be accountable to somebody. Going beyond that, to look into other issues and micro manage through various ways, given the limited autonomy the states now have is not desirable. There is already the FRBM Act and the GST Council. Setting up a Fiscal Council, over and above this too, would be uncalled for. What makes you think that it won't degenerate into further constraining the states? That is my fear.

Lekha Chakraborty

Sir I was talking about state-specific councils and not the Centre. I was thinking about the new trend of emergence of economic councils at the state level now. I was therefore suggesting a state council. There is already an economic council (in many states).

Thomas Isaac

A council of states to look into the Centre-state finances. I don't think that makes sense. That was not the spirit in which the 14th Finance Commission stated it. Their logic was asymmetrical in the implementation of the FRBM. While the Centre can do anything, the states are under a hard budget constraint. Therefore, the Centre has to be held accountable.

It is a good idea but can easily be turned around into something for controlling states further. That is my fear. I would like you to respond to that.

Lekha Chakraborty

I was highlighting the re-emergence of the economic councils at the state level right now. Many states have constituted State-level advisory councils, for instance, with Montek Singh Ahluwalia (former Planning Board Vice Chairman) in Punjab, Arvind Mayaram (former Finance Secretary) in Rajasthan, Sumit Bose (former Finance Secretary) in Madhya Pradesh. There is a re-emergence of the importance of economic councils to analyse and articulate the economic and fiscal issues at the state level. So, I was trying to explore that for Kerala. Why can't the Kerala state government explore that? That was my limited question.

Thomas Isaac

We have been old fashioned. We still have our planning board.

K.N. Harilal

Professor Patnaik was saying states should be allowed to borrow double the limit and the terms should be very flexible. Chandrasekhar and others mentioned the rate of interest. A small borrowing should be allowed at favourable terms. This much is clear.

Then, there is the question of monetizing the deficit. When it comes to monetizing the deficit, most of the participants were in agreement, but there are some doubts about financing it. Nevertheless, there is a problem with the method of financing the deficit. Then regarding the question of inflationary pressure, there is much agreement in the belief that there won't be much inflationary pressure. And, we can certainly produce more. Other participants have talked about supply constraints in the short term. A supply problem in agriculture, for instance.

K.N. Harilal, Professor at CDS, was a Member of Kerala State Planning Board, Government of Kerala on deputation from Centre for Development Studies, Thiruvananthapuram, Kerala. He has adorned key positions in the past including member, of the Working Group on External Sector for the Eleventh Five Year Plan of India, Planning Commission, Government of India, New Delhi, 2006-07, Member, Local Resources and Human Development Research Group (LORC), Ryukoku University, Kyoto, Japan, since 2005, Consultant, Decentralised Planning, Kerala State Planning Board 1996-2000, Member, Steering Committee for Ninth Five Year Plan, Government of Kerala, Member, Working Group on Evolving Formula for Interse Distribution of Plan Grants to Local Bodies, Government of Kerala and member, WTO Cell, Government of Kerala. Prof Harilal works largely in the area of capital-labour relations and has a number of publications to his credit.

We have adequate food stocks now. What will we do after six month? Whether there will be distribution problems particularly in the case of non-cereal food, is something that should be discussed. Distribution to remote towns should particularly be observed and discussed.

Now regarding non-food items. What if factories remain shut and supply chains blocked? Many of these supply chains are globalised and internationalised. So, opening the barriers and allowing them to operate will not solve the problems. In the case of many necessities, there will be problems.

Yesterday, Jayati was saying that this problem can only be solved by planning. You can increase demand by increasing the deficit, and taking the money to the people through various means. However, there should also be planning because global disruption of supply chains will ensure that supply is not going to automatically respond to increased money and income.

Monetizing the deficit requires tackling the possible supply crunch. How can a country like India tackle that? In India we were not closely linked to the international market like many economies. We have lived in some kind of a relative protection, but because of recent advances in globalisation our supply chains are also integrated to the global ones. A block in supply chains is an important problem.

Our demand is that the borrowing limits be eased. Now in the case of Kerala, the Centre was very strict about borrowing limits. That is just one of the issues. The major issue is that all borrowings of the state government, (not exactly borrowings as these include some treasury deposits too, which happened three years or four years ago), are being counted as this year's deficit. There is no economic logic behind this, but it is something that is leading to major problems in the Kerala context.

These are some of the issues that I thought the panel could introspect on. Before I wind up, I would like to draw your attention to another topic, which was partially discussed yesterday. The economic advisor of the Government of India was saying that we will not go for incremental announcements and incremental policy interventions, as that will make the global industrial capital nervous. If we make big announcements, increase borrowing limits and monetize, we will be creating problems as investors may not favour it.

As Nagaraj and others said, while world leaders are monetizing and increasing deficits for various reasons in a big way, why is only India worried so much about investors' feel good factor? We should discuss this.

K.J. Joseph

I understand that Prof Patnaik is not able to connect. May I request Prof Thomas to take over?

Thomas Isaac

I will add one more issue that Harilal raised, for the panel to respond. There has been a consensus that pandemic time FRBM limits are to be relaxed, but there is a more important issue in the medium term. The future of the FRBM Act with reference to the 15th Finance Commission. We have the FRBM review committee, which in principle has been accepted by the Government of India. In the context of the current scenario, how do we respond to that? Do we challenge the need for an FRBM Act itself? Or demand the manner in which it should be modified? I don't think that there can be a debate on raising the fiscal deficit ceiling. That kind of position is totally untenable and even if the Centre opts for it in reality, they will be crossing limits. They only want the states to stick to the limits. This is also an important issue that you have to take up.

C.P. Chandrasekhar

I shall now respond to your questions and also to statements made by Harilal and Lekha.

Let us set aside the pandemic for now. We have to ask ourselves if this experience will enable citizens and governments globally, through their parliaments, to actually work out a profile or projectile of their potential expenditures to occur at different points of time. It will be generated since it is linked to the potential expenditures that are undertaken. As we know, expenditure has a multiplier effect resulting in an increase in incomes and revenues.

It is only a basic saying that we are in a position to judge what would be in some kind of reasonable if not optimal trajectory of what could revenue and expenditures and therefore based on what we think is reasonable to arrive the GDP at a figure which we say should be the maximum level to which the difference between expenditures and revenue would be.

The problem is your borrowing or debt GDP ratio is global. First of all, no one really knows how this benchmark of 3% was arrived at. It is that the figure was manufactured in the post-Maastricht treaty negotiations and was just picked up by international finance. It is now applied all over the world.

Even if we agree that there was a computation on basis of which, the 3% figure was arrived at, our experience even before this crisis, speaks for itself. For example, in 2007-08, or in the interim 2007-08 and now, a reasonably clear prediction has been possible, as to what could be an approximate differential between expected growth of expenditure and revenue. However, this is not practical and the only way governments have addressed this, is by either revising their own fiscal deficit targets or by window dressing their budgets to be actually delivered on targets.

Now superimpose on that the fact that you did not predict a very severe crisis either in 2007-8 and you did not do so during this pandemic. Once you superimpose that, what you are actually saying goes to smithereens. There is no way you can make a prediction. All we can say is, governments have to retain for themselves the flexibility to be able to make decisions.

There has to be ways in which entities, other than global or domestic finance, or corporates would be in a position to be able to monitor whether governments are misusing the flexibility that they are provided with. This can be done through parliaments, institutions and agencies, which can reverse a political decision if they feel it is an unnecessary exercise with respect to borrowing.

In my view, there is no way you can have a viable fiscal deficit target imposed over a long period of time. So FRBM must go. It is important to discuss what we are going to activate in terms of monitoring and disciplinary measures to be taken, at a point of time. A time bound approach to assess whether particular governments are misusing the flexibility should not be adopted.

Hence, the path to be taken, even without experience in handling crises is clear, and with two of them behind us, it is obvious. The FRBM has lost its credibility. Now, it is merely an instrument for the distribution of income in favour of the upper income groups, while oppressing the states. It is not an instrument to ensure fiscal discipline either at the Centre or the states. This is my take on it.

Ram Manohar Reddy

Isaac, I missed out on one thing. Can you repeat what the government has accepted?

Thomas Isaac

The FRBM Review Committee Report logic was going to be built into the 15th Finance Commission report. Now the pandemic has made a mess of the recommendations and it would be ridiculous to suggest something of that kind. Nevertheless, the Finance Commission Report is for the next five years and therefore, I am instinctively certain, they would go forward with the FRBM Review Committee Report and try to make constraints more stringent. I thought we should also respond to that. Nobody with any economic sense would argue sticking to this 3% ratio during the pandemic. That is taken for granted, except by economists who do not want the big bang etc. In the medium term we would also have to look at the FRBM Review Committee Report and their recommendations.

Ram Manohar Reddy

I will speak on a few points. Firstly, I wonder whether now that the Finance Commission numbers have all gone haywire, as Pinaki said yesterday, the states can now ask the Finance Commission to rework its numbers and, in the process, look at its approach afresh. It does not make sense at all if the numbers have no basis.

Also, it is not just a question of tinkering with the numbers, but looking at the post-pandemic world where everybody feels things are going to be very different. Can't we look at things differently? It is not within the remit of the Finance Commission to look at the FRBM, who can re-examine it even if they need another six months.

Secondly, we are talking about getting them to change the FRBM etc. Yes, but what really worries me is the whole approach at present. The economy has collapsed. Lakhs of people are still on the highway. There are reports of starvation and even deaths and yet we are completely insensitive. The Prime Minister was saying yesterday that the economy is doing well. People cannot understand the Government's approach. I am not going to speak again about financial emergency. That is a different thing.

In such a situation, how does one even get them to reconsider the FRBM? What is it that will make them take a fresh look at it? I think right now, we need to get the Finance Commission to relook its numbers and then also at the whole FRBM issue. It is perhaps a battle that has to be fought in the next few years or a year later. Right now, it is a question of getting that flexibility to borrow and spend more.

If we step back a bit, the scenario is really frightening. It is not just the pandemic, but the economy. What is going to happen to the social fabric? Can this be handled using media as a tool? Going by the demonetization episode and the negligible damage it did to the Government electorally, there is a worry that the Government has learnt the wrong lessons from it. I think that the battle on the whole issue of the FRBM Act, has been better prepared for and will be fought later, rather than taken up right now.

I think FRBM should be considering taking the humanitarian crisis as a priority and identifying the kind of medium-term expenditure requirement for the state. It will then be possible to put some numbers there.

The states participating in the meeting must have a document showing FRBM the sort of expenditures and exemptions required to borrow. Concrete numbers should be provided and put out in the public domain. That becomes a useful basis and a platform on which we can take this battle forward.

Having a written document by credible people and political backing from opposition ruled states, would be a good way to proceed. I think many of us can put our heads together and work on the document, to get over the humanitarian crisis. Other issues can be taken up later. This is a requirement we need to work on in the next few months. That becomes a public document on which we can work both at the academic level as well as political level. I think this is a reasonable way forward.

Lekha Chakraborty

I completely agree with you that there is a transition happening in fiscal policy, from using the discretion of the policy maker to formulating stricter rules. I completely agree with that. I would like to share your concern that we should do away with our limited goals as far as numerical limits are concerned. I am hopeful. However, I do not know how pragmatic it will be and given the settings at the Central level, I cannot be sure whether they will let go of the numerical limits altogether. Such things do not happen.

Within the framework, the thinking is to give importance to the medium-term fiscal framework. If you have a sectoral ceiling for education and health, then even when a drastic cut in expenditure happens, we can protect the social sector, if we have a sectoral NTFP. That is the only thing which I think we can do if they insist on a numerical limit.

Secondly, I never thought that you had so much aversion towards councils. I advocate allocations, because the Centre makes a lot of promises but does not act. An important role of the fiscal council is to highlight that what you are promising is not there by allocation and marksmanship. I was thinking on those lines when I was talking about the fiscal councils. But, I do agree that we still believe in planning and the relevance of the Kerala State Planning Board. We do not have to set up another institution.

Thomas Isaac

Chandrasekhar, personally, I would fully agree with your propositions. One of the purposes of this exercise is that we are able to bring together as many academicians as possible, on a common denominator that everybody can agree upon. It means that there is an alternative on how to address the humanitarian crisis.

So, far the Government has been totally silent on what they are going to do and have been coming out with piecemeal things. One does not know what ad hoc decision may be taken in the future and we do not want that to happen by default, because nobody had an alternative. It is not an alternative program or minimum program, or anything of that sort.

It is a set of proposals of the measures to be taken during a pandemic and the democratic response needed, which can be shared by a large spectrum of thinkers and actors. This is the humanitarian response to it. This is something that would solve the present challenges. We don't want to be surprised by somebody imposing financial emergency because there is a calamity and the nation has to be supported. That is unacceptable.

There should be some alternative for the country to look forward to. So, in this context, let us look at the points that Harilal raised with reference to chief economist Sanjay Sanyal's interview with journalist Jayaraman of 'The Hindu.' Sanyal mentioned three important points during the interaction. One, no big bang package would be announced and any such announcement should be incremental. Big developed countries have indeed erred in implementing such a strategy, he says. Two, that this approach has been appreciated by international investors. Three, the economic package will be the occasion for important large-scale reforms.

So, what would the panellists say in response to this?

C.P. Chandrasekhar

Kerala announces a Rs 20,000 crore package. Kerala had decided to do its own thing. And, you want to have an all-state consensus on the limits of expenditure you can go to, in the context of the Covid crisis. Supposing Uttar Pradesh says that though we are a big state, we only want Rs 5000 crore. Are you going to be happy with that? In essence you are demanding flexibility. The larger point is that you must have flexibility, but when you climb down, do what you want to do. Be diplomatic so that you may not have to challenge the FRBM limitations directly but, you can ask for the facility to borrow at an affordable rate of interest.

If not, you won't be able to handle your own situation. As far as the principal economic advisor in the Ministry of Finance, Sanyal is concerned, he is only justifying what the Centre is doing. He is just saying, whatever has been done now is the best thing to do.

Ram Manohar Reddy

I would endorse Chandrasekhar. I don't know what can be said in such a meaningless situation. A Niti Aayog member had said that after May 17 there would be no Covid cases in India. We should respond only to important issues.

R. Nagaraj

There should be a political polemical reply to the economist. We must come up with an alternative supported by numbers. We should be able to come up with a firm solution to the problem. If that was publicly available, we would have a basis for a debate rather than a polemical reply. I think we should work towards an alternative, for at least a few states. Not just platitudes but with numbers and a certain logic behind it.

Lekha Chakraborty

We can highlight the context of Kerala's experience in this case. Kerala is the only state in which the policies have been taken in a simultaneous manner rather than sequential. The Centre has prioritized life, then livelihood and then humanitarian crisis. This is going to be very costly. Kerala took simultaneous decisions on the life crisis, economic crisis, migrant crisis. This is a good model to follow. But, I understand that it has not happened overnight.

Thomas Isaac

Thank you. We will take this forward. We shall have a document within a week, an alternative platform on how to tackle the pandemic. We are not going to accept this incremental approach.

Section 6

Kerala's Health Strategy in Containing Covid-19 Pandemic

K.K. Shailaja Teacher

I think all of you are aware of the strategy Kerala is using to tackle this problem. Our previous experience of an epidemic was the Nipah virus. At that time, it was a fairly new thing and we were not aware of all the pitfalls. When the Nipah incident occurred we discussed with expert teams and also searched literature for operating practices that we could adopt and formed our own protocol, with our own means. Collecting things from all parts of the world, we formed a very good protocol and standard operating practices for the Nipah case.

First of all, we were aware that the most important thing was screening and also isolating these affected people from others, while giving them proper treatment. This included not just physical treatment but also that which stabilised them mentally. Every minute detail was arranged for at that time and most importantly, we also had a very good team for contact tracing.

K.K. Shailaja Teacher is an Indian politician and the Health Minister of Government of Kerala. She currently serves as the MLA in 15th Kerala Legislative Assembly. She was previously elected thrice as the MLA in 1996, 2006 and 2016. She is a Central Committee member of CPIM. Before entering active politics, she worked as a high school physics teacher. Shailaja was honoured by the United Nations for her efforts to tackle the coronavirus pandemic. She was among a few of the world leaders invited to speak on the occasion of the United Nations Public Service Day. K. K. Shailaja was awarded the CEO Open Society Prize for 2021. She has authored two books: *Indian VarthamanavumSthreesamoohavum* and *China: Rashtram, Rashtreeyam, Kazhchakal.*

It was a difficult task, but our team did it efficiently and we were able to trace all contacts on time. Such activities helped us to build up some expertise. When Covid-19 broke out in Wuhan, China, the news was flashed across some sections of the electronic media. It was an anxious moment for me, because the memory of Nipah was still with us. I called my health secretary Rajan Khobragade and told him that a new kind of SARS virus had spread in Wuhan, China, belonging to the coronavirus family, which gave rise to acute respiratory syndrome, just like the Middle East respiratory syndrome virus. I told him it would be a dangerous virus. We started our preparations right then, because we had so many Malayalee students studying in Wuhan University.

We were sure that we would have arrivals from Wuhan to Kerala. As we expected, some students and other passengers came from Wuhan on January 27th. By January 24th, we had formed our control room, had a rapid response team meeting and formed our control room in Kerala. We had these groups not only at the state level but also in the districts. We passed on the message to them that a certain kind of virus was spreading in Wuhan in China and we should be in full preparedness, with immediate effect.

We formed control rooms in all districts, much before the first Wuhan case happened here. As we suspected, on January 27th, a flight with passengers from Wuhan came here and we screened them at the airport. By then we had formed a strategy and also decided we should screen foreigners entering Kerala. If there was a symptomatic case amongst them, we shifted them to hospitals where we had set up isolation wards.

Even if there were no symptoms, people from abroad were shifted home for strict quarantine with advisories asking them to confine themselves to a room and not use a common toilet. If they did not have a separate toilet for themselves, we stepped in to arrange separate facilities for them. We asked them to follow the instructions and we even put a notice on their doors, giving all instructions on how to serve them food, the precautionary measures to be taken and minute details that their caretakers were required to follow.

Such work yielded good results because of our preparedness. All the three Wuhan students who had tested positive were admitted to the hospital, cured and soon discharged. That was the first phase. The virus and pathogens are taking flights from other countries now and that is the worst situation now. We all know about the huge spread of the virus in Italy and other parts of the globe.

So, we again started strengthening our awareness program and preparedness efforts and we decided to have a mock drill in the month of March. We knew the virus would hit us again, not as a mock drill but as the actual thing on the ground.

We did this because we came across infected foreign passengers from Italy and the United Kingdom. We tested and screened them. The method followed was screening, home quarantine or isolation, treatment and discharge. We even followed a good discharge protocol. I am not getting into all the details because I would rather hear from you since we are in the process of looking out everywhere, to get some more advice on how to proceed further.

Now Kerala has flattened the curve. We all know that it is not possible to completely stop the spread but, flattening the curve is the most important thing. In Kerala, we have flattened the curve properly. Our fatality rates are very low and our infectivity rate is still very good in the range of 1.5 to 3.5. The nature of the virus is such that in some places it may progress faster from 1 to 4 or 4 to 16 or even more. We have to break the chain. That is the most important thing. We have started a campaign to break the chain by promoting hand wash and also ensuring social distancing. We did all these parallelly. These activities have also helped us to flatten the curve.

Now look at the doubling rate in India. In Maharashtra it is 7 days, while in Kerala the doubling rate is much below 7. We achieved this, because of our preparedness and continuous work. Until yesterday, we had 491 cases, after testing 23,000 samples with a PCR test. Initially, we tried to have these antibody tests done with kits from the ICMR. However, when we tried to validate it, the results were not reliable. We passed on the message immediately to the ICMR. Several states did the same thing. Following this, the Central Government asked us to discard the kits.

We are now trying to get more kits from other places. If we get them, we will do the antibody tests too. Kerala is ahead of other states as far as PCR tests are concerned, but Maharashtra is ahead in the case of antibody tests. They did a large number of tests using antibody strips, but we have only PCR tests here.

Our main difficulty is the shortage of RNA extraction kits. This would have enabled us to conduct more than 3000 samples a day since we now have more testing labs. Initially, we had one lab in Alleppey, the Alleppey Virology Lab and we have now permissions from ICMR for 14 labs. As many as 12 are testing continuously and 2 are preparing to conduct tests. However, our hands are tied due to this shortage and we are unable to increase the number of tests beyond a limit. I would like to get your suggestions on this.

But yesterday, we took almost 3056 samples as per the instruction of our honourable chief minister, the results of which will be out today. But, we cannot do 3000 tests each day because of the scarcity of RNA kits. We have no way to solve it. That is the situation here. There has been a decline in some districts of Kerala, while it has increased in districts like Idukki and Kottayam.

The infection is not being spread by foreigners, but from our neighbouring states. The major source is now Tamil Nadu with whom we have a common border. Infected people are crossing the borders on foot. The police are trying to stop it. Since we have strong linkages with other states, it is difficult to curb the number of people entering and leaving. We cannot easily identify the traffic. We have been trying our best. This is the situation in Kerala.

Yesterday, we had 481 cases out of which only 163 were in the hospital. All others have been cured and discharged. The recovery rate is also high in Kerala. There were 3 deaths, of which two had comorbidities. There was also a 4-month child with congenital heart disease and other problems.

We cannot predict whether there will be another surge. We are fighting hard with the cooperation of all other departments. We have financial problems. The financial crisis is severe but our finance minister is not holding back funds even for fresh appointments. He is helping us more than anything by giving us money to buy inventories, medicines and other things. The chief minister is leading from the front and ensuring the convergence of all departments.

This is the case in Kerala, but what next? It is exactly for this purpose that we want to get advice from experts throughout India and the world. Several eminent personalities are present in this seminar. I hope we will get more advice from you.

I apologise for the long speech, but I had to explain what is happening in Kerala. The finance minister insisted I do that. I will not speak further, but rather will listen and jot down your opinions in my dairy to convey to my health team. I am sure we will be able to work more efficiently after this discussion. Thank you finance minister for arranging this meaningful interaction with eminent personalities. Thank you everybody. We can start now.

T. Sundararaman

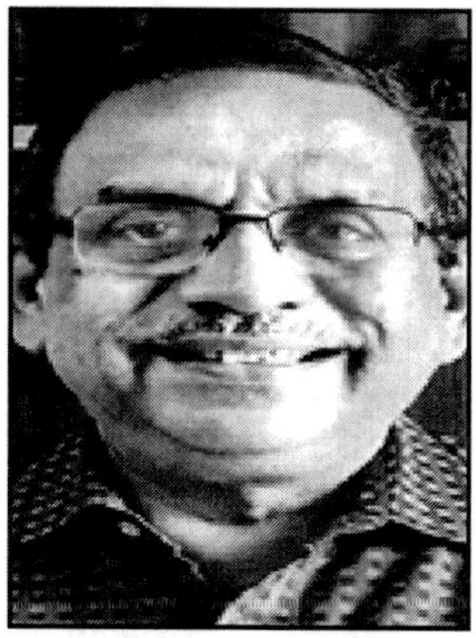

I have been very closely following the good work done in Kerala. By coincidence while the Wuhan outbreak was happening, I was invited to visit Kerala to look at the developments in the Kerala health care sector, and I spent the second and third week of January touring two to three districts in northern Kerala. I had then submitted a detailed health systems assessment report to the government after visiting a number of sites and looking at all programs. So, I have a good background of the health systems context and baselines when the pandemic reached our shores.

The first thing you learn about managing an epidemic is that the best time to start work is 5 years before it happens. Once it happens, there is so little in the nature of health systems strengthening that you can actually do. It becomes mainly a fire-fighting exercise. The epidemic response happened faster in Kerala partly because of the earlier experience in dealing with Nipah virus outbreaks, but let's not give too much credit to just that. There were a whole lot of other things including the palliative care program, the way local self-governments are engaged and the way Kerala had developed a system of outreach to reach the vulnerable. . You actually have a situation where every panchayat member and

---

T. Sundararaman, a public health expert is the former executive director of the National Health Systems Resource Centre, and former Dean of School of Health System Studies at the Tata Institute of Social Science (TISS). He is also former Director of State Health ResourceCenter in Chhattisgarh. He is a founding member of All India People's Science Network (AIPSN) and has been part of the People's Health Movement (PHM) since its formation. Currently he is the global coordinator of Public Health Movement, a global network of grassroots health activists, civil society organisations and academic institutions around the world with presence in 70 countries.

ward member can recollect without referring to notes, the number of cancer patients, kidney patients, post-transplant and paraplegics patients they have. They can tell it just by recall. This is remarkable. I don't think that anywhere in the world, have I seen that ability in local self-governments.

One of the main strategies required to cope with the Covid-19 is shielding. I have heard the finance minister referring to it as reverse quarantine. Internationally, they use the term shielding. The vulnerable people are shielded from this infection. You already have a system in place, by which the system is in touch with each household on health issues and you are actively reaching out to those who are vulnerable. So, when contact tracing is done, Kerala was able to effectively home quarantine a huge number of people. I have seen that in most places they quarantine 10-15 people per Covid patient and here you are doing 200 home quarantines for Covid-19.

That home quarantine system requires a very good system of outreach, which this palliative care outreach and sub-centres had already established. The other major advantage that Kerala had, was that it has implemented over these four years, the National Quality Accreditation Scheme (NQAS) which has been picked up with so much enthusiasm from below. I don't see this program projected at the state level but at the ground level and I saw public providers and facility managers working on it and fine tuning it very well. Thus, in every facility they have looked at the quality process and in the quality process, infection control is the most important thing.

Now in all these viruses, one major source of infection is the hospital itself. You also have a high degree of health worker affliction, including deaths You could see that in Maharashtra and Delhi, whereas Kerala has been relatively spared of that, If it has been spared or had a lower level of infection of caregivers it is because of the work it has put up in the district health system on hospital health care infection control which we call nosocomial infection controlI think this excellence in reduction of nosocomial infections, has been another achievement that has helped Kerala.

I think this is the third feature, not pertaining directly to the healthcare system, is a complete lack of stigmatisation. You see the other states suffering from intense stigmatisation. If the people get fever, the reaction would be to panic and shut the doors, and take a paracetamol, but not get "caught out" and sent to a quarantine or isolation unit.

In such states, there is a breakdown of trust, cooperation and friendliness. Case-detection becomes a policing act. I am very apprehensive about using the police for even inter- border inspections. It only means that people will hide. At some point the people have to self-report. They should report the moment they feel ill and if that was happening in Kerala it owes a lot to the degree of trust that you have built between the local governments, between health care workers and the population. That friendliness that exists, I think, is a resource, whereas we find in many other places there is a huge degree of suspicion and mis-trust.

The other positive feature that Kerala has in its health system, is very good logistics. In my earlier visits I had been critical of Kerala's logistics. They had procurement, but distribution was lagging. This time I noticed very good changes. Now if you have to move a lot of health commodities in a very responsive way to very varying demands, you can easily do it. I think that is to your great benefit when it comes to pandemic response.

So, there are a whole lot of strengths that have actually come together. My sense is also of caution. The organisation of health services is a complex affair and as complex an affair as bringing up a child. You may do very well when the child is below five, but you may lose the game when he or she is an adolescent. You may then not be able to take care. While you may have been a good parent at one time, it doesn't work now. As the game changes, what you need to do changes. What is success at one point, need not translate easily into what you need at another point. It is not just a continuation of the thing, the game keeps changing. We saw that in Covid pandemic, which went through so many different phases. But this is also true of non-pandemic contexts.

One of the fundamental things in pandemic preparedness and response is that the disease surveillance architecture must have a central role. One should not be confident that transmission is occurring in only known chains of transmission and one should not limit contact tracing to only such sub-groups. The point is you will never know where exactly the next cluster of cases will occur. Where it will occur is not predictable, but that it will occur somewhere is predictable. South Korea has had remarkable success in control but still clusters continue to surface. Iceland has also done remarkably well but they continue to generate 40 to 50 cases in a week. If they were able to contain transmission despite it, it was because they picked up the clusters early and took good quarantine measures.

Once essential services are opened people will come in from across state borders and along with that so with the disease. Prevention at the border will never be perfect. This is applicable for international borders too. China gets cases from Mongolia and USSR and has a steady number of cases along their borders. So, I don't think there is a way to impose perfect restrictions. We will have to live with a situation of low level transmission. We should be able to screen, contact and isolate cases as soon as they are identified in any village. It is not a one-time event that we are eliminating but rather preparing for an endemicity. For that, the goal is not complete elimination, but extremely good surveillance.

The key to surveillance is testing people with fever or cough. It is not enough to test people falling in the high risk category, like health care workers and others, but also test all people with fever. At some point, you can even use clinical diagnosis when test kits are not available. The technique called pooled sample testing can also be used, where there are a lot of negative cases. Pooled sample testing will reduce your test kit requirement. However, you need surveillance. Curiously at the National level, the country has a very good disease surveillance program that was developed after the swine flu pandemic and was producing weekly reports of outbreaks ever since. Every week's reports from 2012 onwards, till the first week of February were being put out in the public domain The last report was a brilliant three case study of Kerala's first three Covid patients. And then the reports go silent. The reports have not been seen in the public domain since the second week of February and now actually, the flow of reports has stopped. So now at a time when an epidemic is in full swing, , the central vehicle of managing the data driven response to an epidemic appears disabled. That has great implications for understanding our problems with governance of health.

I will stop with two more points. The other point that I want to make is about Covid care and infrastructure required for it. We have seen that in China and Spain when building Covid-19 management capacity, they built new temporary hospitals. In India, when the Prime Minister talked of an additional 1 lakh beds in the first few months, it was re-purposing of existing, very vital tertiary and secondary care public sector beds, which provide essential services for the poor, that was being referred to. These public hospitals have been converted into Covid-19 dedicated hospitals which can push out patients, with other health care needs.

So, in some sense, how do we continue with non-Covid care? It is indeed a big problem. I have reports from other states, which I don't have in Kerala, of increased newborn mortality, increased maternal mortality, and increased cardiac mortality. At some point without a disease surveillance system, without mortality statistics kicking in, we may be paying an exponentially increasing price for non-Covid mortality. This has to be really factored in.

For example, if a patient does not take his or her anti-diabetic drug for three weeks, the diabetes will go out of control and if they don't take it for six weeks, they are likely to die. So, there is an exponential degree of risk, if denial of health care occurs over a long period of time. There are great dangers such disruption of essential services and such disruption has four major reasons. This is the lack of public transport, there is the closure or suspension of services of many private clinics, there is the re-purposing of hospitals and diversion of staff to Covid-19 duties, and there are administrative orders to cease many health services. Such disruption will show up as excess mortality figures later.

As a public health care professional, I am seriously bothered about this. It is going to be a long phase. This pandemic is going to be there till the vaccine arrives. The good news is that the vaccine is expected to come by the end of this year (2021). But when we say that it will continue for a 6 to 9 month period, we can't continue with this degree of social and economic restrictions, nor health care restrictions. Definitely pushing poor patients in tertiary care to private hospitals is unthinkable for a government which has invested so much in strengthening public health services and for which Kerala has become a role model. Using this pandemic to push a lot of tertiary care to the private sector is neither feasible nor desirable.

Then there is a major challenge. Kerala has done some work in medicine production- in domestic manufacturing. This game is going to last for a long time. There is a good case for Kerala becoming like South Korea or Iceland. The first thing they did before anything else, was to ramp up their own indigenous test manufacturing capacity and their manufacturing capacity in some of these vital areas. And then also enter the area of vaccines.

Kerala does really have to build in such systems during the long run, because pandemics, believe me, are going to be around in different form for some time to come. Look how many pandemics we have had within two decades. There has been the HIV pandemic, the swine flu, the Nipah virus, the SARS virus, the Zika virus and so on. It is not as if we are having it every year but we need to be thinking of some generic capacities that we should be able to ramp up. The capacity for domestic manufacture and even drug innovation takes a long time to build, but we are entering a world where in the long run, we need to be self-reliant on most health technologies, not only medicines, vaccines and diagnostics but even , but even on protective equipment.. I think I will stop with these few comments and pass it on to others.

B. Ekbal

In response to what Sundararaman has said, I would like to comment that the current situation in Kerala can be summed up as, 'so far so good.' We could pick up the Covid-19 patients from the hospital itself and trace the contacts fairly well. For every positive case, we have traced up to 100 contacts and quarantined them very effectively and efficiently. As many as 200,000 of them were quarantined, most of them in their houses and they were regularly monitored. Nevertheless, I have to submit that Kerala is facing a large number of challenges compared to other states.

That is why I am not comfortable making statements like "Kerala is emerging as the model for the country" and "Kerala is performing better compared to many countries" etc. The reason is that compared to other states we have a number of state specific problems. There are a number of issues that need to be addressed in managing a pandemic of this proportion Kerala being a highly porous state, anybody can come in through various routes, not only by the established ones but also by other less utilised channels also. Neighbouring

---

B. Ekbalisa public health activist, a neurosurgeon, and an academic in Kerala, India and has served as a member of the Kerala State Planning Board (2016-2021). He was previously a member of the Kerala State Planning Board from 1996 to 2000, during which he played a vital role in the People's Plan Campaign, a decentralisation moves by the Government of Kerala. He was the chairman of Kerala State Pollution Control Board and is also one of the joint convenors of Jan Swasthya Abhiyan (Public Health Movement - India). He is also the chairperson of the expert committee (State Level Expert Committee on COVID-19 Management) that advises the chief minister of Kerala on all matters related to Covid-19.

states like Tamil Nadu is considered as a hot state because of the high incidence of the pandemic. People from Tamil Nadu have easy access to districts like Idukki, Palghat and Thiruvananthapuram. Since movement by people from Tamil Nadu to Kerala cannot be easily prevented this is a major problem we are facing. We are expecting a large number of emigrants to come to Kerala in the near future. This cannot be prevented for long. Monitoring them medically and quarantining them if necessary are going to be major problems. Most of them will be elderly persons with other morbidities and likely to succumb to the pandemic. The second problem that Kerala is facing is that the number of vulnerable persons likely to have serious health impacts with Covid-19 infections: the elderly and those with comorbidities are high in Kerala, The elderly and those with other health problems like Diabetes and Hypertension are more likely to get Covid infection and related complications and the possibility of mortality is also very high among this group. It is estimated that at least 7.6 lakh people are there belonging to this vulnerable group. That means one third of the population is at high risk. The young persons may also get infected but may not suffer from complications. However, they can transmit infection to the elderly We will not be able to build a Chinese wall between the younger and older people even while we isolate the elderly with reverse quarantine etc,

A large number of people will be coming from other states, mostly youngsters and we have to see that the social distance between the vulnerable people and the young are maintained. We are following such public health measures but there can be loophole here and there and this is going to be major problem. So, we are now propagating reverse quarantine for the elderly and those with other health problems and we are monitoring them at their homes very diligently. Our palliative care units are very active because most of the vulnerable groups are bedridden and lonely in their homes. Such services as providing them with food and medicines are taken care of by the Asha workers or the palliative care team.

The third problem we are facing is in relation to testing for the infection, Sundararaman very rightly pointed out the need for sero surveillance. In fact, we had an excellent protocol for sero surveillance, thanks to the excellent work done by the Achutha Menon Centre for Health Care Studies in collaboration with the National institute of Epidemiology, Delhi. We actually wanted sero surveillance with antibody testing, but unfortunately the anti-body kits received all over India were substandard and could not be validated. So, we could not start the tests earlier, but with the availability of good quality tests we are regularly doing antibody testing.

We have a problem with the other testing methods also. We are fairly comfortable with the kits available for RT-PCR testing. We have about 14 testing centres now and the Central University has opened up their laboratory for testing. Many private medical colleges have given us their RT PCR testing facilities. We have something like 3000 or 3500 PCR kits and the Rajiv Gandhi Centre for Biotechnology has promised another 3000. Nevertheless, you know that when the demand increases, that too will not be enough.

The other options are the anti-body test. Another good news that I have is that the Rajiv Gandhi Centre for Biotechnology has developed an anti-body kit, which has been validated at a very high percentage and they are waiting for a nod from the ICMR. The Sree Chitra Thirunal Institute of Technology and Medical Science has also developed an anti-body kit which they say can test 75 lakh persons a month.

Since that is possible, we hope to get a large quantity of antibody kits in two to three weeks at the most. Now there are other issues also. The major issue in Kerala now is not only handling Covid patients, but also non-Covid morbid patients. We focus on the Covid patient so much so that the morbidity and mortality aspect of the non-Covid patient is largely ignored and therefore, likely to increase. This is a major threat.

We have allowed emergency cases to be managed, especially surgical cases. We also wanted semi-emergency cases to be managed. But the question is how they can be managed because medical professionals are themselves reluctant to take care of these semi emergency cases. We have to first test the patients before surgery. If we go for RT-PCR testing it will take up to 5 hours. We cannot wait so long for the management of an emergency or even a semi-emergency case.

There are other testing facilities. One is the Gene Expert which is available in one medical college. We are in the process of moving the facilities from the TB centres. You are aware that the NAT viral facility was available in the district TB centre. Now, we are moving them to medical colleges, so that we can do the NAT testing that can give the result within 45 minutes so that we can manage emergency and semi- emergency surgical cases without much delay,

Regarding the private sector they are using the TRUENAT testing. Unfortunately, ICMR said that this was only a screening test, because it tests only a single gene and therefore all positive cases should be followed up with RT PCR testing. Since the RT PCR resting facilities are increasing in number this problem could also be solved.

If you look at the history of epidemics all over the world you see that epidemics only settle down after the development of a vaccine as early as possible.

It may take another six months to one year to develop a vaccine. Another way by which pandemics are controlled is by the development of Herd immunity by community transmission. This can be achieved only when at least 60-70% people are infected, but in Kerala it can be a problem as we have a huge number of vulnerable populations. So therefore, when community transmission comes, we will again have to keep the barrier between those who are affected and the vulnerable population intact. In a way that is a double-edged weapon. Once community transmission comes, herd immunity develops, and the disease may settle down. On the other hand, the community transmission takes place and suppose it spreads to the vulnerable section then the morbidity and the mortality will be very high. I am confident and optimistic that because of the large social capital Kerala has, we can tide over these challenges. All the 22 private medical colleges have thrown open all their facilities to the government. In fact, the Kannur self-financing medical college and the Wayanad self-financing medical college have been converted to Covid hospitals. You know that in such a crisis all those with different political views, even though there may be a few controversies occasionally, will all stand together and try to meet the challenge.

Thomas Isaac

Iqbal has two issues. One is on testing and technical details. Second it is regarding the shielding of the vulnerable population. The latter is a very large issue in which apart from health workers, local governments, councillors, palliate care networks etc. are all involved. Well, if we have time, we will come back to it.

K.K. Shailaja Teacher

I would now like to hear Rajeev Sadanandan, my former health secretary's views.

Rajeev Sadanandan

Kerala's current situation has been accurately described by our Hon'ble Minister Mrs Shailaja Teacher, Dr Ekbal and Dr Sundararaman. In the beginning the Hon'ble Finance Minister, Dr Thomas Isaac, said that people from outside the state would be interested in knowing and learning how Kerala handled this pandemic. I shall try to respond to that first. To some extent, I do agree with Sundararaman that Nipah was the beginning and not the end. But I disagree with him otherwise.

Nipah did indeed have an effect on the system. As you know the capacity of a system to respond to a crisis, what we call resilience, is built up overtime and not overnight. Each time a crisis occurs, the system gets tested and strengthened. If the system learns from the crisis and uses that experience to build systems to deal with future crises, health systems will deal with health emergencies better. Successful management of crises also develops the confidence to deal with similar ones later and increases the trust of the population in leadership. This was the impact of the Nipah outbreak and the 2018 floods.

Rajeev Sadanandan, IAS, is the founding Chief Executive Officer of Health Systems Transformation Platform, New Delhi. Prior to taking up this assignment he was a career civil service officer with specialisation in health systems and health financing. He held three terms as health secretary of Kerala. He has been involved with the health system of the state of Kerala and has been active in health sector reforms in the state. He has served as an Additional Chief Secretary heading Kerala's Department of Health and Family Welfare. Currently he is a Commissioner on the Lancet Global Health Commission on Financing of Primary Care and an Honorary Advisor to the Chief Minister of Kerala on management of the COVID Pandemic.

Secondly, as Ekbal said, it is important to keep the core work of the health system functional, even while managing the crisis. These include management of non- communicable diseases, tuberculosis, mental health and so on. The ability of the system to return to its pre-existing state, preferably at a higher level, once the crisis is over is an indicator of the resilience of the health system. But resilience in crises is also a function of the capacity of the system to absorb shocks they are faced with: it is called everyday resilience. Resilience of the Kerala health system is the result of the depth the system has acquired over the years.

Covid-19 is a health emergency. But it is a pandemic that has impacted the social interaction between individuals, communities and nations. It also spreads through social functions like family get togethers, religious meetings and so on, which means this it cannot be controlled by the health department alone. There is the need for coordinated action from many departments like police, transport, among others. Accepting such social and economic restrictions also requires a high level of social capital, transparency and trust in government. Evidently, what has been seen till now, is not only the strength of Kerala's health system but the large social capital that is there in the state, which in turn has enabled the right response to the pandemic.

A health system is resilient if it can protect citizens from disease and get a good health outcome during the crisis. It must have inbuilt knowledge about the threat, an early warning system to alert itself, be able to assess the dimensions of the threat and plan and execute the response to it.

Kerala's economy is heavily dependent on its expatriate population and on international tourism. Hence, Kerala, right from the HIV/AIDS pandemic of the eighties and nineties, has been highly alert to the threat of disease spreading from any part of the world. I used to joke that whenever anybody sneezes anywhere in the world, Kerala reaches for the handkerchief. So, when our minister said that when the unknown virus was reported from China and Southeast Asia, Kerala changed its threat perception. It was almost like an adaptive immune system responding to a known pathogen.

As we have seen the health machinery, drawing from the past experience in handling medical emergencies, began to mobilise itself. At that point, I believed we were over mobilising. In any case, it is always better in such situations to do more than less. This wouldn't have been possible without well-trained and highly motivated health personnel in adequate numbers. Like what happened during the Surat plague, most governments have chosen to respond to Covid through the government health system. For many years, and Sundararaman can bear me out on this, the policy discourse within the health sector and outside has run down the public health system as inefficient and of poor quality. They were starved of funds, understaffed and demoralised.

The resultant shortage of infrastructure, procurement, inventory management systems and so on is evident. When you push that system, which has been rundown and not even able to manage the normal load, to deal with a crisis it will crack. When you look at the way states have responded, I see the way states got differentiated themselves and the most determining factor for me is the importance that the state governments have given to the government health system.

When you compel medical personnel to work without ensuring their safety they get demoralised. When the staff gets demoralised and scared, the quality of care would suffer and this would be reflected in the fatality rate. I am afraid that is what is happening. Unlike in Kerala, in many states, the government health sector has been highly undervalued irrespective of the government in power.

It is history that largely accounts for the depth of the Kerala health system. The princely rulers, the missionaries, the successive governments, civil society and so on have played their role. It has resulted in a good government health system. When the government cut back investments due to fiscal constraints the private sector stepped in to fill the gap. With the government and private sector combined Kerala has a high availability of health institutions and persons. This was true even in 2015. When you look at the national health profile, you will find that the population to be managed by hospitals, beds and doctors is half the national average.

The strength of the government health system was further augmented when the government launched the Aardram mission in 2016. One of its objectives was to increase the percentage of people using government hospitals. For people who are outside the system, it is impossible to realise the huge improvement in morale. The whole feeling of being valued was there for many people in the health system. Aardram got into full steam in 2017 and 2018, largely due to the support of the finance minister. We added 836 posts of doctors, 937 nurses, 444 lab technicians, all created and filled within a short span of .just three years.

Moreover, the investment went up from around Rs 630 crore in 2014-15 to almost Rs 1500 crore in 2018-19. In addition to this, using KIIFBI Fund, the government is now investing Rs 2256 crore of borrowed money for improving hospital infrastructure. . It has been just four years now, but the results have started becoming visible.

When you move from the 71st round of the NSSO to the 75th round, the percentage of people using government health facilities has gone up from 34%

to 48%. In fact, in the rural areas where most of the investments are taking place it has crossed 50% and is well on the way to 60%.

Let us not discount the role of the Nipah episode. My colleagues in the health department tell me that it taught district and lower-level managers how to assimilate a threat, identify the resources that could be repurposed, stand down once the threat was over and keep the other services going during the crisis.

Meanwhile the skill of tracking and tracing, highly applauded in the country, which was learnt during the first Nipah got further strengthened during the second Nipah crisis. The supportive management of critical patients was also one of the lessons that was learnt. The analysis of how the epidemic is progressing, the prevention of health care associated infections, the psycho-social support of the persons under quarantine and treatment were all learnt while managing the Nipah outbreak.

After the Nipah crisis, while the rest of the country and the world was applauding Kerala, the state's health system went back to identify where we had got things wrong. One of the areas identified was that a lot of infections happened within the health care facilities. So, the Kerala anti-microbial resistance action plan, which is first of its kind in the country, was drawn up and the Kerala Anti-Microbial Resistance Surveillance Network was set up. A rigorous infection prevention and control system was started. As Sundararaman mentioned, that has had a good impact on the practices. The face masks and the hand washing had become standard practice after Nipah.

The other thing was that the detractors had predicted disaster during the first Nipah crisis. We were aware of such predictions. But the fact that the government health system could handle it, created confidence and self-belief that is there even now.

The strong community support, which is outside the health system, but is a necessary condition for handling a health emergency, is unlike what I have seen in any other state. The linkage between the external social capital and the health system emerged out of the democratic decentralisation in the state. All the PHCs are under the panchayats. We have to appreciate the role played by the village health, sanitation and nutrition committee. It has the ward member as chairman and the health worker as convenor. It is their job to lead on prevention of infectious diseases. Most of the gram panchayat members realised that this is something that adds up and connects them to the voters and they took it very seriously. They also know that failure or success has political cost or rewards.

So, panchayats have been using their resources for controlling diseases, purchasing medicines and bringing in additional manpower. When the

Kerala government on 20th of March issued a set of directions to the local self-government departments on control of Covid-19, it was a part of the routine for them. It was the continuation of a long tradition of managing infectious diseases in the past.

I would not get into the numbers. Frankly, I believe it is risky to discuss things like the fatality rate when you don't have a scientific surveillance system that is accurate. Now Kerala did get a bonus when the lockdown was imposed across the country. The reason why it helped Kerala, to a large extent, is because of the measures taken earlier when the prevalence of infections in the community was at a lower level. However, more important to me was the demonstrated social capital of the state.

The lockdown to ensure social distancing has been prescribed as a strategy to protect the upper social groups who had no financial worries and could stock up on the essential provisions. But for daily wage earners, poor and migrants the situation was precarious. The Kerala government promptly responded to their plight through community action at the instance of local self-governments. More than 5000 community kitchens were opened and most of them have been funded by local contributions.

In the statement submitted by the ministry of home affairs in the Supreme Court, more than 60% of the approved support units for migrants were in Kerala. Officials in Kerala who could speak the language kept in touch with migrant families and reassured them of the needed support. As I mentioned before, an epidemic of this nature could not have been managed by the health department alone. The coordination of various departments was very important. Full credit should go to the Chief Minister. In fact, the systems that were put in place during the 2018 floods have been made more efficient now. These departments can in fact, now kind of dovetail into each other and present a unified front.

The other important thing is information. During the epidemic most of the news is bad news. Governments generally try to hide them. When you hide the truth, false information gains prominence and dealers in false and malicious information gain upper hand, the phenomenon called infodemic. This was learnt during the 2002 SARS epidemic. Unless the community is co-opted in the prevention and mitigation efforts, it would not be successful. Kerala also learnt it during the Nipah crisis and is being applied today. The moment the social contract is broken, people will turn against restrictions.

During Covid-19, the government has been prompt in providing accurate and updated information to the public. All news, good or bad, is given out.

The Chief Minister's evening news conference was the most closely watched event in Kerala during recent times. The government has won the trust of the people through this.

We know from the Ebola epidemic in Africa that one of the most important ways of managing an epidemic is winning the trust of the people. The people of Kerala believed that their government would tell them the truth and take care of them if they fall sick and support them if they needed. So, they are prepared to subject themselves to restrictions that the government has imposed. Should they ever fail to do so, the people of Kerala are capable of exposing government falsehood.

It is true that the government has been successful so far and the test of the crisis will come if and when the situation turns serious and the state capacity threatens to be overwhelmed. As I mentioned before, and as Sundararaman said, the state capacity is going to be sorely tested as we move forward. The numbers will go up and they have to go up for the rate of R0 to come less than one. It is unfortunate, but it is the logic of a viral epidemic that we have to live with.

What has worked in the past may not work tomorrow. You will have to look for out of the box solutions. Slip-ups will happen. People will lose patience with the government, but finally I believe, the inherent resilience of Kerala's society in general and the health system in particular will ensure that Kerala will come out successful from this challenge. I thank the honourable minister for her leadership she has provided and also for her kind words.

Thomas Isaac

Later we will take up some issues I have identified from your presentation, which are important for the next stage and the health minister will then wrap up the session.

V. Raman Kutty

Most of the things that I wanted to say have already been said. We are in the middle of the pandemic in 2020 and have definitely come out well so far. As they say, the proof of the pudding is in the eating. We have only fewer patients and deaths are in single numbers. So far so good. Even India has not done too badly, even though the numbers are bad in some states. While this is a reason for satisfaction, this is no reason for smugness or relaxation.

Coming to Kerala's performance, the points I want to emphasise again are few. The fact that we were prepared was because Nipah was an important lesson on how to deal with an epidemic and we experienced it twice in the last few years. It was not only Nipah but also the floods which taught us many things. One is how to handle emergencies, how to work under a common leadership and across sectors. The health sector was never alone in dealing with these things. They learnt to work with other departments which was very important.

I think that was a huge benefit for the state and also the very fact that we have a very educated population. The social capital that we have is a traditional asset. Also a good chief minister who is very active in the media, which means

---

V. Raman Kutty, Chairperson, Health Action by People, is an Indian health economist, and epidemiologist, currently Research Director of Amala Cancer Research Centre, Amala Institute of Medical Sciences, Thrissur and an emeritus professor at the Sree Chitra Tirunal Institute for Medical Sciences and Technology. His major publications in the domain of COVID -19 include *Unnikrishnan J, Mangalathu S, Kutty RV. Estimating under-reporting of COVID-19 cases in Indian states: an approach using a delay-adjusted case fatality ratio.*

that correct messages have been spread very fast and the people have responded to that.

Secondly, you already have a very robust public health system as pointed out, even though most of the beds are still under the private sector. We have a well-functioning health system which has been boosted in recent years by initiatives like the Aardram, a very commendable initiative under the former health secretary which needs a very detailed study at some stage. Also, these are factors which act at the primary healthcare level. What is very important is not that you are spending money at the top. But at the bottom the infusion of personnel at the primary level is a very important thing which some of us have been clamouring for quite some time.

Thirdly, I would again point at decentralisation and governance which again has a long experience in dealing with epidemics like dengue and other things. They have always been managed with the help of local politicians, local panchayats and community leaders which is very useful in the organisation of community kitchens and ensuring food security in rural areas and also among the less affluent sections of the population. Let us also not forget the very proactive public distribution system.

There is another feature that has conferred advantage but people are talking less about. It is something we have to acknowledge. Simply the fact that it was by chance, that we had a smaller number of cases. The most likely reason could be that we had a lesser infusion of the virus into the population. This is because if you take countries like the United States and Italy, even after the epidemic was noticed in China and people knew about it, as many as 5 lakh people travelled from China to New York. You can imagine the number of people who carried the virus there.

That fortunately has not happened to us as we do not have flights to the epicentre. We did not have direct access to the epicentre of the epidemic. That probably has contributed too. If we look at the number of cases reported by Maharashtra, one of the reasons would be the huge traffic at the international airport.

Now as we open up, we find a lot of non-resident Keralites from the Gulf states registering to return to Kerala. This is going to be a very important factor as we go forward and we should have a system which will screen them and isolate infected people. I am sure that the system will take care of it. I am just flagging an issue. We can't rest back on our laurels saying that we have managed so far. The game is not over. It is going to be a long time before we say things are under control. This should be remembered.

As Dr Ekbal pointed out, there are many people saying that after the epidemic started, there has not been so much of a rush for other health issues at hospitals. They are saying in some ways that it is an indication that there is over medicalization. I don't think so. As a doctor, I think it is a wrong view to take. I think that people are postponing things. They are probably not getting the treatment that they want. As Dr Sundararaman also pointed out, there will probably be a backlash. We will have to deal with that.

We also need to boost state finances in health. That is probably also a major challenge. Most things have already been said. I will stop here. The only thing I want to emphasise is that the game is not over. We have to be ready for things getting more complicated in the future. But I am quite confident that the system can take care of that.

A.V. Jose

It was a very educational experience, listening to the presentations by Smt. Shailaja Teacher, whose formidable leadership helped the state face the pandemic crisis. She has strengthened the firewalls of the state, made extensive use of a network of professionals in the state, and equipped the state to deal with the crisis. The end result was a very humane response to the crisis. Kerala did an extremely commendable job and I should place on record the appreciation of the entire country for the magnificent leadership provided by the Ministry of Health in Kerala and the honourable Minister therein.

The distinguished panel of members of this session have also given us much interesting insight into what the coming days hold for us. I am not going into the technicalities of it. They are extremely competent specialists who also took on board the instances when shortfalls could have happened and can still happen. We ought to be prepared for contingencies that require a lot more care, because life has changed all over the world. Will we be able to avoid the situation faced by major cities, especially in the west, where people died in large numbers. As it happened such mortality was a heavily urban-centred phenomenon.

A.V. Jose is Honorary Fellow at Gulati Institute of Finance and Taxation, Trivandrum and Honorary Visiting Professor at Centre for Development Studies, Trivandrum. He retired from the International Labour Organisation in Geneva and later served as a Director of Gulati Institute of Finance and Taxation. His areas of interest include Employment, Wages, Labour Policies and Social Protection. He has written extensively on labour related issues and edited some important volumes of the ILO including *Organized Labour in the 21st Century* and *Limited Options: Women Workers in India*.

The fact remains that the most vulnerable age groups of the population just died off, while the societies they belonged to were unable to extend the care which they rightly deserved. We are as much vulnerable to that kind of a situation because compared to the rest of the country, elderly people constitute a big chunk of our population. That does not mean that we are not a caring society. The fact of the matter is, we lack the kind of extensive institutionalised care facilities which still need to be created.

One related point: I think it is time we moved on to creating durable institutional facilities that can ensure the access to good quality health care for all people in the state. All the panellists, including Rajeev Sadanandan, went into the kind of infrastructure creation being done in Kerala with excellent clarity and skill. One is not going into that since it is the well-known story of a commendable achievement. The question then is whether the public sector in the state will ever be able to compete with the private sector in providing qualitatively better health care. That means we have to create a contributory insurance-based system accessible to every person in Kerala, based on which they can become equal beneficiaries of sophisticated medical care facilities without ever facing any shortage of resources. One has to think in terms of creating appropriate institutions and I hope that at a later stage when normality returns, we will be able to take this on this all-important challenge.

Rajeev Sadanandan

The discussions were extremely fruitful. In fact, the best I have heard on Kerala's health response to the crisis and the health emergency. I think the panel should respond to four issues which you have mentioned in your presentation and are going to be very important in the coming months.

The first is, what the health minister and others too touched upon; what is going to be the impact of returning migrants? Any ideas on the preparations made and how you will handle it? Two, one thing that Dr Jose had referred to is; how necessary is to shield the vulnerable population at the time of return migration, which will inevitably happen and three, the shield required.

Dr Ekbal was insisting on increasing the tests given. But the minister was pointing to the lack of availability of test kits. How do the next few months look like? Not the future. Finally, something that Sundararaman said; When we exit from the crisis, what are we going to get? Of course, a much more resilient health system.

Kerala health system now has a brand value upon which the pharmaceutical industry, medical devices industry, perhaps a finishing school of nurses who seek out employment opportunities in the west and so on, can be built. So, this achievement of the health sector becomes a very important launch pad for something larger. Therefore, I would say we need to look at the possibility of harnessing our brand equity for evolving a world class health sector with all its complementarities, including research, which could serve as a booster dose for the state's future development.

T. Sundararaman

I think you are the masters of reverse migration. I am not going into that. I think you will get it right. You are going to set up district centres and let them enter in phases. You are going to tag them, follow them up through. It is a lot of doing. I don't think it is just not the critical volume of what you have to do that is the issue or you break it up into component parts. If anybody can do it, then it definitely is Kerala.

On shielding, I already made my point. Nowhere else in India you have a system that is so tuned. It was built for the palliative care system, but it is actually going to work wonders. Because in some sense you already have people out there. You have to strengthen them, provide them with more kits and I think somewhere, one has to be looking at the details of virus transmission. For example, there is a rule which says that you can take a one hour walk in the park either alone or with your family member. You need not be frightened. Shielding need not be seen in a literal way. Life should be worth living. You don't drop that joy of living. If they are old people, let them meet people. What we need is a very humane approach to shielding. I am sure you will get to it.

What we, from the rest of India, are also looking forward to from Kerala, is also something that can be used for strengthening democratic movements and the right to health all over India. Actually, Isaac, I was talking to Iqbal after my January visit. What we are looking for from Kerala is to promote democratic functioning and the right to health. We need an international conference on primary health care in Kerala to point out something more than I am able to do. Maybe after a year. Now the corona virus is rampant but I think you need to showcase an example of what we can do under such conditions in a neo liberal world. Display a certain model of health care.

Now that global supply chains are breaking down all over, there is a different type of crisis in the international economy. I think Kerala has the possibility of showing a very different model not only in health care delivery, but also in the entire structure of the health industry. With these few words, I will now pass it on to others.

B. Ekbal

There may be yet another problem that Kerala may be facing in the coming months. That is, pre- monsoon showers have begun and the monsoon is on its way. This is the time we have to face infectious diseases. In fact, Kerala is a highly morbid society. We face a double disease model. Non-communicable disease is what we were worried about, but infectious diseases too intermittently crop up in Kerala, especially dengue, leptospirosis and H1N1. These conditions also give rise to fever.

Though clinically we can distinguish between Covid and these conditions when they come in large numbers to the OP, fever being the common symptom, can create problems. We already have a fever protocol and I think we will have to change the fever protocol, taking Covid also into consideration. From the primary healthcare centre upwards, you may have to keep the fever patient separately in the OP, otherwise, a community spread can happen at that level.

The health ministry is already aware of this. They have convened a meeting to discuss the pre-monsoon activities with LSDs and education departments. But, I would request the minister to alert everyone, that during the monsoon, these diseases are likely to come back and mix with Covid. It may be at that time that emigrants will return to Kerala. Then, there will be a lot of things to do. So, I think I would request the minister to once again alert all the required departments about taking care of monsoon related infectious diseases.

We were also thinking about the international conference which Dr Sundararaman was talking about. We have to refer to the Almaty as well as the Astana health conferences. The Astana primary health conference was held in 2018 and surprisingly it moved a little ahead of the Almaty conference because Almaty was confined to health promotion, health education etc. When it comes to Astana you see that even at the primary health care level, they are talking about disease prevention, treatment, rehabilitation and palliative care.

If you look at the primary health care in Kerala, which in fact our finance minister quite openly talks about, is palliative care. I would say he is a palliative care evangelist. In fact, his roots in the monastery has helped him to be an evangelist. Once the Covid is over we will hold the international conference at an appropriate time on primary health care in Kerala. Thank you.

N. Ram

Does Kerala have enough PPE for medical and health workers?

Rajeev Sadananadan

In the beginning of the pandemic there were problems regarding the availability of PPE kits. This problem was faced by most parts of the world as supply chains got affected. We had the same problem during the Nipah crisis as well. PPEs were flown in from Dubai by a philanthropist. In January itself, the Kerala Medical Services Corporation tried to buy the PPEs directly from the market but they were not available. Even the small quantity that they could find was exorbitantly priced. The situation seems to be changing now. Right now, although there is a shortage and costs are high, it is possible to go to the market and get an adequate number of PPEs. As Sundararaman mentioned, things are going to change. The kind of management we did for cases in the past, such as treating each case as if it were an ICU management which increased consumption of PPE kits, will change and as the number of cases go up, the style of management has to change. I believe the per capita requirement of PPEs are going to come down as the style of management will change and at the same time. the availability of PPEs across India will go up. Therefore, it should be a lot easier to get them in future.

First of all, I would like to assure Dr Jose that normalcy will come back. I have lived through so many epidemics where the Armageddon was predicted, but it fortunately did not happen. Many people keep asking me what happened to the disaster you predicted in an earlier pandemic. I guess a year and a half from now when you look back, you will find the answers to your questions. The disease would have become another normal viral infection.

As I mentioned before, we can use this crisis to redesign the way we would do things. It would be a major opportunity. Dr Ekbal mentioned people flooding the hospital for fevers. Can we prevent that? In NHS and other places where there is primary care, a lot of primary care has been shifted to teleconsultation. Can we move to a model like that? Can private practitioners who take care of patients, as and when they walk in, be moved to a prepaid situation where they assume responsibility for the health of the individuals, in return for a capitation-based payment. Can we redesign the way we pay for and provide health care?

So, there are huge opportunities for us to rework the primary health care system and the rest of the health system as we get back to normalcy. That brings me back to the question we missed out. Kerala, during the Nipah crisis and even now, has not invested adequately on research. I think we are depriving India and the world at large of ideas on how to run a system at minimal cost. My request to the Honourable Minister and Dr Ekbal is to use this as an opportunity for research. This is not an opportunity that we will get every time. We missed it during Nipah. We should not miss it again.

As far as testing is concerned, it is also linked to the issue of migrants. With the present expensive RT-PCR mode of testing, it is unlikely that we will be able to manage the loads that come in. What some of us have been pleading for right from the beginning, is that ICMR and NIV should have invested in antibody testing.

ICMR position was that antibody tests would not be enough for clinical management. At some point when community spread has reached certain thresholds, testing for clinical management is going to be irrelevant. More importantly, it would have been a great help had we got the antibody tests for research purposes. What we still don't know is that while the other viruses have been able to confer immunity on the person infected, does Covid do that? The question is still open. Assuming that the question will be answered by the time the migrants come back, one good thing will be to administer them anti-body tests, find out if they have been infected and, subject to feasibility, spread it to the entire population also. Identify people who have developed immunity and use them for your frontline work. Again, that is a question that has to be solved.

Kerala should continue to innovate and collaborate. We heard about the test developed at the Rajiv Gandhi Centre for Biotechnology, and the one at Shri Chitra Thirunal Institute of Medical Sciences and Technology. Have we not been overly deferential to the ICMR? This is a crisis. When Nipah happened, we worked on it ourselves. Hence what are we afraid of now? Why don't we collaborate with research centres in India and validate those tests?

That is a risky decision. I hope the policy makers will give thought to it because when we lead, others will follow. I think we need to invest heavily in trying to validate the different tests that have been developed. We have enough people who are cured to validate antibody tests. So, I request the Kerala government to collaborate with well-known researchers in the country to validate these tests. I will stop with that.

Thomas Isaac

It has been extremely useful. The kind of messages we are receiving. I am not going to read them all. Everybody appreciates what is being done.

K.K. Shailaja Teacher

Thank you, Sir, for such a fruitful discussion. I will keep the major points in mind and make use of the suggestions for further planning and preparedness. I shall now respond to the main points raised here by all of you. The major question is, what exactly is the Kerala model? Is it related to the health department only? We can never say that because, since 1957 onwards we have had separate planning and adopted separate kinds of people-centred methods. We have been implementing them. Despite being a state with a low financial capability, no one is able to believe the social development of our society has been hampered. This definitely is due to people-centred planning methods.

Now the world is discussing what is happening in Kerala. We do not know if they are now discussing socialist or communist planning. But there is something in it. We have been making efforts since 1957. One is the land reforms. Each and every one owns land in the state. The other is public education and hundred percent literacy. Improving the public health sector has also been a continuous process since 1957. We have advanced on that basic structure.

We have been experimenting constantly. When the LDF came into office in 2016, the health sector was one of our priorities. We found that out 67% of the total population was using private sector facilities. This was despite the extensive public health sector, with primary health centres in every panchayat that had sub-centres for every 5000 people. We have general hospitals, district hospitals and medical colleges too. But people were still using private centres.

The out-of-pocket expenditure on health is very high in Kerala. We decided to have some improvement in the health sector and went in for primary health care improvement. One such mission of the government in the health sector was called the Aardram mission. We prepared a very good action plan for Aardram. We held on to some principles upheld at the Astana and Almaty conferences, which gave importance to primary health care and prevention of diseases.

In the Aardram mission we converted more than 300 primary hospitals to family hospitals and 500 more are being converted to such hospitals. Work on them is going on. We also decentralised some activities to the primary hospitals. Not only did we come up with people friendly and technology-friendly infrastructure, but also added some medical practices at the primary level itself. These included clinics to test the COPDs and Ashwas clinics for mental health etc. So, the common people can now come directly to the PHC for health check-ups. That practice helped us to prevent and limit infectious diseases on a continuous basis.

We have done many such things at the secondary and tertiary level too. The KIFBI funds were an important help and I thank the finance minister for it. We got around Rs 2300 crore to build hospitals, install new equipment and improve the infrastructure, as well as the functioning of the institution. We set up super specialties in cardiology, nephrology and neurology amongst others.

These were initially available only in the medical colleges. We extended them to the secondary level also. The district hospitals were provided with Cath labs, angiograms and so on. This helped us to a great extent.

Another action taken was on infection control. More than 60 primary hospitals in our state were awarded for it. All the top 12 hospitals ranked by the Central Government were from Kerala and more primary hospitals are awaiting national accreditation. They scored more than 90%, which was due to improvements made in the primary sector. Hospital infection control was the main area which we focused on, in the last 3-4 years.

I would also like to point out that this was not just due to our efforts, because after decentralisation all these institutions were under the local self-governments. They have some funds for the development of the primary health centres. It was a people centred program. The common people came out in huge numbers and gave us donations to convert primary health centres to family health centres. KIFBI funds have been used only for secondary and tertiary hospitals. For primary hospitals, we collect funds from the people. We got a lot of company CSR funds and also from individuals in the society. That is why we are saying it is a people centred method. A different method adopted by Kerala which everyone can use as a model.

In the case of infectious diseases, we have two threats in front of us. One is the chest diseases and then dengue, HINI etc. We had a handkerchief revolution to prevent H1N1. We implemented them with the help of local self-governments. We also started a campaign that ensured that some preventive activities were conducted every day, to tackle communicable diseases. For instance, the Aarogya Jagrata campaign, the slogan for which was 'My Health is My Responsibility.'

A drop in non-communicable diseases, as everyone here in Kerala knows, is mainly because of change in lifestyle due to improvement in conditions. Kerala is the diabetic capital of India. Life expectancy increased. The population comprises a large number of people over the age of 60 and they are vulnerable. Though it is a positive thing, it is also a threat when infectious diseases occur.

We have been working on this too. We have declared reverse quarantine during the lockdown and with the help of the social justice department and also the department for women and children, trying to protect vulnerable people from the virus.

These department personnel including anganwadi workers are interacting with the old people. Asha workers of the health department are also visiting homes to keep track of the situation and if anyone gets sick, they are being taken directly to the hospitals and treating them even in the Corona period. With the help of our NCD control, we have been doing very good work. NCD medicines are being supplied in their homes. The vulnerable sections are being supplied medicines for at least two months. The outcome of these efforts has been good and older people are getting better protection from Corona because of our efforts.

As the finance minister said, we are looking forward to the future and things to be implemented. Fortunately, I have very good officers like Rajeev Sadanandan, who laid the foundation stone and now Rajan Khobragade who is working hard. So many of them, like the district level DMOs and DPMs, also work hard. At the Kasaragod general hospital, they tackled the situation very efficiently and reduced the Corona cases from 89 to zero and everyone has been discharged. I had a video conference with them. It was excellent team work.

Shielding vulnerable people, not only the old people but the differently abled people has been given priority now with physiotherapy and other things. N Ram enquired whether there are sufficient numbers of PPEs. We did have problems in the early stages with few stocks. We do not manufacture proper PPEs in our state. We have not been getting the raw materials from China. We have two to three lakh masks which is insufficient.

The real scarcity is for testing kits, especially RNA extraction kits. We were asked to examine other test methods too like antibody testing etc. The problem is validating them properly. If we succeed, we can make use of these tests. There are many other tests. We are experimenting with them. We will be in a better situation soon.

What will we do in the post-Corona days? That is the question before us. Our government, under the leadership of the chief minister, is trying hard to meet the challenges. We have to save not only lives but also livelihoods. What happens when the lockdown is lifted? Managing the economy will be difficult. We are trying to tackle them.

We are considering the AMR reduction plan for Kerala. It is a strategic action plan. Again, a novel thing in Kerala on procedure action. We have implemented so many action plans in Kerala. We are working on them and since we have four airports, viruses are being constantly unleashed. We are working on it. We are doing more tests and improving our preparedness. We are expecting the worst and hoping for the best. I thank you all.

We have formed an expert committee to discuss the major problems and Dr Eqbal is working sincerely on it. I want to convey my thanks to Sundararaman.

I call Rajeev almost every alternate day. Dr Ramankutty and Dr A V Jose, thank you all very much.

Thomas Isaac

A clarification. We do not and shouldn't blame other states. Far from it. Only statements. Somebody can even blame Kerala for bringing the pandemic into the country because the first case from Wuhan appeared here. We are good neighbours with Tamil Nadu and we have to live with it. GIFT and KILA are jointly organising a webinar on local government in India and the pandemic. How local governments in the country have responded to the pandemic. Thank you once again.

Section 7

Financing Livelihood in the Context of Covid-19

V.K. Ramachandran

This session is on financing livelihoods in the context of the pandemic. The economic crisis associated with the Covid-19 pandemic is unprecedented. Previous disasters were mainly natural disasters, when the economy suffered damage to its productive capacity over a specific time, with measurable consequences in the short and medium term.

The production of goods and services during the Covid-19 pandemic came to an abrupt and almost total halt. Further, the halt to production during the Covid-19 pandemic is not locality-specific or scale-specific. Its effects are from top to bottom and across all locations. There is uncertainty about the period that it will take to resume production after the crisis is over. There is also uncertainty about how long it will take to achieve previous levels of production. This is because the resumption of production involves national and international supply and distribution chains.

Immediately after the necessary and inevitable lockdown was declared in Kerala, the Government moved to protect livelihoods. It did so in different ways. The Government resorted to Direct Benefit Transfer and ensured food for everybody.

V.K. Ramachandran, Vice Chairperson, Kerala State Planning Board, was Professor and Head, Economic Analysis Unit, Indian Statistical Institute before joining the Planning Board. His areas of study are development economics; the agrarian question and agrarian relations; rural development; issues of labour and workers in the Indian economy; and class, caste, tribe, and gender discrimination and other forms of social oppression in India. He is the Editor of *Review of Agrarian Studies*.

Secondly, the Government of Kerala also ensured safe shelter not only for our own people who are regularly assisted by the Government, but also those who have come in to build our economy, namely the migrant workers.

The third assurance to the people was that there would be access to health services for all. As the lockdown eases, we need to look for other means to support livelihood through forms of wage employment, self-employment and training for modern employment.

This whole gamut of issues, that is, from direct transfers to protecting livelihoods in different ways is the focus of this discussion. I also ask you to suggest how they should be financed.

Pronab Sen

Let me first take up the latter part of your comments which is, what happens when the lockdown is lifted. The fact of the matter is that, we are thinking of livelihoods but what really is important is what we have done during the lockdown itself. If the lockdown has gone on for too many days, there is a danger of productive capacity particularly in the small-scale sector ending and actually dying down.

As far as the medium scale units in India are concerned, they will not have reserves of more than two to three weeks. They have already reached their limits. The real critical issue is that, as we come out of the lockdown, the process of reviving livelihood is going to be extremely difficult. Rebuilding and re-establishing economic activity is time consuming, and that is not going to happen at the flick of a switch.

The issue is, how are we going to continue? At the moment, very little has been done to help enterprises survive. In fact, the only measure that has been taken so far is what the RBI had done within the constraints of its authority.

Pronab Sen is the Country Director for the International Growth Centre's India Central Programme and, until early 2016, he was the Chairman of Indian Statistical Commission. He received his Ph.D. in Economics from the Johns Hopkins University, specialising in open-economy macroeconomic systems, international economics and public finance and his M.A. in Economics (1975) from the George Washington University, USA. Previously, he was the Principal Adviser, Power and Energy, at the Government of India's Planning Commission. He also had positions as the first Chief Statistician of India, acting as the functional and technical Head of the country's national statistical system, as well as Secretary, Ministry of Statistics & Programme Implementation (2007-10).

What has been done is that, banks and financial institutions have been given liberty to give a moratorium on the loan servicing required.

The problem here is who does get the moratorium and who does not. It depends upon the banks. This is problematic because we know that banks in many cases were very risk averse even prior to the pandemic. Today the banks would be even more risk averse. The net result I fear, is a lot of enterprises who otherwise would be viable, will begin to look risky.

If that happens the damage is going to be huge. The problem is, it cannot be solved through exhortation. This requires steps that the Reserve Bank cannot take. In fact, the only entity who can do that, is the Central government. That is, the Central Government needs to tell banks, NBFCs and microfinance institutions that the three-month moratorium that the Reserve Bank has announced is not voluntary, but mandatory.

If you do not do it, then you are taking a call on who survives and who does not, with very little basis for such a step. That is step one. The fact of the matter is that, even with that step, a situation will arise, as we move out of the lockdown and production facilities are opened up, in which working capital limits of all entities will have been used up and they simply will not have the working capital easily.

The second part of it that can come later is that it must be mandatory for banks and other financial institutions to provide additional working capital for their additional requirements. Which of these will survive or not survive will come much later. We should expect a fair number of them not to survive. That is a risk we have to take. That is a cost we have to bear because we do not have the information base. This is something only the Central Government can do.

If you do all this, what will happen is that financial institutions as a collective, will take a severe hit on their reserves and possibly on their capital base also. So, there must be a willingness to meet them upfront and ensure that recapitalization will be done. The amount of recapitalization and the process of recapitalization is something that we can discuss later, but unless this is done immediately, I am afraid we are going to see very high rates of mortality in our productive sector.

Then ensuring livelihoods is going to be a problem. A whole bunch of other problems will also rise because business models will be fragile but that is something that can be handled later. So, I will stop for the moment.

R. Ramakumar

I will not get into issues that have been discussed in great detail earlier. It can be summarised in one sentence. We need to expand fiscally. That is, fiscal conservatism should be disbanded and the FRBM Act should be thrown out. The government should be allowed to spend, by borrowing and monetizing those deficits. There is no doubt about it. Globally the focus of most packages today is not fiscally expansive packages or fiscal revival packages of the sort we have seen in the past. They are basically most in the monetary domain. That is important to understand.

When we speak about the 330 billion pound package in the United Kingdom, we have to understand that at least half of it is not necessarily expenditure from the budget. It is also a monetary expansion by providing more liquidity and more loans from the banks and so on. All these are bundled together into a single package. I think one point that has not been adequately discussed, is the monetary domain.

R. Ramkumar is a Professor in Tata Institute of Social Sciences, Mumbai. He has also been serving as a member of State Planning Board, Government of Kerala, from September 2016. In the State Planning Board, he is in-charge of agriculture and allied services, land reforms, cooperation, irrigation and flood control, tourism, sports and youth service and skill development. Dr Ramakumar's work on agricultural economics and banking policy is among the most quoted scholarly works in India. His research interests are agrarian studies, agricultural economics, development economics, fiscal policy in India and national identity schemes. He is the author of "Note-Bandi: Demonetisation and India's Elusive Chase for Black Money" and has papers in many national and international journals. He is also a columnist in leading newspapers.

What I mean by monetary domain is to premise it on the fact that a lot of small businesses, a lot of livelihoods of small producers etc. are very much dependent on the credit system and the banking system. Therefore, it is fully necessary to exercise the full potential of regulatory forbearance, in order to protect the livelihoods of these sections as well. The interventions should not be restricted to the fiscal domain even as we remain strongly anti-monetarist in the theoretical domain.

If you look at western developed countries, their packages are generally to ensure that producers hold on. They are trying to hold on at the point that they were before Corona, until at least the virus blows away. These are not revival packages and they are not going to invest in infrastructure, or invest in sort of classical Keynesian packages of the sort we have seen in the past. They are basically trying to provide cash and liquidity to small companies in order to help them retain the workers in their payroll. Only when they keep the workers in the payroll will they get a benefit of say 80% of their wages being provided to them by cash, so they could be retained and employment could be protected till Covid goes away. Then, they could restart exactly at the point where they left it.

That is the assumption of most western packages. I basically see most western packages, when you reach a post-Covid era, which are really holding packages, will have to necessarily expand into a classical form of revival packages, which will necessarily be a double of what they have already invested. If they have invested 10% of the GDP on just holding on, I believe that 20% of the GDP would be required to revive in the next six months or so. I see many of these revival packages, which are very large in the western world, as only the beginning of a larger package that may unfold as we go by.

A lot of this money is going into protecting small and marginal enterprises, number one and number two, to ensure that employment is not lost and number three providing a number of tax relief measures to a whole lot of companies. So central banks have stepped in to soften SMEs finance constraints and a variety of financial facilities have been provided in many countries. For example, temporary tax relief, deferred payments, direct financial support including fresh loans, loans at zero interest rates and loans of zero collateral, quick processing of loan applications, government guarantee to new loans, new insurance programs and so on.

These are the multitude of measures that are being attempted in those parts of the world. Lot of penalties have been deferred. In many cases, the utility bills, rent bills, power bills, water bills are all being waived or halved or measures of that sort are being adopted. A whole lot of policies are being adopted to protect small enterprises, small producers and protect employment till the time Covid blows over.

At the same time, (it is again something that has been mentioned in this seminar), the Indian Government's response has been extremely disappointing. The Union Government, it is very important to understand, has taken what they call an incremental approach and not a big bang approach. Their thinking is that we should not peak too early in our response. As a result, the Government has not announced a second revival package, which was supposed to come after the so-called invisible task force meets at some point.

However, what is more important here, is to see a class dimension in this approach of the Central Government. This will be evident if you observe the response of many of their advisors, influential think tanks, like the Observer Research Foundation and so on, who see this as a time of reform. Take Raghuram Rajan for instance, who says, it is said India reforms only in crisis. And he says that it is the time to get into reforms we have postponed for a long time.

Observer Research Foundation has an official note that says Covid-19 is a 'perfect storm,' for deep reform. You can see how the divisive agenda of the Government and the ideological basis of this government and economics in some form, come together here. Economically Covid-19 is a 1991 moment, geopolitically Covid-19 is a Balakot moment, constitutionally Covid-19 is an article 370 moment and together, these are all examples of India's 'spiritual renaissance.'

If you see commentaries of this sort, you can see very clearly efforts to use this as a new opportunity for a further stepping back of the state from the social sector, from different sectors of the economy where you need more government intervention which has receded over the last 20-30 years. So, you basically see an effort by the Government not just to step back, which is one point, but also transfer a lot of the burden on to the working poor in an effort to protect business and so on.

So I see the lack of ability or the absence of a large revival package in this ideological sense, just as they see this as an opportunity for greater reform as in 1991. They also see this as a possibility, where a large part of the burden can be passed on to the workers, while businesses try to survive. Let me state my point in very brief terms.

In my view, basically we need at least a Rs 5-6 lakh crore revival package at this point of time from the Government. When I say this, I would also add that because a lot of this spending is done by the state government, a lot of interventions and investments will have to go into the health sector, as part of our efforts to rebuild livelihoods in the next few years. I assume that Rs 1-2 lakh crore will have to be invested in the public health sector in the next one or two years, to build resilience and also infrastructure and personnel in this sector.

I believe if you have a package of Rs 5-6 lakh crore, about Rs 3-3.5 lakh crore should be passed on to states in an untied format, so that states can decide what to do with the amount. It is very important to insist that aid comes through Finance Commission intervention or through some other intervention by the ministry.

A large package of untied funds should be given to the state governments. I would ballpark estimate it at Rs 4.5-5 lakh crore, out of say Rs 6 lakh crore. Rest could be used by the Central Government or passed on to states to decide what to do to (a) build resilience to the Covid-19 pandemic, and (b) how to decide and format revival packages, which are customised according to the specificities of the case.

The Centre's role is very specific. There is the MGNREGA program and there are central sector health programs, where they should actually convert the sharing formula to something like 90:10 if not 100:0. They have to intervene in areas akin to agriculture where it was last a livelihood protection program, focus on increasing MSPs, expanding the public distribution system, creating price stabilisation funds etc. It is an area where the Centre can come in at a major level.

All this reminds us that we need the Planning Commission back as well. Niti Aayog has been perfectly incapable of doing this. In the remaining part of my intervention, I will focus on something related to Kerala and what would be required from a Kerala perspective, just because we have done some work on it. It helps us to articulate the points better than from an all India picture.

If you look at a state like Kerala, two important areas which I am personally aware of are agriculture and tourism, two major sectors, where people are employed in large numbers both on a self-employed basis and also on a casual regular basis. If you look at agriculture, Kerala has already taken a hit because of the predominance of cash crops and export-oriented crops, in a situation where exports have come to a complete halt. Here we are staring at a loss estimate of at least Rs 3,500 crore till April 30. That is the kind of loss we see in the agriculture sector.

If you look at the areas like rubber, if you take a rough estimate of the amount of stocks that are lying in different parts of the state, the national losses they incur will come to Rs 600 to Rs 700 crore just for one small sector. That is the kind of losses that we see.

The United States for example has this intervention that protects the farmers of all categories there in the following ways. They calculate an average price decline that has taken place between January and April first week and the extent of loss is calculated on the basis of quantity and price. And 85% of the loss is simply passed on to the farmers as a transfer.

Now this is an intervention that the United States has tried. We need not try the same way but we need to look at an MSP increase, some cash transfers through the PM Kisan Scheme. We need to ensure that loans of farmers are provided some sort of relief if not waived completely, fresh liquidity is provided if possible at zero rate of interest. Also, you need to ensure the Kisan Card scheme in the coming season and interest subvention to pander to animal husbandry, fishery etc. which are all currently outside the subsidised crop loan system.

We need to expand the interventions through the rural infrastructure development fund and we need moratoriums. Also, much of these losses of the banks would have to be compensated by the Government through a recapitalization of the banks.

Let me state some numbers here. The total interest income of banks in one year is about Rs 8 lakh crore. Out of this, interest on term loans would come to about Rs 6-6.5 lakh crore. If you calculate on a monthly basis what it cost the government to simply waive not moratorium, not postponement but all the interest payments on term loans, it will cost the government only Rs 60,000 crore a month.

So, if the government completely waives off all interest on term loans for 3 months, March, April and May, it will cost the government less than Rs 2 lakh crore and this would be an enormous relief to all term loan borrowers. It doesn't cost much to intervene in areas like this.

Similarly, let's look at a core area like tourism, which employs as many as 15 lakh people in Kerala. We calculated what would be required if a subsistence payment of Rs 9,000 is provided for one worker, for about a month. It will cost about Rs1000 crore a month for providing a United States style wage supplement to protect employment in small scale industries and enterprises in tourism.

I am wrapping up my presentation now. To sum up, you need to look at both fiscal and monetary domains. A lot of interventions in the monetary domains like waiver, interest rate relief etc. will spill over into the fiscal domain and many of this will possibly come in the Central domain. A lot of it will come under state domain if you have to protect small and marginal enterprises. That is where untied funds of Rs 2 lakh crore to 2.5 lakh crore from the Centre to the states becomes extremely important as an economic revival package of the Centre. Thank you.

V. Bhaskar

I would like to begin my intervention on the impact of Corona on fiscal federalism. This was discussed yesterday, where it was termed cannibalistic federalism and the Centre drawing all power to itself. If there is time, I will refer to it. The basic thrust of my intervention is that while the discussion is extremely relevant and pertaining to the crisis period presently faced, we do not yet know enough to formulate an action plan. So, I will raise a series of questions, the answers to which may be necessary to proceed further in regard to fiscal federalism. If I have time, I would like to raise the issue.

Is it possible that the states are losing sight of the ball and losing fiscal space to the Centre more by apathy, than incapacity? Let me speak about it in the context of Covid- 19. This is a crisis led by the health sector. What action should be taken to alleviate the stress in other sectors including livelihoods, will both be dictated and influenced by progressively restricting Covid.

The primary responsibility for this lies with the health sector. Suppression and medication are being conducted in all states under Central guidance. Some

---

V. Bhaskar, Former Chairman, Andhra Pradesh Regulatory Commission, is a Public policy analyst and administration professional with experience in international, national and regional settings. He has extensive experience in both policy formulation as well as implementation, economic analysis and power sector issues. Bhasker worked as Chairman of the Andhra Pradesh Electricity Regulatory Commission. He was a member of the Indian Administrative Service from 1981 till retirement in 2013 with various capacities including Special Chief Secretary, Finance Department, Government of Andhra Pradesh and Joint Secretary, Ministry of Commerce and Industry, Government of India. He also worked in the management cadre of the State Bank of India specialising in credit to SMEs.

like Kerala are more effective than the others. But unfortunately, Covid seems to be presenting to us some 'unknown unknowns' which we are yet to assess. Are our testing samples biassed? What is the percentage of symptomatic carriers, do people who are exposed earlier acquire immunity? When will we see a peaking? Will there be a second wave in winter? Will we have to wait for 60% immunity, either through exposure or vaccination to finally conquer the virus?

Till then, will India have to have a continuous cycle of lockdowns and liftings? The answer to these questions will tell us how and in what manner the lockdown continues. Presently it may be lifted by 3rd May. Covid has affected different states differently, so their stance in the manner of lifting lockdowns should be equally differentiated.

It was suggested yesterday, that we have smart lockdowns, suppression lockdowns and breaks in between. My basic submission is that, until we know with certain assurance when the lockdown will be lifted and in what manner, we cannot effectively confront a strategy of what kind of livelihood to promote, when to do so, how to financially intervene and support. We need to see the future, beyond two months to decide how to support livelihoods. Until we know more it will be difficult to make a decision. That is my basic point.

Let us now come to our livelihoods. During yesterday's discussions the need to promote livelihoods in agriculture and SMEs was emphasised. Others spoke of the employment intensity of the real estate sector. I agree with the emphasis but more analysis may be required, before we can come up with effective approaches to supporting livelihoods.

The present lockdown prohibits movement of people across borders. In my state Rabi harvesting is on and farmers are facing labour shortage. The forthcoming Kharif operations will commence. Will farmers be able to import migrant labour as before? Most migrant labour is stuck in relief camps, are at a low morale and are more interested in returning home than working. I know a case where a district magistrate offered one thousand migrant labour, double the wage to work as harvesting labour. They refused. They said they wanted to go home. I sympathise with them.

Should we instead support farmers through procurement and immediate payment of the produce and hope that market mechanisms will take care of the labour. MGNREGA was mentioned in the past. MGNREGA has competed with the requirements of the farmers for agriculture labour. Should we relax MGNREG norms to allow work on private lands, which is not currently allowed for agriculture preparatory work, harvesting and so on?

The answer to this also depends upon the state from which the labour is coming from and when the lockdown is to be lifted. If you want to nurture the economy through the crisis, we need to prop up firms, which are faltering in the face of both demand and supply constraints. Though the government of India has instructed that there should be no termination of employment, this is hardly implemented.

SMEs need support. The MHA relaxed guidelines to allow for only small shops to function. If the lockdown is done in a series of cycles, will it be appropriate to assist in the revival of the continuous process industry? Where will they get their labour from? They are not only required to follow the health protocols notified by the Ministry of Health and Family welfare, it also includes provisions on hired workers being physically distanced from one another.

Will these be workable and financially viable? Will the workers be provided with accommodation within factory premises? What is the procedure when a worker is diagnosed with Covid? Will the factory be shut for 28 days? Will the owners and workers have to face isolation?

The answers to these questions are critical to the revival of industry but the answers are not forthcoming despite the MHA and its guidelines of April 23. They claim these are only apprehensions and not facts but they don't tell us what the fact is. Then how do we address the problem of constriction of demand even when industries are supported and supplies are available.

Over the next three months there will be very little demand for white goods, electronics, luxuries etc. Entertainment and tourist industries will be subdued. Real estate demand has plummeted. Government will have to take up massive infrastructure projects to generate demand. These are the issues related to protecting livelihoods. Until we know how we go about it, we cannot look into the issue of livelihoods.

Now I will come to the issue of financing. The states are undeniably on the frontline. They need support for these. States face a triple whammy as far as their finances are concerned. The first is that their own tax and non-tax revenues have come down. For inexplicable reasons, liquor has been put on the banned lists and this prime source of income for states has been removed. GST revenues are down and so is devolution to states.

Over and above this they have the additional expenditure on Covid. That includes free rations, cash grants, payments etc. States want increased borrowing limits, GST compensation, compensation of expenditure on migrants, but one thing missing from the debate is the state's expenditure plan. States are saying revenue has come down, I have expenditure and I need to meet it through an open grant of money. Are the states not responsible for a credible expenditure plan?

Except Kerala which announced a Rs 20000 crore relief package, no one has made a Covid expenditure plan, nor a credible expenditure plan for the next 12 months or a revision of the budgets. It is essentially a revised budget which will become credible, if it contains elements which shows that states are totally committed to tightening the belt. These could include examples like removing the free budget subsidy and implementing the direct benefit transfers.

More important is removing vanity projects in state budgets. It is not only the Centre which has fancy projects like bullet trains and Central Vistas. States also have similar ones like coastal roads and statutes. Is it not time for states to relook at their expenditures, when they look at financing? What about vanity schemes like financing lawyers on graduation, providing marriage expenses, pilgrimage expenses, constructing monuments?

I would argue that Covid-19 is a great opportunity to do deep reform and especially on the size of the government and fiscal expenditure. It is an opportunity to reduce the very large government salaries and pensions. In the face of lockdown, the government has significantly contracted its size and it is working, at least for the duration of the lockdown period. Why is the Government of India and the states fighting shy of reducing the government size? I am all for retiring grade 3 and grade 4 personnel in government who are overpaid in the market and with full pension.

Considering the extraordinary nature of the emergency, perhaps you can also do it and the fact is that most of the government employees are not working. Would they be willing to take a cut? Isaac carefully said Kerala has not cut but only deferred salaries. Why are we not taking this up and saying that the size of expenditure is far more than the governments could bear and it is time that size of government was curtailed. It is a beautiful opportunity.

Regarding financing, I would like to point out that the Government of India has allowed frontloading of borrowings in a remarkable gesture. States were allowed to withdraw 50% of their debt allocation. If states were really short of money and they had a finance problem, I would ask them to borrow, as the Reserve Bank allowed three tranches of borrowings on April 7, 13, and 24. Some borrowed thrice, but relatively smaller amounts. Kerala borrowed Rs 5000 crore in the first tranche. Maharashtra borrowed thrice that amount.

The question I want to ask the chairman is, why are states like Bihar, Chhattisgarh, Jharkhand, Meghalaya, and West Bengal keeping away? These are all Covid affected states. Why have they not borrowed? Are they not short of funds? Is there no Covid expenditure? This is another issue along with the expenditure plan of the states which needs to be addressed before they can go to the Government of India asking for a Covid grant. I will stop here.

Gayatri Nair

I would just like to make one point here. For a livelihood strategy or livelihood revival, we need to focus on three things: sustaining, restoring and reviving livelihoods. The scenarios for the lockdown period and the post-lockdown period are two different scenarios. If we think of the lockdown scenario we are currently facing, we know that livelihoods can be sustained only through direct cash transfers by the Government, which all economies are currently working on through cash dole outs.

Then there are certain voluntary measures also. For example, if we sustain the income of domestic workers or if the non-working units are paying wages to labour. These are voluntary measures that are being taken during the lockdown period. A common thing about all these measures is that they are not sustainable. Even the Government can't continue cash transfers indefinitely and the voluntary measures also have to stop.

If you look at the post-lockdown scenario, I feel there are five scenarios. When the economy starts working, it will almost switch to normal levels, like in the case of formal employment. The income should be restored at the original

---

Gayatri Nair, belonging to the Indian Economic Service, is currently Director in the Department of Pharmaceuticals, Government of India. She served as the economic advisor to vice-chairperson, Kerala state planning board, Government of Kerala from July 2015 to July 2022. Prior to the assignment in Kerala, she served as the Assistant Director in the Labour Bureau, Shimla and Chennai, Deputy Director in the Department of Economic Affairs, Senior Research Officer and Deputy Advisor in the Planning Commission Government of India. She entered into Indian Economic Service in 2004 after securing 1st Rank in MA economics from Kerala University in 2000.

level. The second scenario is where livelihoods will be restored only at lower levels of income. For example, auto rickshaw drivers, their incomes will be much lower initially. For them livelihoods will be restored at lower levels of income.

A third scenario is where livelihoods will take a longer time like tourism, hotels and restaurants, which will take time to open. The workers engaged in these sectors will need more time for revival. The fourth scenario is one where there is complete loss of livelihood as in the case of business which has gone bust or those which find difficulty in reopening.

We also have to think of new avenues of employment. The fifth scenario is where we have new options for livelihood. Currently there are many firms entering into producing, masks, sanitizers, personal protection equipment and there are also opportunities for income from online classes. So, we see new options of livelihood emerging in this crisis.

I believe that these are different scenarios we are actually facing. We need to focus on different categories of workers too. For example, the first category would be the most vulnerable people who are surviving on their daily incomes. Second is the livelihood of women. Many families depend on income from their women wage earners. Then there are the migrant workers who have not gone back. What will happen to them? The sectors they are currently working in will also need time for revival. How do we deal with them?

Then last but not least, is the emigrant population. The non-resident Keralites who will be returning to Kerala and who might have lost their jobs in their respective countries. So, we have to think of livelihoods across several categories and also prioritise them. Coming to the discussion of financing these livelihood options, this is going to be a challenging task.

I have five suggestions to put forth before this panel. The first is, we know there are budgetary constraints. We also know that our annual plans have embedded within them livelihood plans also. There are certain schemes that can play a role. For example, we have the Ayyankali urban employment scheme, which is the counterpart of the NREGA scheme. Then we have Kudumbashree as an organisation. It is a role model for women's empowerment and livelihood. We also have a scheme under NORKA for returning migrants.

All these schemes have to get priority. They can make a change in livelihoods in the coming weeks, when the economy reopens. A second suggestion would be about how we can have increased Central Government support. There are certain schemes that are specifically oriented towards livelihoods. We know the rural employment scheme and the national livelihood mission.

All these schemes need to be pushed aggressively and the Central Government too needs to increase their funding and also their share of the funding, so that the states will be supported adequately. The third option is about sectoral grants and the 15th Finance Commission. Sri Pinaki Chakraborty made a point about the immediate recommendations that the 15th Finance Commission should actually come up with, for livelihood revival and also Covid recovery funds, which they should seriously think of.

We need to explore more about grants under the 15th Finance Commission. All states should push for this suggestion. Fourth, is tapping corporate social responsibility funds. We know that whenever a crisis occurs, we actually depend upon CSR funds. It is very important that we tap this fund and already under the schedule there is a provision for livelihood enhancement projects.

The last suggestion would be on how financial institutions should play an active role in supporting industries and their revival measures. Only relief measures have been announced so far, but we need to go beyond that and need to have policies for revival of industries, agriculture operations, trade and services. So, banks should also have to have a proactive role in this regard.

To sum up, I would suggest a strong intervention by the government, accommodative monetary policy and a very key role for the private sector to finance livelihoods in these difficult times. We should not only focus on direct revival but also indirect revival which should also help. These are my points. Thank you.

Pronab Sen

The essential issue that we are facing now is that there are two things that need to be done. One is survival of human beings and the other is survival of productive activities. Now, as far as the first is concerned, it is the principal function of the state government and that is what states need to focus on. As far as the second is concerned, it is really the function of the Centre, because for us to able to support production enterprises at an individual level is virtually impossible, which is why we need a huge frontend financial sector to get what is needed to keep production enterprise alive.

The fact of course is, there has been very little discussion on the financial sector at all. If such a discussion doesn't happen, then we are going to be in a situation in which much of the SME sector will vanish. I am less worried about the informal sector as we do have some experience from the demonetization episode, where the formal economic arrangements tend to be much more flexible and adjust to circumstances.

I have no reason to believe that something similar won't happen this time. So, the government has to worry about the informal sector to make sure that lives are protected. I think the focus also has to be on the SME sector. There, I would specifically look at the role of the microfinance and the NBFC sectors. They are really the frontline soldiers in economic revival.

Secondly, we need to be very careful when we go in for a proper fiscal strategy. Till such time as we are convinced that the production side has come out of the lockdown successfully, an excessive fiscal stimulus will either be ineffective or precisely produce an outcome that we don't want. A fiscal stimulus as a demand stimulus should come in a graduated manner and really should be backloaded after we are pretty much confident that the productive sectors have started coming on live. Till then, we have to play the waiting game. Make sure that enterprises will survive. That should be the mantra.

In all of this, the role of the centre is clear and I repeat that, if we are going to use the financial sector, we should be putting pressure on the Centre. We have to be led by the Central Government. They are the only ones who have the clout and the reach. Nevertheless, the discussion has to be to be in collaboration with the states as well. The directives have to come from the Centre. How one manages to get that across, is the challenge we are facing.

Mridul Eapen

I don't have to underestimate the relevance of this particular session. It is something we have to be very concerned about. Figures that have come out yesterday, show the extent of losses that have been made in production, in wages etc. So, it is absolutely crucial that we start thinking of how to hold on, as Ramakumar said. There is no question of holding on the employment. There are a lot of people who will have no employment in the post-lockdown period.

I am glad you mentioned that. Firstly, it is important to remember that, for many people there is nothing to hold on to. Secondly, you have to have new types of employment as Gayatri mentioned. The thing is that, the whole issue of generating livelihoods, perhaps would have to be thought out more specifically at the state level. For financing, I think we have to seek resources from the Centre as the state can do very little, at least during the lockdown period.

A lot of finances are required in the post-lockdown period also. The financial sector, as Pronab Sen was saying, becomes more relevant and that has to be brought in, to provide relief to people in a much bigger way. As far as livelihood is concerned, as Bhaskar said, until we know what the process of unlocking the lockdown is, what will be permitted to open/function and what will be under restrictions, we cannot say anything about livelihoods to be promoted.

Mridul Eapen is presently Honorary Fellow at the Centre for Development Studies, Thiruvananthpuram. She was a Member of the Kerala State Planning Board (2016-2021). She works predominantly in the areas of industry, gender, employment and rural transformation.

The states have to start thinking, as they know their own economy, on what are the losses to livelihood that will occur, given the state specificities and how they can be protected in the post-lockdown stage. I think this is a very important thing that we have to keep in mind. The state has to start planning for the revival of livelihoods and then we have to consider how to address issues of fiscal orthodoxy we were talking about. I look upon health and livelihood together.

Like we discussed yesterday, we need to get as much from the Centre as we can in terms of borrowings and of course, the lump sum amount that Ramakumar talked about. This has been on my mind but I have my doubts on whether we will get it through the Finance Commission or can the Central government have a large corpus of Rs 5-6 lakh crore, which is then distributed as untied fund to the states using some devolution criteria.

If that is possible, we don't have to go via the Finance Commission, because I am worried about adding another term of reference to the Finance Commission, as they already have the new defence and internal security term added on. Will it be possible to look at both? They look at defence and if that takes precedence, then where are we? Defence will take away most of the funding. So, I am wary of going to the Finance Commission with this stimulus package. I think it should be the Central Government which could do it in some other way.

The other thing that I really wanted to say about livelihood was what VK Ramachandran started with. It is a much broader concept, but as Gayatri says, she was looking at it in terms of earnings at the moment. That is what I would like to emphasise. Once upon a time, we had thought that the livelihood approach is a better approach because income is too narrow an approach to understand poverty and especially in the rural areas, we should have a livelihood approach. However, in reality it has led to so many multiple activities to be undertaken to survive, that the burden on the women to make a living has become absolutely tremendous.

Livelihood is necessary to make a living. What else is the way to get the basic necessities of life? They have to find many things to be able to do, to be able to make sufficient money. I think at some point of time we have to start thinking that households should have a regular, steady source of income. At least one source of income should be permanent and the rest could be built up around that. That is the sort of thing that is possible.

Here too, in the given situation, we can start thinking of what Gayatri was mentioning, as to what we have in our plan schemes, for instance. There are composite schemes in our plan, where men and women can get employment in industries, agriculture, tourism, and the service sector. We have so many schemes. There is money kept for creating employment. This is how we could create employment, a more decent and regular employment for men and women.

The point is that the women get much more adversely affected and they are also the ones who have to be in the forefront of fighting the pandemic, primarily to care and look after the household. So, these women should not be burdened with too many activities as part of the livelihood concept. The livelihood approach for me should give more emphasis on the earning side rather than other multiple activities people do to survive. This is my opinion having looked at women's work recently and the number of things they do make a livelihood. I feel that this is a big problem in the poorer households.

Thomas Isaac

I would like to respond to the remark made by Bhaskar referring to the cut in salaries. I just met the media regarding the high court verdict on the challenge of some employees to salary deferment. The court stayed the deferment. That is a contractual obligation. I don't know the exact reason, but it has been stayed.

It is only a deferment. Kerala does not want to cut or reduce salaries. We are very categorical about that. We are deferring it to pay it at a better time. There is a salary revision commission and let them take a call. The Kerala government is not going to interfere in that. It is for a simple reason. A government should be a model employer. If the government begins doing this, then what will be the fate of millions of workers in the factories and other areas in the unorganised sector, who anyway have very little protection?

You have raised a very important question. Why are the states not borrowing and spending? There are two reasons. One reason is, I have tried to outline this with Ramakumar, in a paper written about 7 to 8 years back. The title of the paper was 'Why do the states not spend?'. It was a take on the rhetoric of Chidambaram in parliament. The states don't spend because they have certain targets to meet. There is a revenue deficit. Even if you have money with you, you don't spend. True, Rs 1.5 lakh crore of rupees is tied up in government securities. We in Kerala chose a different way. That is the reason that we are doing well now.

We have spent on education and in health care and it has come in good stead during the present crisis. Now if you are spending heavily on social expenditure, your revenue will always be in deficit. We shall not change it for the FRBM Act or anything else.

For most states it is decreed you can't spend for fear of revenue deficit. Therefore, you hesitate to spend, but during the present pandemic, I think states have been drawing upon their securities they invested in. I don't know the exact situation now but the investment of states in Government of India securities must have come down drastically.

Secondly, all the states except Kerala were testing the waters. We were committed to roll out a Rs 20,000 crore Covid relief package, which we could finance only by frontloading of borrowing. Therefore, we went to the market for Rs 6,000 crore. Others went for Rs 500 crore or Rs 1000 crore. They got 6-7%, while we borrowed at 8.9%. Then the Reserve Bank advisors informally stated that the market was unsettled and hence no one needed to go to the market immediately again.

This is an extreme form of liquidity preference. The banks and financial institutions don't want to lend money. Money is the king. Now they are afraid of what will happen tomorrow. Just consider the Franklin Templeton incident. Here is a major hedge fund redeeming their bonds. There are institutions that were downgraded. They are in trouble. Now the Government of India has to pump in Rs 50,000 crore. They only needed a moment to do that. Was there so much discussion to give Rs 175,000 tax reduction to the corporates?

Take the situation today. I am certain that there are a lot of things to be answered. There are two committees. One by the Kerala State Planning Board to look at the impact of Covid on the economy and another, to look at the impact of Covid on revenues. Things are not clear. We don't know for example, the implications of half a million migrant expatriates returning to Kerala.

Here is the reality. The simple reality is that 70% to 80% of India's daily earners, self-employed as well as wage workers, are locked out. They don't have income. This is a simple fact on which there is no debate whatsoever. Now, it seems like all the policy makers who have given Rs 1.75 lakh crore to corporates, without any sort of qualms or written off Rs 84,000 crore of rupees to defaulters just the other day, have washed their hands off this vast mass of India's poor. I cannot stand that. Whether we go broke six months from now or not, the Kerala government intends to support them.

All I am saying is that you need to give immediate relief. That is simple. In some places, petty shops in some small-scale industries, cottage industry, marginal tenements of land, they have been locked out of their livelihood. How do you exit from that? Now you see a small shop owner. After one month you go back to the shop. You find there is nothing left to sell. It would all have been destroyed. A Kharif crop that could not be harvested well in time is gone. Now, how and what do they sell?

Therefore, the minimum that is required for livelihood to begin is extension of the moratorium for a year or more. Ramakumar described the scale of state intervention in many other countries. We may not match them, but, the minimum that is required, is a relief moratorium and a waiver of interest or at least a partial one. The banks too should provide the system itself an additional 20% working capital for the small farmers or the small entrepreneurs. This is the first stage. This is the minimum required for opening up or exiting the lockdown.

Gayatri Nair

The basis of all the discussion depends on whether there is a trade-off between saving lives and saving livelihoods. All our discussions pointed out that the more we endeavour to save lives by putting the economy in lockdown, the more it is affecting the livelihoods of millions. We are unsure of the post-Covid economy, so, all our efforts have to meet those challenges, if you have to have any impact. That is what I want to say.

V. Bhaskar

I just want to add the point about the government that Isaac mentioned. My point is on the need to right size the government, not cut everybody. There are a lot of extra staff. This is an opportunity to do so. Apart from this opportunity to do so there is another set of deep reforms that has not been talked of so far. There are states that feel it is a good opportunity to levy an agriculture income tax. States have consistently shied away. Why can't states levy an agriculture income tax on all persons who pay the income tax and have an agriculture income? You have a cut off right there.

If I pay income tax and have agriculture income, I should pay agriculture income tax. This is an opportunity to try out these things. It is not happening, because a large number of states are not showing expenditure. I have suspicions why the Centre is not coming up with this Covid package. They are looking at the borrowings, but nobody can say where the expenditure is coming from. Except Kerala, which knows what it is doing. A large number of states don't know. The Centre probably thinks this is an issue.

The second is, I would like to support Isaac. The ways and means advances were supposed to be increased by 60% by the Reserve Bank. This increase is a paltry Rs 19,000 crore. Compare it with the Rs 50,000 crore fund opened up for the mutual funds in a day yesterday. The Centre is not actually opening up as much as it could.

On fiscal federalism, my view is that the states are not keeping an eye on the wall. On March 30, the Finance Bill 2020-21, was amended with a single line buried in the text saying that the figure 8 is changed to 18 in annexure 1 of the Finance bill. It basically meant that the cess on road and infrastructure was increased by Rs 10 per litre. The Centre took advantage of the fall in price of oil, to walk into the fiscal space. This amendment was not challenged but passed unanimously.

I agree that since these are Covid times, the amendment was passed without a whimper. States allowed the Centre to occupy the fiscal space. The other issue is the operational space regarding Covid and though I would love to go through the Pandemic Act and the Disaster Management Act, I have to restrict myself due to time constraints. States have the power on working with Covid, but the Centre has assumed those powers through a Supreme Court order.

R Ramakumar

Yes, I think I will make three or four points. The first is that Bhaskar's comment brings an episode of 'Yes Minister,' to mind. It is the story of a minister who sees an opportunity to boost his career when he sees a fully built and fully staffed hospital, which seemed to have no patients. That represented the classic strategy to cut the NHS to size. It is a feature of our attitude towards the public sector. That, I feel, is only a part of the problem.

When we speak of deep reform, it is about right sizing the state and right sizing the state includes a kind of apathy to the informalization of the workforce and the importance of the public sector in providing certain core services. The number of government servants in India, per lakh of population, is actually one sixth or one eighth of what the United States or other countries have. We need a larger public service, which can provide basic services to people. So, I do not think deep reforms mean right sizing the government in terms of personnel, manpower or human power.

Secondly, I had mentioned that you do not have scope for a large demand revival package of the classical Keynesian sense at this point of time. That is because, there is a lockdown and only after it is over and supply chains pick up, can you think of such a package.

However, at the same time, when I say hold on, what I mean to say is, there are also areas where increasing demand and relief converge in their meanings, or in their objectives of providing a small transfer to people, to purchase food at the same time. My way of looking at it therefore, involves a demand revival, as well as a relief measures, which allows them to hold on.

If you look at food price indices coming down, it actually refers to a sharp fall in demand for food for consumption. This is shown by many data sources and in that sense, we need a demand revival package. Relief thereby coincides with demand.

One last point. Dr Isaac, the Central Government decision to cut dearness allowance is also in some sense the negation of reengaging from the contract, if you interpret it the same way. The dearness allowance cut is equivalent to a salary cut of 52 days in a year by the Central Government. So, I am saying that all those measures will be now under question given the high court verdict that you have cited. I have not seen the judgement, but only know what you have said.

Pronab Sen

There is one action of the Central Government that has not been discussed at all. The government has actually asked all departments, except some selected departments, to cut their expenditures by 5-10 percentage points. The inevitable will then happen because the entire cut is going to be reflected on centrally sponsored schemes. State budgets are therefore going to take yet another big hit. That has perhaps not been factored in, but take it from me, it is coming.

Now the real issue is, states are still wary of going to the markets. The borrowing limits of states have not been raised. Front loading of borrowing is all that has happened. When this happens, the states are faced with a very difficult choice on account of centrally sponsored schemes which comes as an important intervention in the states. They may have to prop up it with their own funds, which frankly they do not have. It is a difficult choice they will have to make very soon.

V.K. Ramachandran

We have to wind up now. I just want to say before we end that we do have an expenditure plan, and the Annual Plan is now being reprioritized. Thank you.

Section 8

The Pandemic and the Revival Strategy

K.M. Chandrasekhar

Let us start right away. The subject is 'The pandemic and the revival strategy.' I heard bits of the discussion earlier when C P Chandrasekhar and VK Ramachandran were speaking. The immediate problems that accompany the pandemic have been addressed. We really don't know whether Covid has ended. Probably, it is still growing and we do not know the actual dimensions of the pandemic because testing is inadequate. Hence, it is difficult to assess the real picture especially in some states.

Still, we have to think of a post-Covid world, the current problems of livelihood, migrants, and growing poverty. I think that is something which has come upfront now. Poverty is going to be the most difficult problem that we will have to address in the short term. It has been growing at an alarming rate and I heard Dr Isaac mention that we really do not know what is going to happen.

Now, the point I really want to make is that Covid has only accentuated a problem. There was a problem already existing in terms of the economic slowdown and it was not addressed, because it was never seen as a demand side

---

K.M. Chandrasekhar, the 29th Cabinet Secretary of Government of India from 2007 to 2011, belonged to 1970 batch IAS officer from Kerala Cadre. His past positions include Vice Chairman of the Kerala State Planning Board, Chairman of the Centre for Development Studies, Revenue Secretary of Government of India, Finance Secretary of Government of Kerala, Chairman of the Spices Board, President of Sri Chithra Institute of Medical Sciences and Technology, Trivandrum, Director of Fisheries in Kerala, and Honorary Adviser to Kottakkal Arya Vaidya. Earlier, he also served a diplomatic position as India's Ambassador to WTO in Geneva. He has written extensively on various issues in different platforms.

problem. It was seen as a supply side problem. So, all kinds of things were done like a corporate tax cut which nobody wanted, because corporations will make a profit only when people buy. So, we had to look at the demand side first, and then try to resolve that part of it and then go on to whatever had to be done on the supply side.

Demand has to grow. For that, we needed a sharp self-liquidating kind of stimulus. If you recall, it was done in 2008-09, when we brought forward two successive stimulus packages. This was very successful. The third one, which was done in 2009, was a mistake because at that point of time, the stimulus should have been stopped. Instead we went on for another stimulus and then failed to scale it back, which created a problem of high inflation in 2013-14. However, that failure cannot be attributed to what was done earlier, as it was extremely successful then.

Now, having not injected any stimulus at all, there is some talk about a stimulus, but there is no clarity on when it will come or in what form it will come. All the time, the focus is on the fiscal deficit ratio. I know you have discussed it already.

Fiscal deficit plays an important role in the present situation. If you look at it in numerical terms, the numerator stands for the absolute deficit and denominator for the GDP. If the numerator is increased even beyond the artificial 3% limit (as laid down at Maastricht), the denominator will be affected and the fiscal deficit ratio will correct itself accordingly. Even otherwise, if at a particular point of time you need to scale it back, you find that it again comes back to whatever level is considered normal, and that could be 3% or 4% or 5%. In any case, since we have just accepted the European Commission's 3% deficit rule, we tend to adopt that by default.

We still continue to talk in terms of the supply side and maintain that the fundamentals of the economy are sound. In fact, we keep repeating this. This is strange and it frightens me for it is the same language that was used by Herbert Hoover, just before the great depression. Finally, you had to have a man like Franklin Roosevelt to intervene and create the new deal which is a Keynesian thing. We have to think in Keynesian terms now. That is the first of the issues that we have to really look at.

What is the next step? My view is that it will be the state governments who are more affected than the Centre. The Centre would like to do everything. I can understand that. I have also been participating in several cabinet meetings where the fear was always that the states were getting credit for all the Centre is doing. That is something that has been ingrained in the minds of those at the Centre for a long time.

Right now, however, what is required can be done only by the states. You need to look at the problem of poverty immediately, and how you are going to address it in agriculture and small-scale industry. We need not worry much about corporations. Corporate groups will take care of themselves. They don't need supply side measures. If there is demand, then corporate groups will automatically do well.

On the demand side we need to do something. I do believe that the best way of doing it is to empower the states, who will be able to do what should be done. There probably might be a positive impact if you can have the fiscal deficit and FRBM norms relaxed for the states for some time.

I heard Pronab Sen say just now that even the Central share of the centrally sponsored schemes is going to be cut. There are other measures that can be taken on the demand side both in the private and public sector, like scaling down salaries and amount paid to workers etc.This again will adversely affect demand, which will make economic turnaround even more difficult.

Once we take care of the demand side, we need to look at the logistics of movement because whatever we do, even if there is demand, unless your products are going to move smoothly across the roads without barriers, it is not going to reach the consumer. That, then, is a point at which both the Centre and states have to work together and ensure freedom of movement.

This is particularly so, since people are not going to go out to the shops and buy. That channel which has been blocked now, needs to open up if you really want the revival strategy to work. At the same time, the financial sector will need to be particularly careful about its interventions. In my view the Central bank has been showing more sensitivity than the Government of India during the pandemic. They have been responding better, but there are several areas where they need to do more.

There needs to be some degree of regulatory flexibility on non-performing assets at this point. Immediate reaction to panic situations has helped, like in the Franklin Templeton case, when it decided to completely give up its debt funds. In a timely action, the Reserve Bank stepped in immediately and provided a Rs 50,000 crore line of credit. The problem that I now see on the Reserve Bank side is, perhaps, that a little more flexibility is required to handle situations as they arise.

However, I don't see any great revival strategy being thought of. Small things are being done occasionally .That is not going to bring in the change we need at this point of time. There is also not much thinking done on the strategy. Even the discussions between the Prime Minister and the Chief Ministers, as reported in the newspapers, hardly look at the future. We are thinking of getting out of the present problems and that is justified. You have to first get out of the Covid situation before you can get into the revival plans.

Dates have been mentioned and I don't know where and how they get these dates on when Covid would end. They seem to be more of astrological forecasts. Now at the end, after we have looked at the revival strategy, I feel we have to look at the long term. Has the pandemic taught us anything? Has it taught us to look at our economic philosophy itself? We have been focusing on things like foreign investment, ease of doing business and so on.

But I think we need to look at a single parameter. How are we going to raise the basic minimum standards of our people? If that becomes the focus of our thinking and our philosophy, we can probably achieve more results. This is proven by the excellent example of Kerala also. What have we done in the last 50-60 years? We have really looked at education, health, basic minimum standards. Those are the things paying off today. Our people are educated and literate and they are able to respond a great deal better.

The health system is better organised. We are able to respond better. So, with good management which successive governments have displayed, the results are showing in Kerala. We need to have similar results everywhere and this, I think, is something that we should really look at in the future. How are we going to judge our progress? Is it only through GDP growth or is it by foreign investments or are we going to bring in other factors also? So now I would like to leave the floor open for discussions.

K.P. Kannan

I have been attending these highly informative discussions since last morning. It is heartening to see quite a lot of consensus on what needs to be done. However, as Ram Reddy said, it should not be all talk and no work. There are clear signals about the timing of the revival and the strategy that needs to be followed. A short term crisis has already begun and we have to provide all possible humanitarian assistance. That could lead to a path of recovery of the economy and then there will be revival. These are not to be seen as compartmentalised, but rather as overlapping phases.

In this continuum, if we act fast on the relief phase, i.e., the current phase, providing whatever it takes in terms of financial and non-financial intervention from both Central and state governments, the quicker will be the recovery. If we continue our actions during the recovery period, shorter will be the recovery period and then we could get into a revival phase. So, any kind of slowing down

---

K.P. Kannan, a former Director and currently an Honorary Fellow at the Centre for Development Studies, Thiruvananthapuram and Distinguished Fellow GIFT, is a renowned development economist. He is also the Academic Chairman of the Laurie Baker Centre for Habitat Studies and Chairman of the Centre of Science and Technology for Rural Development (COSTFORD). An academician with a doctorate in development studies from the International Institute of Social Studies in The Netherlands and a people's science activist for years, he is also a Past Conference President of the Indian Society of Labour Economics. A prolific writer, he is a member of the Editorial Advisory Boards of two international professional journals and three national professional journals. A Human Development Report on Kerala, sponsored by UNDP, India, was prepared under his leadership in 2005. He was a full time Member of the National Commission for Enterprises in the Unorganized Sector during 2005-09.

in the first phase, I am afraid, will slow down both the recovery phase and the revival phase.

From that point of view, I want to start by saying that I agree with Chandrasekhar when he says we now have to focus on the demand side of the problem. There is an important part of the demand side to adjust, especially the loss of income of the poor and the vulnerable. As much as 80 percent of workers are informal sector workers. Another 10 percent are informal workers in the formal sector. So, 90 percent of the workers are in the informal economy.

Taking care of the loss of wage income in the informal economy will activate the demand side, even if partially. That demand will activate some sectors now. It will also take care of the local economy through demand for food and other necessities. Addressing the demand side of the poor and the vulnerable will activate, in my view, the supply side problem to some extent. This is especially so since the country has enough food stocks which is three times the required level and we also have inventories of other non-food items. Based on a rough estimate, I find the loss of wage income for 90 percent of the informal workers is around Rs 3.5 lakh crore per month. So, we have already crossed the first month and we are into the second month. If it lasts for three months, the amount will be Rs 10.5 lakh to Rs 11 lakh crore. That is close to 3 to 3.5% of the GDP. I am only talking of the wage income of the informal workers. What public workers, scholars, administrators ask the Government is to provide at least Rs 6000 per family for those who come under the National Food Security Act. That is a proxy for reaching out to the poor and the vulnerable and their families. If we do so, it will amount to less than one sixth of the wage income that they get.

I would like to emphasise the need to address the supply side problem from the point of view of the micro, small and medium enterprise sector (MSME) where most of the informal workers are employed. Basically, there are something like 50 million MSME units in the country with at least one hired worker. Two third of the establishments in the Economic Census are counted as own account enterprises which is a euphemism for self-employed persons. If an amount of at least Rs 5 lakh each is provided as financial assistance to these enterprises, that will call for something like Rs 7.8 lakh crore. If the Government of India gives Rs 6000 per family plus Rs 5 lakh for each MSME it will come to around Rs 11 lakh crore that is around 5.5% of the GDP.

I have argued that we need at least 10% of the GDP as a major intervention. As much as Rs 11 lakh crore to Rs 12 lakh crore will go in this way and an additional sum would be needed to fight Covid and strengthen the public health system which is in a difficult condition except in two or three states like

Kerala, Tamil Nadu, Himachal Pradesh and may be Punjab. In the rest of India, it is in a pathetic condition. We need money for that. We also need money for strengthening the public sector, as well as the corporate sector to respond to the supply side issues.

When I say strengthen the public sector, I am making a big point, in the sense that we are now learning our lessons about the critical role played by it during emergencies. I am not against the private sector, but in an economy when there is a crisis, the first sector which is called upon to face the crisis and take remedial measures is the state and its agencies. In this case, it is the public health sector which has been called upon to shoulder a majority of the responsibility. Some private sector health institutions might have rendered some voluntary assistance. But that is not enough. By an executive fiat, a government can of course summon them to render specific services in an emergency situation. However, it is the state which has a primary obligation to intervene to save the lives of the people through whatever available means.

In such a scenario, you have the public sector which is strong enough to supply goods and services that are required to combat Covid and also provide for the livelihood requirements of the people. Take the case of bringing our own workers and their families from abroad. It is Air India which is being called upon to perform the task. It is the public sector. Not that you cannot use the private sector, but the first call is on the government.

There is a need for rethinking our economic logic. My view is that we have gone too far in the globalisation game. First through external compulsions and then by adopting it as an overarching national economic policy on our own. Going too far into globalisation is not necessarily in the national interest of most countries. Now there is a rightward attack on it. I don't think it is the best way. We may have to go back in one way or another. If I may, for want of a better term, say a Nehruvian middle path is required for building a strong public sector along with such policies and programmes for the growth of a vibrant private sector.

As far as the informal sector and the informal sector workers are concerned, I would like to draw your attention to the final report of the National Commission for Enterprises in the Unorganized Sector (NCEUS) titled *The Challenge of Employment: An Informal Economy Perspective* (Academic Foundation, 2009). It is a comprehensive report for providing universal social security and national minimum floor wage, as well as promotional measures for livelihood enhancement and a package for financing the MSME. I think it is the right time to revisit the recommendations of the NCEUS and adapt it to the current conditions. It will also serve the country in the long term, when it comes to revival of the economy to provide broad-based growth and development.

Public employment, in my view, is a crucial link between the crisis-recovery-revival continuum in the economy. The Mahatma Gandhi National Rural Employment Scheme should be strengthened to explore its full potential for employment creation linked to the development of productive capital. That will also, inter alia, take care of the livelihood requirements of the poor and vulnerable. It should also be extended to urban areas. That is what people want and that can also be banked on for revival of the local economy, especially agriculture, animal husbandry and so on with the help of the panchayat raj institutions. A national lesson that India could learn from its State of Kerala is the central role of the panchayat raj institutions during the time of crisis and responding immediately to panic situations.

As a final point, let me say that we need to take care of the situation at three levels. One, India should jealously guard its strategic autonomy in international economic relations and not put all its eggs in the globalisation basket. Second, national economic policies should explicitly take into account the long term national economic development by protecting the livelihood security of the poor and the vulnerable. Third, there should be adequate autonomy – in terms of policies and financial resources—for the state government to address regional-specific situations and challenges. At the core of all these is the inadequate attention paid to raising financial resources through enhancing the tax collection efficiency both at the central and state government levels. There is considerable room here given the low ratio of tax-to-GDP ratio at the national level and low tax-to-GSDP ratio at the state level. There is considerable scope for research and policy-oriented work here. I am sure the Gulati Institute of Finance and Taxation will pay enhanced attention to this challenging issue. Thank you.

G. Vijayaraghavan

Thank you, GIFT. I heard some of the discussions. One of the things we all need to realise is people are talking of a new normal. It is going to be very clear that the world is not going to be what it was before. That means the way we live, the way we work is going to be completely different from the past. This, we need to keep in mind. We cannot go on in the way we were doing, whether in the government or the private sector we work. We have to change and there is no other way.

One of the things you notice now is, there is the Central Government telling the state governments to do a lot of things but there is no money being passed on. The state governments continue to do a lot of things that it can do. It is just like the state governments telling the local governments to look after a few things. A very similar thing. The state government is telling the local government to run the community kitchens and take care of that. You have the Central governments telling the states to look at the migrants and take care of them completely. Only there is no funding happening.

So, what is happening is that those who have the money are keeping it with themselves and spending it the way they want, but not passing them on. This is

---

G. Vijayaraghavan, Honorary Professor, GIFT, is the founder CEO of India's first software technology hub –Technopark and former President of International Association of Science Parks (Asia Pacific). He has held key mentorship and advisory roles in both the government and in the private sector. Some of his earlier positions included Member, Kerala State Planning Board and the Kerala State Council of Science, Technology and Environment. He is also the Hon. Director of Trivandrum International School and the National Institute of Speech & Hearing.

exactly the way it is happening in the private sector also, where the companies are also trying to do the same. They are trying to keep the money with them and not giving it to the people, whom they have taken services from. They don't know how long they will be able to hold on during the crisis.

So, this is something happening across the country. Indirectly it is not the government or the private sector, it is actually the human way this is happening. Dr Bhaskar and Dr Isaac replied to this point in the earlier rounds. One thing is clear. The governments cannot continue to do things the way they do today. We need more governance and less government.

So, we need to look at ways in which we can cut government expenditure. When I say cut government expenditure, I am not asking to cut down government expenditure in the social sector. In fact, I remember that when Chandrasekhar was the vice chairman of the planning board, an additional substantial amount was given to the health care, social justice sector and tourism. Substantial amounts we got from the Government of India was allocated only to two or three of these departments, in such a manner that we could improve the services provided there and governments have been continuing that very clearly.

So, it is necessary for state governments to decide on where its money should go. It should clearly chalk out what it wants to do. Clearly health is something we want to do. When we do health, we also need to be clear that there is a private sector in health. Unfortunately, what is happening is that the private sector has been completely ignored, though I would not like to say that.

Nothing much is happening in the private sector, even though we hear people say we will use them when we want. At the same time, the amount of money that the government has been giving to the private sector hospitals as reimbursement in the past has been high.

The hospitals in our state today are in very good condition. I know if you really look at it in terms of the quality of doctors, the quality of infrastructure etc. the hospitals are very good. The government should take a firm decision on the state government hospital insurance schemes and assert that there will be no reimbursement in private hospitals. Any state government employee, any MLA, any minister, any politician can take insurance of their own and utilise the facilities if they want. The government should clearly say they are not going to reimburse expenses in the private sector.

Indirectly, you will increase the money coming in. Today what is happening with the insurance schemes is that they go to the private hospitals and spend their money there and come back to the government hospital when all their money is exhausted. The most important thing is that you have to look after the poorest of the poor. You have over 40 lakh people on welfare pensions. If my memory is right it was during R Shankar's time that the welfare pension was fixed at Rs 15. It was an old age pension or something on those lines. I have done a post-on this sometime back,

At that time the primary school teacher's salary was around Rs 30 and that Rs 15 pension has now gone to Rs 1200. The salary of the primary teacher has not gone to Rs 3000 or Rs 3500 but it has gone to over Rs 40,000. What has happened is that in spite of the fact that all the governments have always said that they are for the poorest of the poor, unfortunately they are unable to have some kind of balance even in the area of welfare pensions.

The second thing here is that the welfare pensions have never been paid on time. I know that Dr Isaac has now taken the initiative and given the last six pensions together. You are also talking of an additional two months, which is good. What we want is that the government should allocate money for welfare pensions first whenever any money is available. What is left should be used for government salaries and government pensions.

If this pension of Rs 1200 can be increased by 3 or 4 times, where do you get the money? I know you talked about deferment and that you won't cut salaries but, you should remember that you are talking of only 5 lakh employees and 5 lakh pensioners. Kerala has a population of over 3 crore. This is not even 4-5% of the population which the government says will not be touched at all. The rest of the population is spending for themselves.

So, if you look at a 25-30% cut in the government expenditure on salaries and pension without touching people with salaries below Rs 30,000 or pensions of below Rs 20,000 and without touching people in the health sector and the police, you will be able to generate enough money to multiply the pensions. You don't have to do this for ever. You just do it for a few months and you will see the impact this will have on society is going to be substantial. Because you are actually going to take it from the haves and give it to the have nots. Which is what I think all political parties talk about. I fully agree with you, when you questioned the reduction in corporate taxes. It had no impact on the economy at this point of time.

I will talk about the poorest of the poor. If the government can use the money saved from the government expenditure on salaries and bring in another 60-lakh people in on the welfare numbers, you will have one third of Kerala's population get a minimum income of Rs 5,000 to Rs 6000, a month. You do not need to mobilise it from somewhere else. You can cut it. It should not be made an executive order. You have an ordinance to cut it. Once you pass an ordinance, the court can't go beyond a point. I know the efforts you took to enforce a voluntary cut in salaries. The teachers took to burning the order which was terrible. You should cut 40% to 50% from those who get the highest salaries.

Next, unwanted government expenditures should also be cut now. We will cover two sectors which are important for the revival of small businesses, which Kannan talked about, and about which we definitely need to do something. When we talk of 60 lakh people, many will be employees of these small shops and small businesses. Get the ESI to pay the salaries as during medical emergencies and they will get that.

Two sectors have been very badly hit. One of the badly hit sectors is tourism. Tourism sector may have 14 lakhs to 15 lakh people working in the sector and the salaries are not huge. In fact, this sector will not have any income coming in for the next seven months and it will take another four months even before they start stabilising. Imagine you close down the hotel for six months and try to calculate the amount of money needed to make it functioning again. You will find that many of our resorts and hotels will have a serious problem there.

It will take at least 12 months for them to get back to somewhere near normal, if things don't worsen further. So, we need to do something for the sector. I am not saying that the government should pay the private sector. I do not know what the government has already done. You do need to have a clear outline on how to revive the tourism sector.

We must also consider the IT sector. It now employs around 2 lakh people. Salary levels are much higher. Their annual revenue in Kerala is around Rs 20,000 crore to Rs 25,000 crore. Unfortunately, neither the government nor the associations have clear figures. These are based on what I tried to get from companies and my own calculations. The loss will vary from Rs 3,000 crore to Rs 5000 crore by the end of April, because most of them continue to pay salaries.

This sector has been completely hit by international events, not domestic. The big customers do not want to give money to these people. They will hold on, ask for deferred payments, they will talk about cutting down expenditure. Already, the number of people who have lost employment in the United States is huge. You're going to find a similar number here. My estimate is that Kerala will see 2000-3000 jobs lost in the IT sector.

If you look at what has happened in the industry during the 2000 dotcom bust or the 2008-09 financial crisis, around 75% to 80%, will get back the jobs. Another thing that has been happening in this sector is the gig economy there. Many of these people will become entrepreneurs and I hope that within a span of six months, of the 20,000 odd who lose jobs 4,000 -5,000 will become small employers. You will find that the sector is revived. It will take them a few years to recover the loss that they make in the next six months and come back to normal. This is another area where one needs to look at specific things.

I am aware that yesterday too, the government passed specific orders that say that companies who have taken up to 10,000 square feet of space from the government IT parks, will not have to pay rent. However, it is not the small companies alone, but the bigger companies too that will have to be supported or they also will have problems.

So, one thing is clear, business is going to be very bleak in all these sectors. Now I will come to the overall picture. One of the things that the government needs to look at is the way of the new normal or the way we are going forward. What kind of people should be looked after most and what would be the kind of priorities we would lay down. The poorest of the poor should come first. The priority sectors should be the health sector and education. We should continue to do what we are doing. For social justice, we should continue to do the same.

In the case of many public sector undertakings, I don't think we should continue with what we are doing. Find out ways, we can actually give them off. Also remember that there are more than 1,000 companies ready to set up manufacturing facilities in India. Japan has announced a $ 2.2 billion program to move manufacturing out of China. How do we capture those? Can we capture them with the kind of thought process we have and the time it takes to set up or do business in Kerala? We have to remember that we are competing just with other states. We will first have to compete with the rest of the world, for them to look at India and only then can we compete with other states. We will have to take a deeper look at our labour laws.

I know it is very difficult for some to accept such changes, but we need to decide whether we need to create an environment which would allow people to create jobs. We can set our norms. We can talk of minimum wages and other things, but there should be deep thought on all these before we do it. So, these are all the things which are absolutely necessary for us. I just covered two major sectors and the poorest of the poor.

The other segment that requires special attention is, (and I know that Isaac also knows), people with disabilities. We need to do something there, because unfortunately when the cut comes in plan areas which is done on a department basis, the cuts will kick in also on the welfare and pensions of the disabled. So, it cannot be cut across the board. You will have to look at it sector wise. Whom do we invest our money in.? It is a very scarce resource. We will be borrowing for that. It would only make sense, if we do not use this money for salaries.

Rather, it will have to go to the poorest of the poor or to programs that will create employment. Though it may be difficult for people to agree, I think just like the Niti Aayog has replaced the Planning Commission in the country, in Kerala unfortunately, KIFBI and the rebuild Kerala mission has replaced the Kerala State Planning Board. I know that it is a very harsh statement. We need to ensure that the planning board, which has a certain level of expertise should get consulted in this entire process in whatever Kerala is going to do. It must be noted that for most of rebuild Kerala, the planning board was not consulted. You cannot do it the way the Government of India has done and apportion funds, depending on who is the stronger ministry. The planning board was the big balancer, where they used to discuss and decide the government's priorities. That is something which we need. I will comment later.

K.M. Chandrasekhar

Vijayaraghavan was talking of the expectation of a lot of industries moving from China. I saw some statistics from Nomura. Of the 56 countries relocating from China, 26 are going to Vietnam, 11 to Taiwan, 8 to Thailand and 3 to India. If we don't really apply our mind it will be difficult to bring them here. It is important to make this an opportunity for attracting industry from the Kerala point of view. The second part is of course, how to stimulate demand. It requires some bold action.

George Mathew

The discourse on Covid-19 pandemic and fiscal federalism in India is highly relevant today. From the deliberations, we can conclude that only the Kerala state has taken the lead in facing the crisis. Many practical suggestions and revival strategies have emerged. I shall underline three issues. First, the unorganised sector. It must be our prime concern. According to the Arjun Sen Gupta Committee, the unorganized sector contributes 60% of the national economic output, out of which 120 million are women.

How do we intervene in this sector, which is the most hit? Revival programs of the unorganised sector can be implemented by the local governments - panchayats and municipalities. They are nearer to the people and understand the sufferings of the rural and urban population. Here we must distinguish between the micro sector and Micro Small and Medium Enterprises. It is important to focus on the micro sector. The state should take it as a very important concern and support MSME marketing and technology.

George Mathew is the Founder Director and currently the Chairman of the Institute of the Social Sciences, New Delhi. He received his PhD in Sociology from JNU, New Delhi. He held many academic positions including Visiting Fellow of the University of Chicago South Asian Studies Centre (1981-82) and Visiting Professor, University of Padova (1988). He is a member of several committees of the GOI, and on the board of governors of national and international organisations. He has contributed a number of books, research articles and papers to national and international academic and research journals. Based on a true story, Dr. George Mathew produced the film: 'Swaraj: The Little Republic' which won the national award for the Best Film on Social Issues (2002) for 'its strong depiction of women's empowerment in rural India'.

Secondly, we always refer to the human capital of Kerala. Because of the investments in education, we have created social capital, through human capital. Today around three million Keralites are living and working abroad. Of course, the government has the responsibility of taking care of their well-being. We have to foster international migration in the post-Covid world by taking steps to protect them from the problems they confront.

Of course, our Kerala government continues to take extraordinary steps in this direction. However non-resident Keraltes must develop a program/plan on an international basis. Kerala has now evolved as a model. In this context Kerala needs the cooperation and support of the Union Government. Most important, is the Kerala strategy for development of the human capital in the years to come.

Thirdly, inside and outside India, there are many philanthropists from Kerala. Presently Kerala's finances are not in good shape and that is a worrying factor. How can the philanthropists of Kerala origin, come in; not as charity, but as partners in the revival process? A good number of people working outside, have returned to their motherland and settled in Kerala. They have rich experience, innovative ideas, excellent human network and scholarship. This human capital will have to be tapped and thus the emerging human resources will result in a quantum jump.

Many of these issues are central to our deliberations. The local governments should come forward and with the support of the present government, these ideas could be deliberated upon and thus Kerala can prioritise the revival strategy to go forward.

N.J. Kurian

The Covid crisis is a crisis of multiple dimensions. It created a health crisis; the lockdown created a humanitarian crisis and there is now a huge economic crisis. An ordinary fiscal conservatism will not work. We should remember that the great depression was created by fiscal conservatism and the world came out of the depression through expansionary expenditure. At present the Government of India has a lot of fiscal conservatism and this has to go.

States are in the forefront to fight the crisis and have to be adequately funded. There is a need for strengthening state fiscal capacity and to a large extent this has to come from the Centre because the economic crisis has led to significant reduction in revenues of the states. The Centre's revenues too have also gone down, but Centre should think of something which most developed countries have already done. The first instalment of fiscal support in the developed countries has been in the order of 5-15% of the GDP, and remember these are

---

N.J. Kurian is a well-known social scientist and economist. He is the president of Action for Food Production and was a former advisor (financial resources) to the Planning Commission, Government of India. He is a Ph.D. in Economics from University of Western Ontario, Canada. As an economist, he has a long experience of over 40 years, of which over ten years in teaching and research at university/research organisations. He served as chairman/member of various committees, study groups, working groups set up by the Planning Commission, Ministry of Finance, Government of India and Reserve Bank of India. He has also served as Consultant with international agencies such as Asian Development Bank, UNDP, FAO and UNICEF. He was the Director, Centre for Social Development (CSD), New Delhi and President of Indo-Global Social Service Society (IGSSS), New Delhi.

mostly conservative governments. They are giving away their fiscal conservatism. This is point number one.

Point number two is about the revival of the economy. You have to seriously think of gradually opening up, because the lockdown has virtually shut down 60-70% of the economy and it has to be revived now. In this context, we have to consider a significant aspect of our labour. That is, the vast majority of labour working in industries and services in cities, are migrants who are daily wagers and they are the victims of the lockdown. Most of them are stranded in host states, who have not provided adequate social protection.

So once the lockdown is over these migrants will return home and will not be available to work in the developed parts of the country. That is going to be a significant problem. Kerala has an additional problem. Around half a million migrants will return to Kerala and many will be unable to go back. Remittance to the state will come down.

So, fiscal support from the Centre is a must but, if the centre does not work out institutional ways to meet the requirement of states, they will definitely feel the absence of the Planning Commission. The Niti Aayog is not in a position to step in as they do not have the expertise or data base of the Planning Commission or even the objectivity to work out the requirements of the states. The Planning Commission had all the information in one place. There is a huge gap. The Finance Commission can do something. They should definitely ask for a revised memorandum from states and their term should be extended, so that they can rework the report and also the revival strategy.

Some of the areas where the Centre can save money are the Central Vista project, the bullet train and other fancy projects that can wait. Similarly, in states also many projects can wait. My feeling is that states should revise the expenditure budget as things are not going to be sold immediately after the lockdown is lifted. Another thing is the Centre is monopolising CSR funds, which is very unfair. States should have been allowed to take advantage of these CSR funds.

Sunil Mani

I thank both the Finance Minister and Professor Joseph for this chance to take part in the discussions here. I will actually talk on revival strategies not just for Kerala, but also India in general. As the chairman correctly put it, the pandemic had come at a time when the economy was already slowing down. Indian GDP has been steadily decelerating over the last seven quarters continuously and then the pandemic struck. There is a general consensus, as the chairman has pointed out, that it is more a problem than anything else.

Most of the policy measures or strategies that have been put in by the Government of India are on the demand side. I would also argue that we need to look at the supply side as well. The supply side aspects of certain kinds of products and services, especially technology and innovations, are very important. The very fact that we are actually able to conduct this webinar is because of technology. These discussions indicate that a number of technologies are becoming very important, not only in containing the pandemic but eradicating it completely.

Sunil Mani is Director and Reserve Bank of India Chair Professor at the Centre for Development Studies (CDS), Trivandrum. Formerly, he was a member of the faculty and head of graduate studies at the United Nations University-Institute for New Technologies (now known as UNU-MERIT) at Maastricht in the Netherlands. He obtained his M. Phil. and Ph.D. in Economics from Jawaharlal Nehru University, New Delhi and has done postdoctoral research at the University of Oxford on a fellowship from the Ford Foundation, New York. He has held visiting professorships at Bocconi University —Milan, National Graduate Institute for Policy Studies—Tokyo, and University of Toulouse —Jean Jaures. Currently, he is a member of the drafting committee for India's new Science, Technology and Innovation Policy 2020.

There are two characteristics of this technology which are extremely important both for India and Kerala. What are these two characteristics? The first characteristic is that these technologies have to be available very cheaply. In other words, if the cost of technology is very high, the diffusion will be very low. Let me bring to your attention the discussions on N95 masks for instance.

If they are priced at what they are now, diffusion will be very low. We need to have huge numbers of them. Also, if you are going to have vaccines, because the only proper solution is to have a vaccine, the dosage should be within the reach of a common man. So, you need to have frugal innovation and frugal manufacturing. This is an area where India has a definite advantage. That is the first aspect.

Secondly, the kind of technologies that the pandemic has raised our attention to. Basically, there are two kinds of technologies. In the first category are various kinds of technologies starting from vaccines, therapeutic drugs, medical devices, personal protective equipment and so on. In all these health-related industries, India has a comparative advantage and I will pick up each one of these. Let me explain why this is the case. In some of this Kerala too has an advantage and it is quite important that we take these projects seriously.

The second category is a whole host of digital technologies including the one we are using now. A wide variety of digital technologies have become very important because of social distancing which is now going to be practised for a number of months and years. If I am not mistaken then we are much more online actually rather than physical activities. When people get used to online activities they are unwilling to let go and so there is going to be a great demand for various kinds of digital technology.

Now let me start first with the health-related technologies and I start with vaccines. Now vaccine production as we know in terms of research shows that there are 80 different research and development projects which are going on all across the world and this number is increasing. A lot of organisations and institutions are getting into vaccine research. Many Indian institutions and firms are also into vaccine research.

The most important thing is that, when you come out with a product you need to make millions of doses of it, because you are talking about inoculating the whole world population, the numbers of which run to billions. So, you need to have billions of dosages that have to be sold at prices which can be easily borne by public health systems because ultimately, it has to be diffused by the public health system. Hence, it is necessary to have cheap doses of vaccines. That is where India comes in because we have a large number of firms.

According to some counts we have at least six very credible firms, which have the capability to manufacture vaccines at very minimal costs. Suppose the General Institute of Oxford University trial, which is the first one to be tried, is able to come out with a successful vaccine today, there are firms in India which can actually make millions of dosages and supply them at less than 50 US cents per dosage. That is an important part of our revival strategy. We can make a big headway if we encourage that sort of contract manufacturing. Contract manufacturing in vaccine production is a very important activity that needs to be encouraged. Next is therapeutic drugs. Of course, we know that game changer drugs that some of the leaders have been talking about have turned out to be a hoax. For instance, Hydroxychloroquine and Remdesivir, have both turned out to be ineffective and they are both not going to be useful as far as this pandemic is concerned.

After a whole discussion on HHCQ Hydroxychloroquine therapeutic drugs, I got to know that these therapeutic drugs could be used in treating certain kinds of non-Covid diseases afflicting a large number of people. I would say that it is actually a blessing that hydroxychloroquine is not useful for treating Covid because it will be very useful for treating other non-Covid diseases which are now getting relegated to the background. Here again, India is the largest producer of Hydroxychloroquine and hence the leader of one country 'twisted' our leaders' arm to get large doses exported from India to that country. So therapeutic drugs is an area in which we can actually play a very important role because it has raised the importance of not just our capability to make this drugs, but also produce them extremely cheaply so that it is well within the reach of public health systems and could be used a lot in terms of the pandemic.

Third is medical devices which again is another area that people have been discussing. They include a wide range of devices starting from ventilators to a host of other kinds of small devices. This is an area again in which India can play a very important role. Work has already started on a commercial scale ventilator, which costs only about Rs 1.5 lakh when the normal invasive type of ventilator would cost something in the rage of Rs 7.5 lakh.

That is what I mean by frugal manufacturing, that is, making it available at a cost which the public health systems can actually use and then diffuse. That is again another area where we can play a very important role and there are a fair amount of other cost effective research and development products, which are being produced at the moment. These in turn will help produce various kinds of low cost medical devices that can be used quickly and very cheaply, not only for this pandemic but also for other kinds of non-communicable diseases, which we have to worry about.

Next is about Personal Protection Equipment (PPE) and I would especially raise the importance of N95 masks, because if you remember when we talked about PPE, the initial discussion was that these masks were not important since the WHO was saying that there was no need for them. But, the current feeling is masks should be basically used by frontline workers like health workers who are in very close proximity with the Covid patient. The kind of masks they should be using are not the reusable masks that you and I are using, but N95 masks which are also covered by patents.

This is another important issue that I will talk about later. So there is a fair amount of scope for making frugal innovations. Several experiments of this nature are going on in India and hold great potential for large scale manufacturing. This is an area where both India and Kerala can get into. Therefore, in all these health-related technologies, vaccines, therapeutic drugs, medical devices and PPEs both India and Kerala have an important part and that should be made an integral part of the revival strategy. This actually raises the importance of the role of the government because some people were talking about the fact that we need to reduce the size of the government. I would say it is not about the size of the government. Size does not really matter. It is the kind of intervention that you are actually talking about.

The role of government with respect to technology promotion in these industries is different and we cannot continue with the old modes of promoting. The primary role of the government is actually financing this activity. Now this activity was largely financed, as far as India is concerned, by provision of tax incentives for research and development. According to the Ministry of Finance, which computes the revenue impact of tax forgone, through various incentives given to industry, (which they have been doing very religiously since 2005-06 until now), the only thing is, the name has been changed from tax forgone to revenue impact. The amount of tax forgone as a result of research and development incentive is one of the largest and it ranges from Rs 8,000 crore to Rs 11,000 crore.

We also know that research and development of most firms in the country have not shown any increase of any kind. Studies done both in India and abroad have shown that these tax incentives are not very effective in terms of promoting additional investment in research and development. So, if you are going to use the traditional methods of promoting innovations, especially in the health-related technologies it is simply not going to work. It would be a waste of tax resources and instead I think it should be used essentially for provision of research plans.

So, this research plan can be directed to the particular industries that I talked about since you can have tangible results which are forthcoming. So, research grants for frugal engineering and frugal innovation are the technologies that I talked about. Another important area, in which governments have shown interest is one in which much more international participation is required as they relate to international governance rules with respect to intellectual property rights.

We know from recent discussions that one of the reasons why N95 masks were short in supply is because there is only one major company making these and this an American company called 3M. They hold some 440 patents for this particular technology. So, it is not just availability of raw material that the health minister was talking about, but also the fact that intellectual property rights is a major barrier to entry.

You need to have a situation of open science or open innovation, where we need to completely rehaul the role of patents in the area of pharmaceuticals and medical equipment. That should promote innovations. In fact, in a limited way this is happening in certain sectors. So, I think that these are the kind of revival strategies I will put on the table. We need to have revival strategies in terms of promoting innovations in health-related technologies, such as changing international governance rules which will allow you to do that.

K. Ravi Raman

Thank you Chair. Let me begin my comment with a different kind of foundational statement about Covid-19 and the economic situation. Covid-19 is not just a public health crisis or an epidemiological crisis or even simply an economic crisis; rather it is a moral economy crisis. I trust the chairman will allow me to return to this point after making a couple of comments on the observations made by the presenters in this session.

I find a high degree of consensus among scholars who presented their papers despite the difference in emphasis. For instance, K.M. Chandrasekhar, K.P. Kannan and N.J. Kurien have focused on the demand-side problems, while Sunil Mani placed more emphasis on the supply-side but not excluding the demand-side; Vijayaraghavan has also taken a closely related position.

K. Ravi Raman, Member, State Planning Board was formerly a senior fellow at the Nehru Memorial Museum and Library, New Delhi. He was also a Director, Institute of Applied Manpower Research, Planning Commission and a visiting fellow in Oxford, Cambridge and Manchester for varying periods. He is also honorary research fellow in the Department of Development Studies, SOAS, London and affiliated researcher on Egalitarianism, University of Bergen. He works on a range of themes with a focus on agrarian and labour studies, social movements, policy and development, business and labour history and environmental studies. He is the author of Global Capital and Peripheral Labour, editor of *Development, Democracy and the State* and has contributed to various journals. He is in charge of transport, labour and labour welfare, public works and civil supplies in the State Planning Board.

We all know we had a double hit both on the demand-side and the supply side. In this case, it is important, as Dr Kannan has rightly pointed out, that the income loss and wage loss for the workers and the marginalised social sections have to be taken into consideration. We also have some observations from our own study in the state planning board on the loss of employment and the loss of income among workers. It is quite significant in the sense that the wage loss is about Rs 13000 crore, which may be an underestimate, but is still a huge amount, a loss which may continue for some time to come.

So, it is quite important to find measures to boost the demand of the poor and vulnerable social sections. But apart from that, I would imagine classifying the areas into three, in terms of the gravity of the impact of Covid19: the severely affected, moderately affected and the least affected industries.

The severely affected are the automobile (both public and private transport, for instance), hospitality, logistic, tourism sectors and particularly MSMEs. We know that the credit absorption ability of MSMEs is very high, which according to some officials is about Rs 60 lakh crore to Rs 70 lakh crore. But, the financial flow to this sector as credit is hardly Rs 10 lakh crore to Rs 12 lakh crore. There is so much capacity for absorption and if the banks are willing to give up their risk-averse approach, they can make available funds to MSMEs and others. The moderately affected industries include banking, textile etc.

Therefore, what I am trying to say is that, once we classify these industries along these lines, we should also be able to have a time frame to make recovery possible. The next aspect is about the amount of resources we need in each of the sectors. We should be able to work it out at the National, state and regional levels and we in the planning board are trying to do this.

Apart from the three categories, their time frame and the resources required would allow us to link the issues discussed yesterday, on resource mobilisation. There were one or two issues which remained outside the discussions yesterday. Those issues where there is a consensus like FRBM devolution etc need not be discussed again but I am surprised that we are not able to discuss the reintroduction of inheritance tax. We had it till the mid-eighties. We have to think of its reintroduction. It is equally true with respect to the wealth tax, as part of tax reforms in the country.

This is again a suggestion, particularly considering the fiscal situation in Kerala. How about making a very special request to foreign loan agencies? It is time for us to make a very specific request at different levels: for instance, lowering interest and also rephasing the repayment schedules. Right now, we need to begin negotiations with funding agencies, as we will have to be able to repay the loan from 2021. Let me come to my last point. We need to learn two lessons from history. The first is, whenever there was a crisis in the economy, it was transferred to the poor and vulnerable and whenever there was plenty it was retained by the propertied classes. I would like to assert that this should not be the case as we work towards a new normal.

The second point is with respect to the differential impacts of the crisis on various social sections. I have studied the 2018 floods and have found that the crisis is not neutral in its impacts on caste, class and gender. It is non-neutral in its impact on all three categories.

I would argue that we should go for a moral economy package, as the Covid-19 crisis is not just a public health or epidemiological crisis but a moral economy crisis as well. We should demand a moral economy package from the Government of India, with a focus on the livelihood issues of the marginalised social sections and workers. We should also request that the state should consider the creation of a unique moral economy package, the first of its kind in the world; the details of this would form the subject of yet another seminar.

Thomas Isaac

The theme of the session was 'Strategy for revival of the economy.' We had an earlier one on livelihoods. Now we are looking at a slightly longer-term strategy of development. Very useful and interesting suggestions were made, which in fact means that we have to find out areas or sectors which have potential for post-pandemic growth. Sunil Mani, Vijayaraghavan and all have identified the particular sectors, technological, medical and so on.

We now have to work out the sectoral programs. That is well taken, but Vijayaraghavan would have liked us to go much further. He wanted deep reforms to be brought into the discussion and strategy. We can have a separate discussion on that. As you know these are highly divisive issues. There will be strong opposition to some of the proposals.

I want you to understand that the kind of pandemic situation we are facing is one where we have to rally everybody. This is not a situation where in the name of reforms, you alienate a large section of the population. Even a suggestion of deferring the salary has aroused so much resistance.

I am more interested in having a wider front to resist the spread of Covid, to prepare ourselves for the return of at least 5 lakh of migrants from outside, devise ways to shield our 30 lakh old and vulnerable in the houses and provide a minimum support and succour for those who have totally lost their livelihoods. These are the issues to be settled.

Do not use this as an opportunity like the Central Government, which I think is taking people for a ride. Their argument is that the crisis is also an opportunity. That I think is highly divisible and creates all sorts of problems and undermines all the efforts we are making. I am not passing a verdict on anything. Each of us has a perspective. Valuable suggestions have been made by Vijayaraghavan, Mani and many of you.

Yes, there are problems with the public sector units. However, we know it is the revival of the public sector which has enabled Kerala to increase the share of manufacturing in the last few years. I, being a leftist, know that the public sector in Kerala is not creating socialism but rather this is a part of the larger left political alternative.

I will stop now. This is precisely what we are trying to do. We are trying to have the broadest possible platform where whatever is agreeable among all of us will be the common minimum. The least common denominator. We will choose so that there is a viable alternative statement on what is to be done in the country. We can speak about it in the concluding session. Thank you very much.

Section 9

Media in the Time of the Pandemic

Sashi Kumar

Good evening and welcome. I was listening to the sessions and was increasingly worrying and wondering why there is a session on the media at the end of it all, because it is obvious media is a part of the problem, as well as the solution. We have panellists with different backgrounds in the media. I will just make some preliminary observations and give 6-7 minutes each to the panellists.

I think it would be fair to say that the media was already in a crisis, an identity crisis really speaking more than an economic crisis, when Covid-19 hit us. The business model was up in the air and revenue models were no more available. Retrenchments were taking place. The shift from the legacy media to digital media, was catching people unawares. A lot of adjustments and readjustments were taking place in the industry to cope with these huge tectonic technological shifts, as well as the growing absence of a market model.

When Covid-19 came, it worsened the scenario. We have to look at it at one or two levels. One is in terms of the sustainability, the business model of the

---

Sashi Kumar, an Indian journalist and media personality from Kerala, is currently the chairman of Asian College of Journalism, Chennai. He is the founder of Asianet, the country's first regional satellite television channel. He founded and chairs the Media Development Foundation, the not for profit public trust which set up and runs the Asian College of Journalism in Chennai. He was the first West Asia correspondent of *The Hindu* in the mid-eighties. Sashi Kumar started his career in Doordarshan (DD) as a newsreader and producer. Later he worked in PTI-TV as chief producer and general manager of PTI. He authored and presented independent programs on the economy, politics and culture on Indian television. Sashi Kumar is a well-known filmmaker as well.

media which continues to be hard pressed in search of a model in some sense and two the performance of the media itself which has not been financially or altogether very good. Their media and media and media and a section of the media has been a problem for the other sections of the media, and also perhaps vice versa.

There has been a kind of redefinition of the role of the media itself. We had thought that the media speaks the truth to those in power, has an adversarial relation with the state, afflicts the comfortable and comforts the afflicted. All these definitions, all these noble thoughts about the media have gone out of the window, because we have a substantial section in the media which has willingly laid itself supine before those in power and chosen to become, so to speak, "his master's voice."

Worse, this sizable section of the media has become more like a prosecutor attacking anyone who attacks the Government. The whole process of othering and stigmatising becomes a media plank. I am referring here to a good chunk of the mainstream media. The social media, which is an unregulated space - some would call it an anarchic space - is replete, is awash, with the worst kind of diatribe and poison. It is difficult to understand and counter it sometimes. Apart from all this, there is also the absence or lack of a clearcut business model.

One development we have seen during this pandemic is that, irrespective of where the media comes from or what it is doing, there has been a sudden spurt in the engagement with the media, particularly digital media. So, you find a paradox in the digital media, particularly in the non-legacy and even in the legacy digital media. On online portals, there is a huge spurt in engagement, page views and that too without a compensatory or commensurate monetization. There is no monetization or any hope of monetization in the foreseeable future. Yet more and more people are flocking to the media.

This is a very paradoxical situation that the media is facing and as we emerge from Covid-19, I wonder whether or how the media will reconcile the paradox. The other aspect that I think must be noted about the media is that it clearly failed to call out and hold those in power to account. There has been this creeping idea, a dangerous idea in my opinion, that in times of crisis the media must rally around, endorse, support and enable the policies and programs of the government.

I think the media needs good will. The media needs to act in good faith but it is the task of the media particularly in times of crisis, to be the watchdog of society, to speak truth to power, to reflect, to invigilate what happens, on behalf of its viewers and in terms of the larger public good. That should be the primary criterion for judging the role and relevance of the media. A part of the media, sometimes and not as often as required maybe, has been at the receiving end of a small subset of the media itself - say, in calling out misinformation, disinformation or fake news ; this whole new genre of fact checking journalism. But generally media practitioners are thick as thieves; the press club syndrome which becomes a habit of consensus creation, of manufacturing consent on not embarrassing the government.

I think it is more important now than ever before for the media to be investigative in its thrust. For instance, the criminal underbelly of this whole Covid-19 phenomenon has been, what we have done to the livelihood of the people and to migrant labour. They have been displaced, uprooted from their jobs, their homes and their families and they are in a state of rootlessness. They are almost in a state of suspended disbelief. .

Media has of course thrown important light on this largest displacement of our population since the partition. Some of the legacy media, some television channels have exposed some of what has been happening out there. But, I think it needs better and bolder investigation because the depth and breadth of the crisis has remained indefinite and elusive.

Much of the media seemed preoccupied with prescriptive cosmetic behavioural detail - what kind of masks we should wear, whether we should be shaking hands, whether and how and how much social intercourse is kosher and so on. Not that all this is not important, but when they are in lieu of, when they substitute the in-your-face humanitarian crisis that unfolds before us, it is inexcusable. Because they become tantamount to a concerted act of distraction. That , I think, has been a big failure on the part of the media. I think the media needed to be more vigilant, persistent and conscientious about looking squarely at the obviously more important and impinging issues and not being sidelined by preoccupation with the more cosmetic aspects.

The media continues to work like health workers, doctors and frontline social workers do and continue to be out there in the field. They have a sense of what is happening as it happens. Were they alive and responsive to this designated role? The designated democratic role is not what the government of the day expects of the media. We had a taste of the implication or consequence of such expectation on media freedom played out in Kerala, where two television channels were abruptly and arbitrarily pulled off air because of the way they supposedly reported the Delhi riots. One after the other both were allowed to resume their telecats, but meanwhile we got a good sense of the method behind such madness.

The information minister said there had been some mistake or misunderstanding; but interestingly, even if not surprisingly, the official notice issued to these channels said something to the effect that it was not only that they did not factually report the riots, and also that they bad mouthed the RSS—as if that was a criminal offence.

So, you know that the media was already facing threats from all sides and to add to that, there is this unfortunate fact that public trust in the credibility of the media is at an all-time low. The credibility of the media in the UK and USA continues to be rather low and in India, I don't think it is going to be any different. So, the media is facing a crisis of its own making even as it copes with the crisis brought on by Covid-19. I will now invite the panel to come in.

Sukumar Muralidharan

This is a time unlike any other and the nature of this meeting itself tells us a lot about what is unusual and specific about the situation we are in. We are dealing with the phenomenon of social distancing, which means that all the rituals of community life have been disrupted. Vishu has gone by, Ramzan is on as we speak, Easter, Good Friday—all these observances passed in a completely new mode of observance.

What does this mean in terms of the current experience and what does it mean for the future? One aspect of this is, of course, the physical community, which was in many ways underwritten by our common participation in the cycle of rituals, has become less a part of our daily lives. In terms of the media, there was in Kerala, this early morning ritual of the collective reading newspapers in the tea shops - that sense of community underlined by the consumption of news has gone missing.

News consumption now occurs in isolated bubbles and people consuming very different menus. More and more people are dependent on what is called the

---

Sukumar Muralidharan is a Professor at Jindal School of Journalism and Communication. He was a print media journalist for over two decades. Since 2004 he has worked as a freelance journalist with no formal attachments to any media organisation. He has worked in areas of science and technology, economics and current political affairs. Since 2004, he has held a year-long visiting professorship at the Jamia Millia Islamia in Delhi and worked seven years as South Asia programme manager for the International Federation of Journalists. He has published research papers on the media industry, contemporary politics and worked in the area of conflict analysis, both domestic and global. As a fellow at the Indian Institute of Advanced Study (IIAS), he worked on modes of theorising on technology in the Indian planning experience.

virtual community. We are more now, like in this gathering today, in a virtual coming together and that is perhaps going to be more important in the days and months ahead. It is only natural then that we are concerned about the kind of changes we have been witnessing.

There is also the fear that perhaps there will be large scale exclusion of particular people from this virtual connectivity. This is likely to be true because, India is kind of unique in the sense that in the last ten years or so, we have seen a doubling of the population using cell phones from roughly half the total population to close to the total population. What is also remarkable about the doubling of the cell phone numbers is that a huge proportion of that is smart phones which keeps on increasing with each day.

According to the Ericsson Mobility Report, as against 100 million smartphones in 2010, today we have 600 million odd smartphones. Though it is a rough report, the indications are clear. Also, the kind of data consumption on each of these cell phones has been increasing enormously from approximately 1 GB in 2010-11 to something like 13 GB or so now.

In fact, overseas visitors to India are completely flummoxed and taken aback by the kind of data services we have here and the ridiculously low rates at which these are available. This has happened after the arrival of an entity called Reliance Jio in the market and their highly predatory marketing strategies.

In this respect we should also take note of the recent acquisition move by which the global digital giant Facebook acquired a stake in Jio, breaching one of the red lines in media regulations between content and carriage. We have had a relaxed framework over the years in regulation of media ownership. The normal conventions have not been honoured. So, we have increasingly seen the ground being altered by these monopoly players.

The kind of information that we have access to is getting to be more and more exclusive, though the explosive growth of social media gives it an appearance of being inclusive. So, in the specific context of Covid, of course, we have to look at certain recent developments. Sashi Kumar mentioned the mass exodus of our working people from teeming cities and small towns to the villages. This was triggered by the three week long shutdown, which was imposed with just 4 hours' notice. Just prior to that, the Prime Minister had a video conference with some of the heavy hitters in our media industry, without revealing the intent to implement the lockdown.

A lot of observers were shocked by the abruptness at which the lockdown was announced and were certain that a catastrophe was imminent. The media did a good job trying to track the scenario and brought us poignant human stories when people trekked back days together to the security of their homes, rather than opting to stay back in alien urban environments where they had no stakes.

We also know of the warnings issued to some of the media houses to tone down their coverage and exercise some caution, which they did. So, it is evident that there is an effort to impose a particular and a singular view on the media, so that we the public as a whole are co-opted into a consensus. I believe so and I also believe that the media, in the particular kind of vulnerability it is in right now, is going to have very few resources to resist that. This is because over the last 20 years, certain strategic choices have been made by which media became more and more dependent upon advertising and commercial patronage, rather than audience loyalty or subscriptions.

We have become more and more dependent on official favours in the sense, every time there is a big shake-out, as in the 2008 global financial crisis or the 2016 demonetization shock, we have had to line up before the ministries to seek various kinds of concessions. The same thing is happening now. There is a demand for a 2-year tax holiday, removal of import duties and increase in the rate of Government advertisements.

Frankly I don't know where this is going. The first two demands are obviously going to trigger similar demands from elsewhere and there is no basis by which media can be made a separate entity subject to a different set of rules. There is a traditional argument that this is a public institution and hence it deserves a treatment distinct from any other industry. But then, there is also an obligation to organise in a manner that justifies that claim of being a public institution. Obviously, we have not been witnessing very much because in practice it has functioned very much like any other industry, being profit oriented and everything else.

Of course, these are tough times and one wouldn't have a complete understanding of what is happening here without also looking at the rather shabby and ignominious manner in which the media tried to scapegoat particular communities after the fallibilities of the government strategies were exposed.

This was the topic foremost in the media agenda in the first few days of the lockdown, when it emerged that there was a religious congregation in a particular part of Delhi, in which several hundred people including some from abroad had gathered. Some of them who turned out to be Covid positive, dispersed to various parts of the country and became potential carriers of the virus. This was a cue for the media to switch to demonization of an entire faith and propagate a very toxic narrative about 'jihad' by other means. We have paid a very high price for it.

I would also like to draw your attention to a story in the editorial page of 'The Hindu,' written by a scholar a few days back that Kerala's strategy to deal with the crisis placed great emphasis on securing public trust. He had underlined repeatedly that public trust or social trust is the key to the whole thing. In the rest of the country, or at least in large parts of it, we had adopted exactly the opposite strategy. We had adopted a strategy which undermined the unity and trust among the people and created scapegoats. Once trust is destroyed in this manner, it is not easily regained and that is going to cost us very dearly.

So, we may surmount the crisis in the next few weeks, though predictions can be inaccurate and hazardous. Let us hope we do that. Most importantly, the greater job of repairing the economic damage and the damage to the social fabric needs to be attended to. In both these respects, the media has a fair share of the blame and hence should bear a fair share of the burden. Thank you so much.

K.G. Narendranath

It is too early to make a definitive assessment of how the media have responded to a rare occurrence like a massive and prolonged pandemic. However, on the question of fiscal federalism, as a member of the economic media fraternity, who believes in the virtues of decentralisation of the custody and use of fiscal resources, I wish to make a few observations. There has been a sharp erosion of the fiscal powers of state governments in recent years. This, I think, should be checked. I find no reason to accept the proposition that the Centre is invariably a more responsible and efficient manager of fiscal resources. In fact, its track record on fiscal consolidation and transparency hasn't been more impressive than that of many of the state governments. Also, the parameters of fiscal rectitude, as defined by global rating agencies, cannot be treated as sacrosanct, because implicit in them are vested interests of dominant sections of the world economy.

A provincial government could have legitimate interests at odds with these entrenched principles of fiscal policy and would often know better how to generate public resources and use it for its people, while guarding against the prospect of debt traps.

The formulation of the Goods and Services Tax (GST) was a complex affair. It involved the states losing their powers to determine tax rates on sales

---

K.G. Narendranath is an economic journalist with nearly three decades of experience. He has reported and written extensively on macro-economic, industrial, trade, tax, energy and infrastructure policies as well as on economic regulations. He worked for the Indian Express Group in Mumbai for over four years, before moving to New Delhi. He has been holding leadership roles for the last two decades, and is currently Executive Editor-Economics at *Financial Express*. He worked previously for *The Economic Times*..

(transactions). At the end of a grand bargain, the states gave up these powers in lieu of a direct share in the taxes on manufacturing (excise) and services and a five-year revenue guarantee. States wanted a larger share of GST proceeds but ended up getting only half of it. The administrative set-ups for collection and appropriation of indirect taxes were also redefined, to the satisfaction of both the Centre and states.

During these Centre-state negotiations, the business media I think played a role, in giving currency to the states' interests. That some of the state finance ministers like Dr Thomas Isaac and Dr Amit Mitra have been the most vocal and articulate among the members of the GST Council also stood federalism in good stead. The media coverage of the statements of these state FMs, I think, helped in securing a semblance of balance in the structuring and evolution of GST.

When the Narendra Modi 1.0 government came to power, it promised a highly decentralised federal structure and said that the varied ideas and aspirations of the diverse Indian people should be reflected in the fiscal policies. It seemed to walk the talk initially as it accepted the 14th Finance Commission's awards which increased the share of the taxes devolving to the states to 42% from 32%.

But thereafter, amid the overall revenue decline caused by the economic slowdown, which got accentuated in the last financial year particularly, and with the tax buoyancy also sharply falling, the Centre apparently began a rethink on the (increased) share of tax revenues to the states. This is what resulted in a rather unusual mandate (TOR) to the 15th Finance Commission, which effectively included the task of looking to restrict the states's share and also, to increase the Centre's heft in fiscal response.

Also, the Centre on its own attempted to increase its share of revenue by increasing the cesses and surcharges, which the Centre directly implements and appropriates the proceeds of, without having to share any monies with the states. The share of cesses and surcharges in the gross tax revenues (GTR) of the Centre has increased from 8.8% in the FY13 to about 16% in FY20. The Centre has ramped up its own resources and this is evident in the decline in states' share in GTR, despite the FC's favourable award.

In the context of the Covid-19 pandemic, the Centre is being very economical with its fiscal packages. It is actually becoming too ungenerous to the states.

While this is the fact, many states like Kerala have their own social development policies and political economy objectives, which may not be in sync with the Centre's. These states need more fiscal leeway. A study by

National Institute of Public Finance and Policy says that, after the 14th Finance Commission award, the social sector expenditure of many of the states have actually declined. So has the share of the states in overall public capex.

The argument against more fiscal freedom to states is that since many states are not very efficient in spending, the Centre needs more resources at its disposal which would serve horizontal equalisation for a national development plan.

If you see the off-budget financing of the Government expenditure through various Central government entities like the FCI, the actual fiscal deficit is even higher. The Centre is trying to protect its headline fiscal numbers to the extent possible. In the process, the inevitable strain in Government finances is being shifted to states and Covid-19 and the economic slowdown have exacerbated this trend.

The Centre has asked the states to borrow more from the District Mineral Fund (DMF) for Covid related expenditure, Forest Funds and also the Corporate Social Responsibility Funds. It has also restricted the use of DMF by states. So, in every way an attempt is being made by the Centre to reduce the fiscal space of states.

The social-sector expenditure of the states has declined after the 14th Finance Commission award, a fact the Centre uses to create a rational basis for its attempts at centralisation. Of course, many states with poor spending efficiency have been laggards in producing tangible social and physical development outcomes. The argument is that in their case, the Centre has to take the lead.

The point is that states that have performed well on sustainable development like Kerala should be given more leeway. The additional fiscal freedom should be linked to a dynamic index based on the spending efficiency of states and the tangible outcomes on certain acceptable development parameters. The concern that higher transfers to the states will lead to low multiplier effect on the economy can be addressed in this manner.

For example, Kerala has long-term development plans and wants more fiscal and spending freedoms to implement them. It is ready to borrow at comparatively higher rates from the market, being confident that planned use of these funds will prop up economic activities and growth, and thereby, government revenues. States like Bihar, on the other hand, have higher dependence on the Centre for their tax revenue needs. Around 60% of Bihar's tax requirement, for instance, is met from Central transfers.

States with higher spending efficiency may be incentivized with greater borrowing freedom, subject to overall considerations of public debt management. If this policy is adopted, the Centre will no longer be able to hold the view that more fiscal freedom to states will lead to economic inefficiencies or reduced multiplier effect or capital expenditure, citing that states don't spend according to the right priorities. Given the diversity of our country, states ought to be incentivized to perform better, without foregoing the objective of achieving horizontal equity in terms of Central resource transfers.

Anil Padmanabhan

Sashi Kumar set the context with his stump speech right at the top. I just want to make four broad points. It is a no brainer. The current crisis is a once in a lifetime opportunity for journalists to cover a crisis of such gigantic proportions. It is an enormous challenge and an experience to be a journalist at this point of time. Personally, for me, my career in journalism started when the economic reforms were beginning and those were contentious issues then. Now at the sunset of one's career, we are seeing such a tremendous challenge that is testing all of us and testing the world in fact. That is the larger point.

The other is the enormous business challenge. Sashi Kumar dwelled on it briefly. On the one hand, the business challenge has worsened. Things have gone from bad to worse. On the other hand, there is an enormous demand for good content. It has just gone through the roof. So, there is an opportunity, but funding that opportunity is not going to be very easy and that is something for which there is no business model. There is no institutional memory to address this. We are actually addressing it on the fly. Obviously, it will hurt different

---

Anil Padmanabhan has been working as a journalist for the last 36 years. After receiving a master's degree in Economics from Delhi School of Economics in 1986 he entered journalism. Since then he has been working in various news outlets including Press Trust of India, *The Afternoon, Business Standard, India Today* (New York) and *Mint*. He has served as the *India Today* Chief of Bureau in New York and until recently (2020) he worked as the Managing Editor of *Mint*. Among other things, he used to write a weekly column, Capital Calculus, focusing on the intersection of politics and economics and anchored a podcast with the same moniker. *Kalpana Chawla: A Life* was his debut book.

people differently, depending upon your own resources to begin with and how the media companies react to the crisis.

A point I want to make is that, what we have learnt, is an enormous learning experience for us. I mean I can speak for Mint. We never thought we could produce a daily newspaper remotely. We did not have the opportunity to do mock drills like the *New York Times* did. Like Sukumar previously said, it blindsided us and we had to just scramble. Our office was shut down and we had to put the paper together virtually.

As you all know a newspaper is a bunch of moving parts. To produce 14 or 18 pages every day in a remote manner is an enormous task. But I am glad everybody stepped up to the plate. Of course, we have discovered new acronyms like WFH or work from home. We are all learning but the notion of WFH is exaggerated. It works for people like us. It is not a workable option for people who actually engage in physical labour. Right now, there is a little bit of romance around it as Sukumar alluded.

Another thing to be considered is the rapidly shifting ground. It is so rapid and it requires some expertise, which unfortunately most newspapers in this country never cared to develop. So, we are actually learning, many of us are actually jumping into it with such energy and just using our wits and instincts. It is revolving around a nucleus which for us, includes two health reporters, and a science writer. So, these three form the nucleus for us and everybody else is rallying around. I have a colleague also who is listening in on this who is doing some outstanding work based out of Kerala. You would have read some of his stories.

Finally, I want to address what Sukumar and Sashi were raising. I can tell you what we try to do at Mint. You can judge us on what we do or don't do. We just try to report facts. Try and avoid the news trap which seemed to have set both of you off and we go the extra mile to look for the stories.

It is a misnomer when we call these people heroes and throw them in the front and we guys sit in the back and tell them it was a great show. It was actually started by my colleague Nidheesh, who is based out of Kerala. He launched the first part, and it was a fantastic story of a nurse in Kerala who was working with Covid and could not go home. And, when she did go home, she could not embrace her kid. That was the moving part, which showed us the reality of what we are dealing with here.

What we at Mint are trying to do is tell you that it is a reality that you can't ignore. It is an economic reality as well as a humanitarian issue, an example of which is the migrant issue, as well as a raft of other issues. In fact, it is just beginning. Humanitarian challenges are yet to hit us. It is still to unravel. I dread to think what will happen. That is why I spoke about working from home and all the things that delude us to believe that these are all resolvable issues. It is in fact not so. We all know, we have spent our careers reporting India's development challenges and we know how tough it is. An epidemic like this pandemic, given our high-density population with pathetic health infrastructure can be simply overwhelming,

For us at *Mint* we are just trying not to get overwhelmed by the challenges but just keep our head above water. Like everybody else we have limited resources. We are a business daily pivoted to look overnight at Covid as the central piece of our coverage. So far, so good. But these challenges, like I said, are just the beginning.

T.K. Arun

When you say media, it is not a homogenous thing. There is nothing you can identify as *the* media right now. It is segmented and different segments show very different characteristics. When people talk about media, primarily they actually mean what appears on the screen, what screams at them, what abuses them, what confuses them. That is what they identify as the media. But, this is not the only media that is consumed. People are also subjected to myriad social media every day.

Today we have a situation where whatever little time people have to consume news about the world around is saturated with images that accuse, sensationalise or try to bring humour or bring out the so-called human condition when people are locked down, whether at home or in hospital or on the street or whatever.

At the same time, the media also has a responsibility to highlight the policy challenges that arise from the present situation and examine the alternatives, look at the right choices being made or the wrong choices being made. Now the Economic Times, being a business paper, deals more with policy rather than with the actual developments on the ground like what is being done, whether

---

T.K. Arun is the Editor, Opinion, of *The Economic Times*. He writes a fortnightly column on the paper's edit page, Cursor. He has been the paper's Resident Editor at Delhi, headed the economy bureau and looked after the editorial page in another stint in the past. He has been with the paper since 1994, except for a two-and-a-half year stint with the dot com world during 1999-2001, when he edited an online portal called Narad online. He has worked as a technical advisor at the Kerala State Planning Board, before beginning his career in journalism in 1992 at the Observer of Business and Politics, New Delhi.

the Government should increase the fiscal deficit or not. The pandemic presents a huge challenge. If the government is prepared to increase the fiscal deficit considerably as we think it should, how should it be financed? Should it be raised locally, should we tap the local markets for funds? Should the RBI take a part of the deficit, meaning printing money?

These are all vital issues that matter when we look at ways to deal with the pandemic. The public at large have a right to know this, as well as keep themselves updated on all the options available. Similarly, keeping abreast of global developments about possible vaccines and cures is also an issue. All this involves the multidimensional activity of mediating information of the disease to the public, so that enriched public discourse can, sort of, lead the Government and policy makers to take the right decisions.

Recently, the Reserve Bank has come out with various liquidity facilities which seemingly are very robust. Large measures to address the problems we face. Now, it has been our judgement, which we carried in the editorial of the Economic Times, that these are actually very inadequate responses. Now it is the job of the media to demystify actions by agencies like the Reserve Bank, which are removed from the day to day activity of the ordinary man in the street, who would not ordinarily understand what the implications of the various policy measures being taken by the Reserve Bank could be.

So, it is our duty to decipher what it actually means. When the Reserve Bank says we are going to conduct a targeted long-term repo operation and give Rs 7 lakh crore to the banking system, fund companies, fund non-bank financial companies (NBFCs) and fund mutual funds which are under redemption pressure. What does it mean? We are pumping money into the banks in the hope that banks will actually pass this money on to the intended borrowers. But, banks are not doing that.

Prior to the lockdown banks were returning to the Reserve Bank, on a daily basis, some Rs 2.86 lakh crore every day. After the RBI pumped so much money into the banks under different liquidity facilities, the banks have been returning some Rs 7 lakh crore to the Reserve Bank every day. That is all that is happening. Money comes to the Reserve Bank from the banks and the Reserve Bank returns the money back to the banks and the banks deposit the money back with the Reserve Bank, without the funds actually going to the companies, NBFCs and thereon, to small borrowers and small business.

So, this futile operation of the RBI has to be explained to the people in the hope that the response of the people will somehow be incorporated in the Reserve Bank decision making process and finally compel them to do something more creative or more radical perhaps.

Perhaps the Reserve Bank needs to buy the bonds of companies and NBFC in India, as the Federal Reserve is doing in the United States and the Bank of England is doing in England and as the European Central Bank is doing in Europe. Only then, will the fear of the banks about lending money and the banker being accused of doing this for a commission be sorted out and transcend this particular hurdle. This will also finally push money into the hands of businesses which desperately need it to meet their fixed costs as well as payment of wages.

So, these are the different challenges the media faces and it does not help that the media's viability is far from certain. The media has to sustain a very serious drop in revenue. Newspapers that rely on advertising have seen the number of their pages shrink. The bulk of the morning paper has come down, it has become very thin, and media consumption is moving online. Online where there are lots of readers, and little revenue.

How does the media survive, how does the media fulfil its core function of creating an informed public discourse when it is financially not viable? This is the current situation in which the media finds itself. It is trying to do its job but I don't think they are doing a great job. That is the sad reality. I will stop here. Thank you.

Sashi Kumar

Very interesting presentations. Sukumar was talking of the whole deal where Facebook was buying into Jio, making it a humongous media kind of entity appearing before us. Simultaneously we hear about media organisations now demanding from Google and Facebook that they should, based on the news they use, share the revenues with them. So, one of the fallouts is going to be a lot of people vying for the same piece of cake.

We have to consider whether advertising as a model is sustainable at all. We do not know if it will lead to some other model, maybe more subscriptions. Newer forms may have to emerge. A whole paradigm shift seems to be in the offing. Sometimes as a response to this, the political players come back with the wrong signals. Congress president Sonia Gandhi has asked that the government should stop spending money on advertising. That is like throwing the baby with the bathwater when newspapers and legacy media are struggling without that. Underlying that is the other fact that this whole process of advertising by the government, particularly the Central government, was being used as a carrot and stick policy because it is highly discriminatory. Even big newspapers were being starved of advertisements. The policy is you scratch my back and you will get some ads.

We have seen processes like that and somebody was pointing to the situation of the information commission. The Central information commission office seems to be working. But at the state level very few of them are working at all. It was the link that the media would have had with the Government. There is a kind of handout journalism. This is where you interface with the governments at the state or the Centre.

The fact that these information commission offices have literally ceased to function, points very poorly to the vibrancy of the media. It is a dangerous kind of trend. In a right to information society, successive Supreme Court judgements have said, right to information is a part of article 21, just like the right to life and right to know. It is almost seen as a corollary of article 21. Therefore, that aspect of the right of the people to be informed is a larger causality that is going to emerge from Covid-19 and the centralising process.

The whole assumption that the media is there only to put out stories that we would like you to put out in order to communicate with the people, the view of the world we would like to convey rather than you writing what you like and creating mayhem as they call it, causing confusion in the minds of viewers and readers and therefore creating unrest in society. These are the kind of scenarios that are not explicitly but implicitly put before us.

So, this is a very difficult situation which the media is handling on the one hand, as Arun pointed out. The job of the media is to demystify and it is fragmented and also calling out disinformation and misinformation within the media itself. Media can't exist in a situation where we find a section of the media is deliberately lying, deliberately stigmatising, deliberately creating a situation in order to create a communal divide. All these are challenges, internal and external that the media is facing.

Any questions?

K.J. Joseph

These are questions from YouTube.

Sir, the problem we find with the media is the new generation journalist trying to innovate, forgetting the basic role of journalism, being the critical fourth pillar of society.

Sashi Kumar

I have a personal problem with the question, as it is not the role of the media.

You cannot be prescriptive of the role of the media. This is the whole problem. The media cannot be prescriptive of what people should do. Unfortunately, we find many television anchors telling people what to do; sit, stand, walk. Short of saying eat, they say everything else. They tell you what to do. The job of the media is to describe the world, not prescribe to the world. It is not the job of the people to prescribe to the media what they should be doing because that comes from the understanding that the media should play second fiddle to the Government, since it is in charge of the process of development and so on. I think others will want to speak up on this.

T.K. Arun

I have been in the section of the media that (prescribes). Writing editorials, we comment on developments in society, government action, policy, say whether they are good or bad and what they should do. So, having a viewpoint is also a part of the media. It is true that a part of the media has relegated the work of raising questions.

Sukumar Muraleedharan

There is always a prediction of doomsday when new technological platforms come along. Somehow or other, the print media surmounted the challenge from cable television and satellite channels in the 1990s and the early days of the internet – Internet 1.0 as it is called. Internet 2.0 has changed the entire scenario and it is an algorithm-based internet which has to do not so much with exploration as with expectation. Every person goes to social media expecting to find something he already has in mind. He is not looking for information but for confirmation of something he already believes in. It is not an open-ended exploration, which is what the traditional media can do.

You look at the pages of a newspaper. You find so many different things there, some of which would be contrary to your established way of thinking. That gets you stepping out of your comfort zone, but here you are more and more eager to stay within the comfort zone, within the established entrenched beliefs you have. That is where WhatsApp comes as a perfect way of communication. Here you create groups. With 400 million users of WhatsApp, you can imagine the number of networks that are possible between each of these and how many can be organised into varying kinds of groups.

You just stay within the bubble listening to the kind of information that you want to hear. Modi after his re-election last year, at his meeting with the parliamentary party, explicitly said stay away from the media. His first meeting with a global visitor was the chief operating officer of Facebook, Sheryl Sandberg. After that he advised his party that they should use social media to get the word out. There is a specific intent there.

Unfortunately, the media because of its weak financial fundamentals does not have the resources at this time to combat that and pose a credible alternative. It is a tough place that the media finds itself in and I don't envy the people who take the decision on how to dig yourself out of this hole. There is no obvious strategy here. There are apple pie and motherhood kind of prescriptions that we can give but in the current context not many of them will be workable.

Sashi Kumar

I think what Arun said about fragmented media, that is media and media and media is at once fascinating as well as problematic. When we say that the Prime Minister does not give a press conference, it is one function that is a lapse in the function of the media because the press conference in the old world of the media is a formal arrangement, where the head of state speaks to the journalists so that they can question them, interrogate them and so on.

On the other hand, he is very media savvy. He is speaking to his constituency on 'Mann Ki Baat,' on Twitter on Tweet. So, if there is one other kind of media, he will argue that he is in constant touch with this constituency, with the people. So is the media abrogating to itself the right to play the mediatory role and is the mediatory role becoming superfluous and redundant in the age of social media? These are some of the questions that are challenging us. However, one thing is certain is that as long as we believe in democracy, we must be able to say democracy in one breath and a free media in the next breath. Otherwise democracy is a sham.

There are many vaulted democracies which have a track record of great participative democracy and yet it is for the first time the media is itself becoming the arena to undo the media. In other words, hijacking the power of social media or hijacking the capital in the realm of the media, in order to undermine basic tenets, the cardinal principles and values of the media.

That is unfortunately what I see is happening before us and therefore, I think as they say, when the going gets tough the tough gets going. The role of the media and the challenge before the media is tremendous and I am sure that in the months and years ahead there is going to be a huge paradigmatic shift and the new age media, as a questionnaire said, is going to come on its own. That is my sense of where the media is headed. With your permission, shall we close this session?

Section 10

Summing Up

K.J. Joseph and Pyaralal Raghavan

The online discourse on fiscal federalism and Covid-19 in India, an issue of immense contemporary relevance for theory, practice and policy, organised by the Gulati Institute of Finance and Taxation (GIFT) during the last two days is coming to a close. The discourse could not have been more insightful and policy relevant, thanks to the participation of eminent personalities, with immense competence in their respective capacity as finance ministers of states, leaders of political parties, scholars of eminence, influential practitioners and doyens of the media. Before proceeding further, I would like to place on record our immense gratitude to all those who participated in this discourse and indeed to Professor Thomas Isaac who mooted the idea of this discourse and passionately participated throughout the discussions. We are also thankful to the Hon'ble Chief Minister Shri Pinarayi Vijayan, who set the tone for this dialogue in his inaugural address.

Highlighting the takeaways and summarising such a rich discourse is not an easy task. We were expecting that Professor Isaac would take up this responsibility. Unfortunately, he has now been called by the Chief Minister for an important meeting and will not be available to do this job. Hence you have to bear with me, a poor substitute. In what follows I shall try to briefly highlight the insights and takeaways from this rich discourse drawing up on the inputs provided by my colleagues.

The two former directors of GIFT, Dr AV Jose and professor D Narayana, whom I consider the two wings of GIFT Jumbo Jet, have participated in all the sessions. Hence, I encourage them to intervene by highlighting what I have missed.

Fiscal Crisis of the State Governments

The Chief Minister of Kerala, Shri Pinarayi Vijayan, who inaugurated this discourse, raised concerns about weakening fiscal federal setup in the country. This is clearly evident from the conditionality on fiscal targets imposed in the terms of reference of the 15th Finance Commission. The Chief Minister set the tone for the discourse by emphasizing the need for further strengthening the fiscal space of states as a means of empowering them to address the challenges of COVID-19 pandemic. Considering the unprecedented financial challenges on account of the pandemic, the Chief Minister demanded that the fiscal rules need to be relaxed and the borrowing power of the state governments need to be enhanced.

The common concern raised by the chair of the session, Shri Manpreet Singh Badal, Finance Minister, Punjab and the panellists, Shri Manish Sisodia, Deputy Chief Minister, Delhi, Professor Thomas Isaac, Finance Minister of Kerala, Shri Haseeb Drabu, former Finance Minister, Jammu and Kashmir and Shri Jairam Ramesh, Member of Parliament, centered around the emerging challenges to fiscal federalism as manifested, among others, in the shrinking fiscal space of states. The centre has been squeezing the states from the top and the panchayats nibbling at their heels resulting in an unprecedented contraction of the fiscal space of states. The panel also has been highly critical of the manner in which the centre implemented the lockdown.

The pandemic has added to the pre-existing fiscal stress. With the delay in the payment of GST compensation, the states find it even difficult to pay the salaries to employees. The states are being for forced to borrow at market rates as high as 9% with an impending danger of heading into a debt trap. The panel also recognized the additional constraints for the union territories like Delhi that cannot resort to direct market borrowing and are not entitled for any direct support from the finance commissions.

The panel made wide ranging recommendations to facilitate the recovery from the crisis. This included, but is not limited to; raising the borrowing limit of the states, keeping the FRBM ceilings in abeyance, raising the deficit ceilings, immediate disbursement of GST compensation and COVID grants and ensure a minimum guaranteed devolution to the states. Converting the MGNREGA to a universal basic income by taking last year's list of users and disbursing money in their accounts which will create demand in the economy has also been proposed. An automatic increase in the ways and means advances from the RBI with an extension of the repayment period from 3 to 12 months was yet another proposal. The temporary suspension of capital expenditure and its diversion towards health and education along with impounding the dearness allowances, deferring the interest payments are other important suggestions for mobilising the resources. A need for a revised budget during mid-July of 2020 has been highlighted since the budget presented on 1st of February has become almost irrelevant considering the pandemic induced economic disruption. Further it was felt that there has to be an increase in the limits of ways and means advances by the RBI, along with a higher fiscal deficit ceiling of 5% of GSDP and also the right to monetize the deficit. The panel felt an impending danger of a declaration of financial emergency that has to be averted at any cost. This is the time for fiscal expansion with reduction in GST. It is also possible for leveraging foreign exchange reserves for a three-year period as an alternative way to borrowing from the IMF.

COVID-19 Pandemic: The Context and the way forward

The chair of the session Shri Sitaram Yechury, and the panellists, Shri Jairam Ramesh and Shri D. Raja firmly highlighted the importance of strengthening state governments during this pandemic. This necessitates financial assistance of at least 5% of GDP. The fiscal package announced so far has been less than 1% of GDP as compared to 15%, 20% or even 25% of GDP in some countries. A 2% tax on the super rich will ensure more resources than the promised fiscal package by the government of India.

The panel dealt at length on how the COVID-19 crisis has exposed the class character of the Indian society. The unplanned lockdown with hardly a 4-hour notice has brought untold misery to the millions of migrant labour. There were neither buses nor trains available for these migrants to return to their villages whereas Indians abroad were brought back on flights from foreign countries.

Another issue addressed by the panellists was on the credibility of the PM CARES Fund, about its functioning and its objectives. The PM CARES fund needs to be audited as it contains one day's salary deducted from government employees.

It was felt that the recessionary trends already set in the economy are expected to get worse further with the pandemic. The growth is already low and is estimated to be negative which is going to impact the Centre's devolution to the states.

As a way forward the panel proposed the following; States need to be paid their GST dues, the borrowing limits of states should be raised to meet the crisis and there has to be huge transfers from the PM CARES fund to the state governments. State governments have to be liberally assisted to procure PPEs for health workers, test kits, provide for cash transfers, free supply of food and make arrangements for the transportation of migrant workers back home.

Taking cue from the first session, the panel called for resolutely opposing a plausible financial emergency. While the state had to give way to private enterprise during 1991, the 2020 crisis necessitates the state to re-enter, especially in health, which needs an absolute priority.

As a recovery measure, the panel felt that there are no alternatives to increasing the FRBM ceiling to 5% of GSDP for the short term and timely payment of GST compensation.

The expectations are that fiscal federalism is going to take a knock and there is the need to resist the movement towards greater political centralization and financial authoritarianism. The general tendency of the central government has been more in centralising everything. In the context of the pandemic, the threat to democracy became more visible. The centre should have consulted the democratically elected state governments instead of grabbing all powers and unilaterally announcing the lockdown.

Even before the crisis, investment was sluggish; there has been a downward trend in GDP growth in six consecutive quarters along with stagnant exports and tax revenues. The three years data prior to COVID reveals that devolution to the states was only 31-32%, which is far lower than 42% as recommended by 14th Finance Commission and accepted by the government. There is an urgent need to reinstate the fiscal capacities of the states, which has been eroded even before the COVID-19. It is also quite unfair to completely blame the pandemic for the slowdown of the economy.

Covid-19 Pandemic and the First Report of the 15th Finance Commission

The chair of the session Professor M Govinda Rao and the panellists Professor Abhijit Sen, Professor Sudipto Mundle, Shri Rajesh Kumar Singh IAS, Professor Geeta Gouri, Shri R Mohan, Professor Pinaki Chakraborty, and Professor D Narayana deliberated on how Covid-19 has affected the center-state relations. The panel also dealt with the implications of the interim awards of the 15th Finance Commission and how additional resources can be mobilized to bridge the gap between falling revenue collections and rising expenditure needs.

The panel expressed concerns about the interim awards of the 15th Finance Commission. They noted that first, there is a huge difference in tax devolution because of the difference between the Finance Commission estimates of revenue for 2020-21 and budget estimates to the tune of Rs 71,000 crore. It was suggested that the states should approach the Finance Commission for a revision of estimates for 2020-21. Second, states' vertical devolution share will further reduce if the 15th Finance Commission creates a cess for defence expenditure. Third, after the implementation of the GST, states' fiscal/performance has become irrelevant and thus, its weight in the devolution formula should be reduced. Fourth, the union government tries to throttle the Fourteenth Finance Commission's higher devolution award to states by adopting ways and means, which is not in the right spirit of cooperative federalism. They are creating new cesses or upending the cess rate, and increasing the surcharge rate. Similarly, while the international petroleum prices have declined, the union government raised additional excise duty without raising the basic excise duty. Since revenues from additional excise duty and cess are not sharable with the states, this reduces the states' share in vertical devolution. As the states cry for additional funding in the post-pandemic situation the Center should share this money with the states through some mechanism.

Some estimates show that the GDP growth of many states will be negative. In addition to this, the rising expenditure and depleting revenue of states will push the combined fiscal deficit of the centre and states to 10-12% of GDP. For meeting expenditure, there is a need for additional money. Most of the panellists expressed their concern about the philosophy and rationale of the FRBM Act and urged the Finance Commission not to be guided by it. To facilitate more borrowing by states, the panellists felt that the fiscal deficit target needs to be revisited and raised to 5% of the GSDP. The FRBM Review Committee of 2017 had suggested the need for an 'escape clause' to meet financial exigencies. However, this is not going to help in the current crisis. Similarly, the debt limit should be raised to permit the states to borrow more to meet the expenditure needs. Finally, there has been a general agreement that Covid-19 grants should be given to the states through the finance commission . At the same time, states should focus on revenue expenditure and the slowdown in capital expenditure to make existing resources available for the pandemic related expenditure.

Cooperative federalism demands that equal treatment be given to CMDRF of states, PM-CARES, and PM National Relief Fund. However, the Ministry of Corporate Affairs has given a different treatment to PM-CARES and PM

National Relief Fund on the one hand, and CMDRF of states on the other hand. The latter is not eligible for the 2% of the CSR mandated by the Companies Act. This goes against cooperative federalism and does not conform to the basic tenet of federalism.

Finally, the panellists felt that fiscal federalism has been seriously compromised and damaged as is evident from the handling of the Covid-19 pandemic , health crisis, GST compensation, vertical devolution, and so on. The union government must take into confidence every state, discuss with them, and form an objective criterion for disbursing post-Covid-19 grants. Importantly, there has to be coordination not only across states but also between the centre and states.

Covid-19 Pandemic and State of State Finances

The Chairperson Professor Jayati Ghosh and the panellists Professor Yamini Aiyar, Professor Balveer Arora, Professor Praveen Jha, Shri S M Vijayanand, Professor Sushil Khanna, and Dr John Samual deliberated on the state of state finances and the relevance of improving coordination between center and states and among states in the wake of the Covid-19 pandemic. Resource mobilisation of both the center and states is in 'intensive care unit', it was opined. Since there is going to be a shortfall of 25-50% of what has been presented in the budget, states must demand a share of cess and surcharges from the centre. A part of that must be shared with states at least as an emergency provision. Similarly, to support states' provision with respect to financial easing vis-à-vis the central bank must be taken into account. For additional resource mobilisation of states, serious consideration should be given to issuing some kind of pandemic bonds, which the RBI can buy, and it can be repaid by taxing the super-rich. Further, the FRBM limit must be relaxed and states must be allowed to borrow beyond the set limit. If the borrowing ceiling is relaxed, learning from the Kerala experience, the states could explore bilateral and multilateral borrowing. The Finance Commission must extend financing of revenue gaps to all states, instead of only a handful of states. Importantly, the states must endeavour to increase the efficacy of expenditure, which will bring down the cost by 10-20%. Finally, at least 50% of the funds needs to be transferred to local bodies, without any further delay, through the state exchequers.

States have very little leeway in the financial market. It is completely a centre's prerogative. Since states have no leeway at all, the deficit can be monetized and the banks must pick up a part of the bonds that the states will have to list. RBI can buy up all the state government bonds and a big portion of all the other debts as well. There is a strong precedent for it. The US Fed has already bought up every available debt in the last few months. Inflation at present is not a concern since capacity utilisation has collapsed. So, in the wake of the expected GDP contraction of 5-7% in this year and plummeting revenue collection, most of the panellists argued for a fiscal stimulus to the tune of at least 7-10% of GDP.

Local government finance is very critical at this point. In the wake of the pandemic, local government revenues will shrink. For additional resource mobilisation, local bodies need to tax the untapped areas: property and profession tax. The states can resort to tax mapping and organise rigorous collection drives. Similarly, local governments can massively adopt MGNREGA. If they can increase the efficacy of MGNREGA expenditure, it can substitute much of the agricultural investment.

The centre and states should coordinate to find an appropriate solution for providing food and cash security to return migrant workers. The issues raised include; the fixing of responsibilities for feeding them and ensuring their safe return home. Importantly, no finance commission has considered the needs of migrant workers in its devolution. Given that this is a new reality, it needs to be assessed by the commission. One of the big flaws in the existing design of NDRF and SDRF is that it does not include pandemics. So, it was suggested that a new conceptualization of NDRF and SDRF is required.

The speakers expressed concern about the low healthcare expenditure by both the center and states. Currently, fiscal transfers to the states in the areas of health infrastructure and social protection is through centrally sponsored schemes and central sector schemes. States have used the National Health Mission (NHM) funding and have complemented it with their own health expenditures. However, it was felt that, spending from NHM has been overloaded with paperwork and red-tapism. This makes speedy and effective expenditures extremely difficult, particularly during the pandemic time. It is suggested that the NHM should go back to its original design which had more flexible funds and allowed the states to spend the funds they require, without some 2000 line-items and 22-35 desk clearances. Some experts suggested that Kerala should have a proper expenditure management and financing strategy. One financing strategy could be to raise a substantial amount of money from NRIs by floating a special bond for 3-5 years.

Covid Pandemic and the Future of the FRBM Act

The discourse chaired by Professor Prabhat Patnaik and the fellow Panellist Professor C.P. Chandrasekhar, Dr C. Rammanohar Reddy, Professor R. Nagaraj, Professor Venkatesh B Athreya, Professor Lekha Chakraborty and Professor K.N. Harilal felt that that the FRBM Act is devoid of any theoretical base and that it makes fiscal interventions pro-cyclical while it should be contra-cyclical. The Act circumvents the political process by imposing a specific ceiling for the budget deficit and given the pandemic conditions it should be suspended at least for the time being. The panel also highlighted the asymmetry between union and state governments in terms of fiscal flexibility. Getting rid of the pandemic induced recessionary conditions calls for a huge boost in public expenditure and inflation should not be an issue of much concern. The panel felt that the union government's strategy of transferring the responsibilities related to pandemic management to the state governments is unacceptable. The states should be allowed to borrow from the central bank at the prevailing repo rate to tide over the situation. It was also pointed out that the notion of fiscal federalism has already disappeared. Resonating the discussions in the previous sessions, it was pointed out that much of the power is concentrated with the union Government that makes use of the pandemic as an excuse to centralize more power. What is more, the union government is deviating from the FRBM targets while the states lack the flexibility for the same. The panel was highly critical of the government for their fiscal conservatism while the governments all over the world, even conservative ones, are increasing their spending. Considering the structural character of the economy, there was a call for providing support to the agricultural sector and exploring the possibility of suspending corporate concessions for the time being and for more non-discretionary transfer from centre to states. Finally, there was a call reframing fiscal rules in the backdrop of Covid-19 and highlighted the importance of correctly identifying the operational parameters in a new FRBM framework and bringing out innovative models to finance the deficit.

Kerala's Health Strategy in containing Covid-19 Pandemic

The discourse began with the opening address by K.K. Shailaja Teacher, the minister of health and family welfare was taken forward by the panellists Professor T. Sundararaman, Professor B. Ekbal, Shri Rajeev Sadanaandan, Professor V. Ramankutty, and Dr A.V. Jose. Shailaja teacher highlighted the various measures taken by the Government of Kerala in order to tackle the Covid-19 crisis, as well as listed out the constraints faced by the state government in terms of testing kits and testing labs. It was felt that Kerala has been more successful in managing the Covid-19 crisis on account of the experience gained from handling the Nipah Virus, which has attracted global accliam. The panel also underlined the need for increasing the manufacturing capacity in medicine production, even in a generic capacity in the long run. The panel also dealt with the issues in shielding the vulnerable population from Covid-19 and maintaining the non-Covid healthcare along with the constraints faced by the state in relation to Covid-19 testing – the availability of testing kits and testing centres. It was felt that the elaborate institutional architecture built-up by the state through democratic decentralisation and the local empowerment backed by the strong healthcare infrastructure helped in managing the pandemic situation. The panel lauded the community support and termed it as the external social capital of the healthcare system. On the whole, it was felt that Kerala's social capital, public healthcare system, and democratic decentralisation were instrumental in efficiently managing the pandemic situation. The panel also pointed towards a plausible backlash in terms of increased number of non-Covid related health issues due to postponement of hospital visits and underlined the need for boosting public investment in the health sector.

Financing Livelihoods in the context of Covid-19

The discourse chaired by Professor V K Ramachandran and taken forward by the fellow panellists Dr Pronab Sen, Professor R Ramakumar,Dr V Bhaskar, Dr Gayatri Nair and Professor MridulEapen felt that the Government of Kerala had promptly responded to the inevitable lockdown through direct benefit transfers, ensuring food for everyone, including the migrant workers, apart from ensuring health services for all. But reviving the means of livelihood - wage employment, self employment, especially in the hard hit informal sector units in sectors like tourism and transport among others - is bound to be extremely difficult. The focus of the discussion has been on supporting livelihood during and after the lockdown, which is uncertain, with special attention to their mode of financing.

There is much to learn from the developed countries that expended large scale assistance mostly through fiscal and monetary measures and came up with COVID packages to the tune of even 25% of the GDP. There are also instances wherein the utility, rent, power, and water bills are all being waived or halved. These measures have ensured liquidity and demand. But, except Kerala, which announced a Rs 20,000 crore relief package, no other states or the centre has made a COVID expenditure plan, for the next 12 months or attempted a revision of the budgets. The central government, apart from the fiscal domain, also needs to intervene through monetary measures. Special attention is needed for women as they are much more adversely affected, less privileged and also the physically challenged.

Livelihoods of small and marginal producers, including the rural and agrarian, is dependent on the credit from the banking system. Since the implementation of the moratorium, declared by the RBI, would be at the discretion of the banks, it has obvious limits. The central government needs to ensure that it is not voluntary, but mandatory and the working capital requirement needs to be met. It was also argued that what is needed is not postponement but the waiver of interest payments on term loans.

The states, being closer to the people, are on the frontline and needs financing, but they are under a triple whammy; their own tax and non-tax revenues have come down; liquor has been put on the banned lists and this prime source of income for states has been removed; GST revenues are down and so is devolution to states. In a sense Covid-19 is a great opportunity to do deep reform and especially right sizing of the government and fiscal expenditure. A case was made for retiring grade 3 and grade 4 personnel in government who are overpaid in the market and with full pension or a cut in the salary of highly paid employees. Since the states are fiscally constrained, they should also be enabled to borrow

The Pandemic and the Revival Strategy

The discourse on pandemic and the revival strategy led by Shri K M Chandrasekhar with the involvement of fellow panellists Professor K P Kannan, Shri G Vijayaraghavan, Professor George Mathew, Dr N J Kurian, Professor Sunil Mani and Dr K Ravi Raman observed that the pandemic hit at a time when the GDP has been steadily decelerating over the past seven consecutive quarters. Poverty and misery of the masses, which COVID has accentuated, is going to be the most difficult problem that will have to be addressed in the short term. History tells that whenever there was a crisis the burden was ultimately transferred to the poor and whenever there was plenty it was retained by the rich. Unfortunately, the current crisis was never seen as a demand side problem, instead it was regarded as a supply side problem. So, all kinds of things were done like a corporate tax cut which nobody wanted, because corporates will make a profit only when people buy. So, the emphasis has to be on the demand side first, and then try to resolve issues on the supply side. The three phases, that is the current crisis, the recovery and the revival are sort of a continuum. Effective interventions in these phases could be done only by the states. But the states are to be supported by the centre; Some of the areas where the centre could conserve resources are the Central Vista project, the bullet train and other fancy projects, which can wait.

From the demand side, we need to address the loss of income of the poor and the vulnerable. As much as 80% of workers are informal sector workers. Another 10% are informal workers in the formal sector. So, 90% of the workers are in the informal segment. Here there is the scope for reaping the full potential of the MGNREGA by giving a wage that is fixed scientifically. At a time when the primary school teachers' salary was around Rs 30, the welfare pension was Rs 15. Today's pension is only Rs 1200 while the salary of a primary school teacher is over Rs 40,000. Hence, we need to raise the welfare pension, although it has been raised recently to Rs 1,200 along with clearing all the arrears in payment. About 25-30% cut in the salaries of those above a certain level will bring the needed revenue. The challenge of such a strategy in Kerala, where the government order has been burned by some of the service originations, has also been highlighted.

From the supply side, addressing the concerns of MSMEs and the informal sector units, especially those in the badly hit sectors like tourism, travel, hospitality and others should receive the highest priority and a major intervention package should be provided, which will cover at least 10% of the GDP. There is so much capacity for absorption and if the banks are willing to give up their risk-averse approach, they can make available funds to MSMEs and others. The revival program for the unorganised sector should be implemented by local governments as they are nearer to the people and understand the sufferings. A number of companies are leaving China; and strategies must be devised to attract them. Attention was drawn to technology and innovations, with an open science/innovation perspective especially in the area of pharmaceuticals and medical equipment.

Media in the Time of the Pandemic

Shri Sashi Kumar, moderator of the discourse and the panellists Professor Sukumar Muraleedharan, Shri K G Narendranath, Shri Anil Padmanabhan and Shri T K Arun dealt at length with the varied challenges, both internal and external, confronted by the media. The job of the media is to demystify and also to callout disinformation and misinformation within the media itself. It can't exist in a situation where we find a section of the media is deliberately lying, deliberately stigmatising, deliberately creating a situation in order to create a communal divide. Thus, the media is a part of the problem as well as the solution. It faces an identity crisis, especially during the pandemic. It was felt that unlike mainstream media, social media is an anarchic space where it is difficult to understand things and counteract. The media consistently work with the health workers, doctors and frontline social workers and continue to be out there in the field. Although the media works facing threats from different sides, the public trust in the credibility of media is at an all-time low.

On the one hand, the media did a good job trying to track the crisis scenario. On the other hand, it faces some kind of vulnerability, as there has been a constant effort to impose a singular view and also because it becomes more dependent on official favours.

A conflict exists between centre and states on fiscal leeway. The centre has been very economical and therefore, there is practically no package given to the states during the pandemic. However, many states have their own social development policies and political economy objectives, which is not exactly in line with the centre. The centre was initially in favour of cooperative federalism and a more decentralised federal structure. But this outlook has changed significantly over the last four years as they are trying to protect their headline fiscal numbers to the extent possible.

Media is not a homogeneous entity; it is segmented with different characteristics. Whatever little time people have to consume news, about the world around, is just saturated with different images. In fact, the media has the responsibility to highlight the policy challenges that arise from the current situation and examine the alternatives. It involves a multidimensional activity of mediating information connecting various development aspects. It is a bit challenging for the media to sustain in this manner. Interestingly, the volumes of the newspaper has come down and has become very thin and the traffic is moving online where there are lots of readers, but no revenue.

Social media is not the space for an open-ended exploration, which is what the traditional media can do. One can find so many different things in the newspaper, some of which would be contrary to the established way of thinking and way out of the normal comfort zones. As long as we believe in democracy, we must be able to say democracy in one breath and free media in the next breath. If not, democracy is a sham.

Index